The Home Therapist

A practical, self-help guide for
everyday psychological problems

Edited by Dr John Barletta and Jan Bond

www.
AUSTRALIANACADEMIC**PRESS**
.com.au

First published in 2012
Australian Academic Press
32 Jeays Street
Bowen Hills Qld 4006
Australia
www.australianacademicpress.com.au

National Library of Australia Cataloguing-in-Publication entry:

Author:	Barletta, John.
Title:	The home therapist : a practical, self-help guide for everyday psychological problems / John Barletta and Jan Bond.
ISBN:	9781921513916 (pbk.)
	9781921513923 (ebook)
Subjects:	Self-help techniques.
	Self-management (Psychology)--Handbooks, manuals, etc.
	Psychology, Applied--Handbooks, manuals, etc.

Other Authors/Contributors: Bond, Jan.

Dewey Number: 158

Cover design by Maria Biaggini. Cover illustration by ©iStockphoto/Rebecca Grabill. Authors' photo courtesy Ed Siwicki.

Disclaimer

The information in this book is intended to help readers make informed choices about the wellbeing of themselves and those around them. It is not intended to be a substitute for clinical treatment by, or guidance and care of, any professional person. The advice is general in nature and readers should obtain their own tailored, individual advice about any matters of concern to them. Whilst the editors, contributors, and publisher have endeavoured to present the information contained in this book as relevant and accurate, they are not responsible for any adverse effects or consequences alleged to have been sustained by any person consulting this book. By referring to this book, any and all readers release the editors, contributors, and publisher of any claims for alleged loss or damage alleged to have been sustained by that reader as a result of relying on the content contained herein.

The Home Therapist is great title for a very special self-help book. Families, couples, singles, and elderly people could read a page of it at breakfast or before going to sleep and learn about themselves and their most precious relationships. Following the wisdom and the richness of this book written by many hands (90 Australian experts!) and beautifully assembled by Barletta and Bond, the reader can reflect on lifecycle critical events and cope with the adversities of life with more hope and resilience. Counselling is a very useful experience when families or individuals have to face serious psychological problems, but a book like *The Home Therapist* can help people to prevent them and to believe in their own professional and relational resources.

> — *Prof. Maurizio Andolfi, Psychiatrist and Founder,*
> *Accademia di Psicoterapia della Famiglia, Rome*

Since throwing myself back into the world of acting, my mental strength is one of my best assets. Sometimes we know what we need to do to fix ourselves, but we are not equipped with the right tools to do so; this book is my roaming toolbox. When dilemmas come across your path, big or small, it's nice to have something to draw on and written in a way we can all take in. Do yourself a favour and keep a copy on hand.

> — *Kelly Atkinson, Actress, Sydney*

The Home Therapist offers a wonderful collection of practical and useful concepts and suggestions for leading a more healthy and fulfilled life. Clinicians and laypeople will find that this book will serve as a useful tool for everyday living. As I read from the many talented scholars in this book, I was reminded of what I often tell my graduate students in Counseling; you don't have to be sick to get better. *The Home Therapist* is just the tool to aid so many in taking control of their own lives as they help themselves to a better life.

> — *Prof. Thomas Davis, Counselor Education, Ohio University, Ohio*

I like the KISS principle, Keep It Simple Stupid, and this book is so easy to read because of the layperson terms, and these days it's so hard to find information when you are in need that is so easy to read and understand. I strongly recommend it, even though I dislike reading.

> — *Joe D'Ercole, Managing Director, Hercules Properties, Brisbane*

This book is a timely response to an ever increasing need for distilled wisdom that a collective of professionals present. I suspect it's almost a pocket version of a Wikipedia for busy people used to getting all their information in one place. It would be hard to imagine a reader who would not find something of great value in this book.

— Jelenko Dragisic, CEO, Volunteering Queensland, Brisbane

A go-to guidebook for navigating the most important journey ever: Your life. Highly recommended.

— Dr Leah Giarratano, Author and Clinical Psychologist, Sydney

A concise, yet thorough, source of information for many of the issues that arise in schools today. As educators, our roles include many incidental counselling situations. This book is an excellent resource to equip us with what we need to know and how to deal with such issues.

— Ursula Jamieson, Educator and Administrator, Canberra

We face many difficult challenges throughout our lives, the majority of which are covered in *The Home Therapist*. This book is unique in its comprehensive yet user-friendly design, and I believe it will be a valuable addition to the bookshelves of families, therapists and GPs.

— Dr Tania Jardine, General Practitioner, Brisbane

The Home Therapist demystifies and educates people about mental health and provides a wealth of practical skills, tips and strategies to understand and manage this often complex area of health. Everyone will find this book informative and useful and it will stimulate conversations at home as well as providing an invaluable resource for challenging times.

— Petrea King, Author, Your Life Matters, Sydney

This wonderfully practical book offers a wealth of solid information for anyone who is interested in improving quality of life, personally and in relationships. Numerous insightful tips are presented in a clear and concise way, and classified into sections so people can easily select and apply them. Written by recognised experts, Barletta and Bond absolutely found a way to bridge the gap between science and everyday life in this era of information.

— Dr Liz Pluut-van Dingstee, Child Psychologist and Family Therapist, Amsterdam

Some say that a little bit of information is dangerous, but I say a little bit of information leads to us to question and seek answers. This book, *The Home Therapist*, is a welcome resource as it empowers everyone of us as it gives us simple and basic knowledge. This knowledge will open us up to new possibilities and understanding.

— Fr Chris Riley, CEO and Founder, Youth Off The Streets, Sydney

About time! Quality, well-researched professional information, brought together in an easy enlightening approach, across a wide range of common concerns—a triumphant first aid manual that will improve the wellbeing of all who use it.

— Santo Russo, Psychologist, Brisbane

The Home Therapist is a very useful guide in providing basic information on a wide range of psychological issues. It is easy to read and should provide a very accessible tool for many people who work in the care and health professions. Like the authors, the book is practical, relevant and geared for a diverse audience.

— Andrew J See, Barrister at Law, Kilkenny Chambers, Brisbane

about the editors

Dr John Barletta

John, a Counselling, Consulting and Clinical Psychologist in private practice in Brisbane, enjoys providing therapy, medico-legal reports, clinical supervision, psychometric assessments, consultation and corporate workshops. He holds qualifications from Ohio University (Doctor of Philosophy), University of Queensland (Master of Educational Studies), Australian Catholic University (Bachelor of Education), and Queensland University of Technology (Graduate Diploma in Counselling; Diploma of Teaching). John is responsible for over 200 contributions to publications and presentations in psychology, education, health and pastoral care. He has been a teacher, high school counsellor, primary school guidance counsellor, relationship educator, and professor. He is a nationally registered Psychologist with the *Psychology Board of Australia* (and board-approved Supervisor), and a member of the *Australian Psychological Society, College of Clinical Psychologists, Australian Association for Cognitive and Behaviour Therapy,* and *Australian and New Zealand Association of Psychiatry, Psychology and Law.* John has made contributions to associations in Australia, the United States and Italy, including the *International Scientific Committee of the Accademia di Psicoterapia della Famiglia* (Rome), editorial board roles for the *American School Counselor Association* and *Association for Counselor Education and Supervision,* the foundation of the *Psychotherapy and Counselling Federation of Australia,* and was twice President of the *Queensland Guidance and Counselling Association* (www.johnbarletta.com).

Jan Bond

Jan is a Clinical Counsellor in private practice on the Gold Coast, Queensland. She holds a Master of Counselling degree from Bond University and has published research from her thesis, Public Perceptions of Counsellors, in the *International Journal for the Advancement of Counselling.* With over 35 years counselling and life experience in the field, Jan has worked as a carer for disadvantaged children, drug and alcohol counsellor, project manager and counsellor working with offenders, court support group counselling coordinator, and a grief and loss counsellor for a number of community agencies. Jan currently provides counselling for a diverse range of issues to private patients, and is an Allied Health Professional with two major hospitals providing staff support, employee assistance counselling, and is a team member of a Lifestyle Management Program. Specialising in grief and loss, she facilitates a group for parents who are grieving the death of a child. Jan was recently awarded a SIDS and *Kids Hero Award* for her contribution to bereavement support. She holds Clinical Counsellor status with *Queensland Counsellors Association* and is a member of the *Psychotherapy and Counselling Federation of Australia* (jan@janbond.com.au).

foreword

Mental health, along with the economy and climate change, is among the top three concerns of Australians as reflected in a global survey in 2010. Yet it was Thomas Jefferson who, on the eve of American independence, enshrined life, liberty and the pursuit of happiness as no less than basic human rights of a civil society. Conversely, the greatest threat to happiness, fulfilment, productivity and a strong society is mental ill-health. Mental ill-health is also one of the top three contributors to the burden of disease, just behind cancer and cardiovascular disease. Moreover, when we focus on people in the prime productive years of life, rather than towards the end, we find that mental ill-health completely overshadows all physical illnesses, making up 36% of the disease burden in 15- to 44-year olds, and over 50% in emerging adults. How should we respond to this serious threat?

We certainly need to reengineer and scale-up our system of mental health care so that Australians of all ages have equal access to quality health and social care for mental ill-health as they do for physical ill-health. We made a first step towards this in 2011, and fortunately all sides of politics are now committed to this reform which must continue over the next decade. We are still only halfway there. Complementing this effort, every Australian needs to learn more about what constitutes mental ill-health and how to respond to it in themselves and those close to them. This means better mental health literacy and acquiring the competency to practice mental health first aid. Everyone can also strengthen their own mental health, improve their resilience and learn to cope effectively with the challenges and crises that life and the process of human development places in our path.

The Home Therapist, assembled by an amazing array of experienced professionals, is a comprehensive attempt to better equip all of us to meet so many of these challenges, to reduce the risks of mental ill-health, to guide help-seeking, and to set us on a path where we and those around us might actually flourish. The book reflects a faith in the human spirit and the inherent resilience of all people given the right conditions. Happiness is an elusive goal, however, as Thomas Jefferson asserted, its pursuit is noble and essential. Every journey requires careful preparation, skills, luck and social scaffolding. This book will be an invaluable guidebook for the pursuit of mental health and happiness no matter at what stage in life the journey is commenced.

Professor Patrick McGorry AO, Psychiatrist
Australian of the Year 2010
Executive Director, Orygen Youth Health
Melbourne, Victoria, Australia

contents

Chapter 1 Personal Wellbeing

Chapter 2 — Couples Issues

Chapter 3

Family and Parenting Issues

Chapter 4 — Children and Adolescent Issues

Chapter 5 — Health and Wellbeing Issues

Chapter 6 — Ageing Issues

Chapter 7 Mental Health Issues

Grief and Loss Issues

Chapter 9

Sexuality Issues

Chapter 10

Stress Management and Time Management Issues

Chapter 11 Addiction Issues

Chapter 12 Abuse, Neglect, Violence, Bullying and Crime Issues

Chapter 13 Education and Careers Issues

Chapter 14 Communication, Relationships and Friendship Issues

preface

A life which is managed well is one where the individual is happy, healthy, connected intimately and socially, contributes to the lives of others, and has purpose. The reality is that we all have struggles at numerous times in our lives, and how we deal with those challenges will determine what quality of life we experience. As Elbert Hubbard (1856–1915) once remarked: "Life is just one damned thing after another". By implication then, people need to remember that they will deal with a succession of trials and tribulations across their lifespan.

This unique self-help manual was conceived and developed with three major goals in mind. First, it is designed for general education, the kind of book a family might have in their home library. With a preventive and educational focus, it can familiarise family members with a variety of emotional, social, psychological, relationship, and health struggles most of us are exposed to across our lifetime. Next, this book has an early intervention focus, a first port of call when challenges inevitably arise. Finally, it may be used as a resource when consulting with a professional therapist for help. Although professionals offer heaps of suggestions and strategies in sessions, the reality is a lot of work needs to happen out of sessions. This book can provide supporting information and useful tips to help people between professional therapy sessions.

You will find this book is practical and easy-to-read, while being readily accessible in times of crises. We acknowledge that although it is quite comprehensive in its coverage of topics, like any text, it cannot address every conceivable issue. If you can't find a specific issue covered in this book, find a similar or related topic and explore if the ideas for that subject might be of any help to you.

This book is also easily accessible by professionals such as doctors, psychiatrists, psychologists, mental health nurses, occupational therapists, social workers, counsellors, and coaches. It can be used as a broad reference text by these professionals for their own continuing development, and also as a friendly resource for patients and clients to enhance their treatment and recovery.

The 138 contributions were written by over 90 professionals and are informed by both research data and clinical wisdom. Each contributor was specifically chosen because of their particular interest and recognised expertise. As editors we are dearly indebted to them for their goodwill and their most valuable contributions to this comprehensive publication.

This book should be viewed as a tool that can be effective if it is used in the way it was intended, that is, as a general supportive text in the early stages of a challenge, or an addition to ongoing contact with an appropriate practitioner for more significant issues. If you ever have doubts about what you should do in a situation, consult with a relevant trained professional. This book is not intended to be a substitute for professional care, but to enable people to take more control in their life. Ultimately, individuals are responsible for the actions they choose, and we believe that what is presented in this book has enormous potential to add quality to your life.

We wish you all the best

John Barletta, PhD
Clinical Psychologist
Brisbane, Australia

Jan Bond, MCouns
Clinical Counsellor
Gold Coast, Australia

*To my gorgeous wife Sandra, whose unwavering love, support and
encouragement enables me to do things that are fun,
meaningful and challenging. To my faithful parents who model
love and optimism. And to my patients
who privilege me with their stories, teach me about life,
and impress me with their capacity.*

John

*To my husband Lloyd, our children, their partners, and grandchildren
whose unconditional love and laughter have enabled me to nurture
my individuality. To those who have shared their lives, loves and
losses. Your courage in the face of adversity is tribute to the resilience
of the human spirit. You have touched my soul!*

Jan

1

Personal Wellbeing

- Work–Life Balance
- Positive Psychology
- Optimism
- Personal Energy Audit
- Building Resilience in Children
- Enhancing Happiness and Wellbeing
- Emotional Intelligence
- Enhancing Motivation in your Child
- Creativity to get Through the Tough Stuff
- Assertiveness
- Managing Financial Challenges
- Confidence and Self-Esteem
- Problem Solving and Decision Making
- Living the Life You Want
- Laughter
- Perfectionism
- Home Organisation — Avoiding Clutter
- Christian Spirituality and Religion
- Shedding Guilt and Shame
- Moving House

WORK–LIFE BALANCE

Work–life balance is a concept that refers to assessing and prioritising your time, resources and effort given to work (i.e., career, vocational ambitions) and life (e.g., family, health, fun, leisure). This is the process of getting the lifestyle balance you want, based on your principles, values and goals. The term 'work–life balance' can be used to explore the unhealthy life choices that some people make as they neglect important areas of their lives (e.g., self, family, friends) in favour of work-related duties and aspirations.

In getting the work–life balance right for yourself, it must be remembered that:

- although it can be *tough*, it is not impossible.

- getting the balance right is really *worth* it for many reasons.

- for things to change means *you* have to make some changes.

- *happiness* will be the ultimate outcome.

To help you start thinking about how to restore or regain your work–life balance formula, consider a time in your life when things were in balance:

- Who noticed first?

- What were the signs?

- How great did it feel?

- What were you doing?

- What did you do to get on that track?

- Who helped you get in such good shape?

- How long did it ultimately last?

- What ongoing impact does it have on you?

- What did you learn (i.e., about yourself, about others, about how you changed)?

- Is this something you would like to develop again?

Answering these 10 questions will enable you to review the *information* and *process* you already know about getting in balance, and potentially increases your *motivation* and *commitment* to do the work to again get to that stage. I learnt a long time ago that you cannot tell the shape of a violin by the sound; whether it's a traditional style, asymmetrical, trapezoidal, or whatever; they all sound exactly the same. Even with an inconsistency of wood thickness, a Stradivarius sounds great. Just like violins that are all different in various ways, we all have the amazing potential to do well. There is no one right or perfect way to get the life we want. It is about knowing we all have the capacity to do well, irrespective of where we have come from or what we have. It is up to us to play to the tune that is meaningful.

Current realities of work–life issues

- We work more hours, have more demands, are more competitive, and have less security.
- With minimal free time, we are torn between the pressures of employment and personal life.
- Work is necessary to earn a living, but we also need *quantity* time for ourselves and others.
- We make unhealthy choices and neglect important areas of our lives.
- Burnout is experienced due to stress and overwork.
- We get to breaking point and experience a range of physical and emotional problems as a result.

Spheres of life that need to be considered

When planning for developing areas of your life, these spheres will be worth considering:

- Work — paid, voluntary, home duties, study.
- Personal development — self-esteem, emotions, thinking style.
- Social — partner, family, friends, groups, community.
- Spiritual — rituals, values, beliefs, purpose.
- Physical — exercise, sport, diet, health.
- Relaxation — leisure, rest, hobbies, fun.

Striving for wellness

- What many people strive for in life is a state of wellness. This can best be thought of as being in positive health, comprising a sustainable balance (i.e., mind, body, spirit) as an actively sought goal, and making choices toward a more successful existence that results in an overall feeling of quality of life and wellbeing (e.g., healthy, happy, prosperous).

Benefits of balance

The reasons people actively work toward getting an improved work-life balance is to:

- reduce stress and prevent burnout.

- increase health, energy and motivation.

- stimulate the immune system and promote recovery from illness.

- increase wellbeing via calm assertiveness.

- encourage perspective-taking in life.

- promote self-esteem, social support, connectedness, and happiness.

- increase productivity; employers too are very keen on this aspect!

The following signs may result from, or lead to, an imbalance in life:

- Decreased energy, motivation, flexibility, connection with others, health, performance.

- Increased stress, frustration, worry, negative attitude to self/others/work, alcohol and drug use.

Tips on how to thrive, not just survive:

- Assume responsibility for your own survival (i.e., be proactive).

- Use your strengths to cope.

- Consider your positive times and do more of what you've done before.

- Don't accept what others define as inevitable; and accept what others define as inevitable.

- Be hopeful, not helpless (remember — what you focus on, you amplify).

- With low mood, appraisals are distorted, therefore you must focus on positives.

- Develop a caring approach to yourself (being stressed is self-abuse!).

- Recognise when you are choosing to do too much (or being exploited) and be assertive.

- Use time management approaches to identify use of time and be more constructive with it.

- Set clear goals, then maintain and evaluate them.

- Increase your ability to delay gratification (make sacrifices).
- Set attainable standards for yourself and others.
- Identify the skills you need to work more effectively and acquire them.
- Have the courage to say and do what you believe is right.
- Cultivate positive relationships with colleagues and managers.
- Establish a supportive network both at work and beyond.
- Leave work behind when you are not there (distance yourself).
- Balance work commitments with responsibilities beyond it.
- Take all the time off work that you are entitled to (employers don't like this one!).
- Take care of and spoil yourself with nice things.
- Identify job stress factors, and activate change where you can.
- Postpone major life changes if you are not feeling great.
- Resolve personal conflicts as they arise.
- Continue to do the things you enjoy.
- Control your work.
- Exercise and meditate regularly.
- Seek help when needed (e.g., family, friends, GP, priest, coach, counsellor, psychologist).

Tips for the workplace:
- Know your role and responsibilities and focus on these areas.
- Accept limits (time, energy, skills).
- Take proper breaks to energise.
- Manage workload (i.e., prioritise and delegate).
- Slow down at times; and speed up at times.
- Talk with colleagues (get support and opinions).
- Cultivate a sense of humour, fun and creativity.
- Learn to say "no" as necessary; boundaries are critical.
- Think ahead and set achievable goals.

- Maintain interest and curiosity in work; stay fresh by learning and problem-solving.
- Focus on the positive aspects of work and your personal life (recall these often).

Fear of change

If we take risks there will be fear, and the only way to get rid of fear is to be active. Don't wait for fear to go away before you make changes. As Nike's advertising slogan encourages us; *Just do it!* You need to behave as if you can do something, and you'll be surprised how successful you will be. 'Fake it until you make it' is what I have always encouraged my clients to do. It's easy to put off change until we feel better about ourselves. But self-esteem won't magically improve; it improves after we've made desired changes. Everyone experiences fear in unfamiliar territory, even those who have achieved and are successful. Pushing through fear is less frightening than living with the underlying fear that comes from helplessness and inertia. People who refuse to take risks live with a more severe sense of dread than if they took the risks necessary to make changes.

Life's Sat-Nav!

My belief is that the process of making changes in life should be like a car's satellite navigation system. It needs only two pieces of information: Where are you? Where do you want to be? It does not need to know what your mother was like, what school you went to, what happened when you were seven, what you are afraid of, or how crazy your boss is!

Finally, I encourage you to consider *The Serenity Prayer* (Grant me the Serenity to accept the things I cannot change, Courage to change the things I can, and Wisdom to know the difference). This allows you to pick your battles, step up to challenges, and to be okay with yourself and others.

Dr John Barletta

POSITIVE PSYCHOLOGY

Are you always looking on the bright side of life? Or, do your thought patterns prevent you from trying new experiences, enjoying yourself, or making new relationships?

Psychologist Martin Seligman focused much of his efforts in the late nineties and early naughties in collating research on the positive side of life. He was the catalyst in igniting interest in further understanding how positive emotions such as joy, contentment, and optimism affect individuals, groups, and even whole organisations.

Everyone, regardless of his or her life circumstances, can experience positive emotions and increase the amount of these emotions in their life. Science clearly links our emotions and our mindset. Evidence shows that the heart sends emotional and intuitive signals to, and aligns, many systems to harmoniously function in our body. As well as communicating constantly with our brain, it also makes decisions of its own.

So what does it mean for you? How can you increase the amount of positive emotions in your life?

Raise your own awareness:

- Be alert to when happy moments occur in your daily life.

- Be on the lookout for simple, small things that bring happiness, and a feeling of contentment, gratitude and appreciation — the loyalty of one's dog, or for those with children, amidst all the challenges that parenthood throws your way, it is the small achievements and milestones each child makes.

- When you realise you are in a happy moment, *stop* and take note to self that 'this is good, I am enjoying myself, this makes me *feel* good'.

- Share your happiness with someone. By sharing, you get to relive the happy moment, and in doing so, provide the listener with a happy moment themselves.

- Truly *value* the times you have that are happy.

- Endeavour to replicate the happy moment … what were you doing or thinking when you experienced the positive emotion? Who were you with?

- When appropriate, take a souvenir or photo of the moment, so it will be remembered and appreciated vividly in the future.

Make your life a work in progress:

- The *energy* you put into making your life positive will correlate to the energy you receive from life. Make an effort!

- Invest your time and energy into positive friends and family relationships.

- Identify your *strengths* and determine if you are living your life utilising them. If you are not, then why not? You will be expending a lot of energy if you are living your life outside your core strengths.

- Find an interest in which you can completely *lose* yourself. The expression 'in the zone', or 'flow' encapsulates this feeling. You are so deeply engaged in the activity that time seems to fly by, you perform well and your thoughts are focused on the task at hand. Some people run, others paint, do yoga, read — what is your special flow zone? Find it and schedule it into your weekly activities.

Find your life's calling:

- At various stages of our lives we ask ourselves different questions. At some point we start to really look for the meaning of our life. Why are we here?

- Think about the legacy you wish to leave behind

- What are you truly *passionate* about? What do you *value* in life?

- Be grateful for all the positive aspects of your life. Maybe it is your health, or the relationships you have with your family, the country you live in, the freedom you enjoy.

- Keep a regular diary. Reflect and debrief on moments in your life. Write down the things you are grateful for.

- Take a bird's-eye view of your life, and visualise it as a pie divided into a number of slices, each representing significant roles you play — partner, parent, work colleague, community member, self. What areas of your life are travelling well, giving you joy, contentment, and providing you with energy? What areas of your life are *energy thieves* and need more attention so they are positive energy sources for you?

- Be courageous and walk away from or change the aspects of your life that are not positive. Steer your life toward the things that you are passionate about and truly believe in and value.

The road to living a positive life that follows a clear path guided by your *Values, Passions* and *Strengths* is taken one step at a time, and is a most rewarding experience.

Bronwen Edwards

OPTIMISM

Scientists believe the human mind processes up to 60,000 individual thoughts every day. The ratio of positive to negative thoughts (*green thoughts to red thoughts*) varies between people, as do the skills with which different people handle the negative thoughts. Broadly speaking, thoughts fall into two categories — those that relate to external factors and have what is perceived to be an external locus of control, and then our own internal self-observations. Our self-esteem and self-worth are influenced by the messages we constantly send ourselves about our competence and performance.

Given that the brain likes to learn based on pattern and repeatability, be careful what you practise!

Science also informs us that people have a variable disposition toward optimism or pessimism. Being aware of your natural tendency and accepting it, with the knowledge that you are able to influence the way you perceive your natural thoughts, is the key to living a more optimistic life.

So, how can you frame your negative thoughts so that you can view them objectively and create a more positive mindset?

It is important to note that we are not trying to deceive ourselves in this reframing process, nor are we trying to make ourselves feel all warm and fuzzy. We are starting the process of replacing the energy-sapping thoughts we can experience with constructive, positive ones.

Catch the thought:

- Be aware of your thoughts.

- Ask yourself: *How did I come to think about this matter in this fashion?*

- Is it my belief, or have others *helped* me form this belief?

- Is this thought changeable or do I need to accept it?

- How passionate am I about this thought? How important is it to me?

If a thought is not changeable, it needs to be accepted, and you must move on from the thought, to avoid it draining your energy. For those who are visual people, imagine a stream with a myriad of autumn leaves floating gently by towards a dam wall. Place the thought on a leaf and watch it float away, knowing you can retrieve it later if you want to, but that it is okay to let it go.

Connect to what the thought relates to:

- Does this negative thought relate to any recognisable emotion — anger, fear, jealousy?

- Is the negative thought grounded in past experience?

Often when we take the time to really look at our core values we discover we have adopted one or more of the values passed to us from our parents throughout our childhood. In many cases the value is congruent with us as an adult; however, in others we can find ourselves in constant battle with a value we simply don't hold but think we *should*. It is the same with negative thoughts. We may find ourselves harbouring negative thoughts closely linked to an inherited value that we really do not *own for ourselves*, or they are linked to strong opinions of other influential people in our lives that we have not taken the time to challenge our thinking on.

Look for evidence supporting the thought:

- Are there real facts supporting and justifying the negative thought?

Be the *Evidence Police* and seek out the facts that will help you determine if the thought is justified or not. If the facts suggest that it is justified, then decide if it is changeable or if it needs to be accepted. If the facts simply don't add up, then challenge your thought and look to reframe it in a more constructive, realistic way.

Reframe the thought:

- Find another way of expressing your negative observations/thoughts.

- Check out if your negative thought a result of over-generalising? For example: original negative thought — *I am hopeless at all ball sports.* Reframed thought — *My hand-eye coordination needs some work so I can play tennis more competently, but I am great at soccer. It all comes down to practice.*

- Find a constructive way of expressing the thought, acknowledging specific limitations associated with the thought (perhaps skill/behaviour/opportunity), and being sure to find possibilities for success. Recognise and incorporate what you need to do in order for the negative thought to be no longer justifiable.

- Consider when you are most confident: How do you sound? How do you feel when you are confident? Incorporate these confident emotions into your reframing process.

As with everything to do with you being a *work in progress*, reframing takes practice and a lot of awareness. Every time you reframe a negative into a constructive positive your brain is making new synapse connections and learning the positive route. Why not adopt the mindset of optimism whenever you find yourself *stuck*, or feeling burdened with negative thoughts or feelings? Look at each situation as an opportunity to learn, and find positive, optimistic alternatives to your usual thought patterns. Choosing an optimistic mindset opens your mind to additional opportunities and feelings of wellbeing. Isn't this the kind of advice you would give your best friend, or your children?

Bronwen Edwards

PERSONAL ENERGY AUDIT

Energy ... Vigour! Liveliness! Get-up-and-go! Oomph!

Call it what you like, energy is something we all need and, in many cases, wish we had more of. It affects how we think, feel, act, and make decisions. What a lot of us struggle to realise though, is that we can control our mental, emotional and physical energy levels by how we choose to live our lives.

How do you serve your energy levels?

Below, place a tick in the left box beside each statement that you do actively devote time to, and one in the right box of the statements that you know you do not devote any time to.

Mental energy is concerned with our psychological perspective and state. It requires a stable platform to operate effectively. Poor mental energy can often reduce sleep quality, goal clarity, attention span, decision-making, time management and overall effectiveness.

I currently devote mental energy and effort to:	Yes	No
• having a positive state of mind	☐	☐
• avoiding frequent procrastinating and multi-tasking	☐	☐
• consistently learning, adapting and setting challenging goals	☐	☐
• being engaged in a hobby or strong personal interest	☐	☐
• being open to change	☐	☐
• mentally relaxing ... taking time out	☐	☐

Emotional energy relates to the emotional and social connections being built in your life, and exists between family, kids, your partner, friends, work relationships, neighbours, and community.

I currently devote emotional energy and effort to:	Yes	No
• controlling my negative emotions and thoughts	☐	☐
• having and being a trusted life partner	☐	☐
• frequently spending time with inspirational friends	☐	☐
• having positive family relationships	☐	☐

- having positive and supportive work relationships ☐ ☐
- having daily habits and skills in life, aligned with my goals ☐ ☐

Physical energy is the quality and quantity of energy we have to live the life we want consistently. It includes the quality of our sleep, rest and recovery periods, exercise, strength and endurance, our mobility and fuel choices.

I currently devote physical energy and effort to:	Yes	No
• being physically mobile, fit and active	☐	☐
• eating a well-balanced diet	☐	☐
• having appropriate amounts of sleep	☐	☐
• having frequent rest and recovery periods	☐	☐
• drinking caffeine and alcohol in moderation	☐	☐

If you have five or more ticks in the right-hand column, there may be an *energy leak*. Some aspects of your life at the moment may well be thieving energy from you, and distracting you from important relationships, roles and goals.

By working on removing these *energy thieves*, and changing how you are approaching certain aspects of your life such that they are transformed into *positive energy sources*, your mental, emotional, physical health will improve.

Bronwen Edwards

BUILDING RESILIENCE IN CHILDREN

The concept of *resilience* has become a buzzword when it comes to raising young people. There are concerns that young people today are not as resilient as they used to be, or are not resilient enough to cope with the demands and pressures of modern society. When used in this context, resilience refers to the ability of young people to *bounce back* or recover when they are confronted with a challenge or adversity.

Biological models can be very helpful in understanding how the concept of resiliency works. For example, childhood immunisations are well recognised as preventing the spread of serious and potentially life-threatening diseases such as measles or smallpox. Immunisations introduce small doses of disease into the body. The body finds this biologically stressful and develops antibodies in response to this small-scale threat. It is the development of these antibodies that facilitates the body's ability to later resist the much stronger threats from these same diseases. This same concept can be applied to emotional resiliency in young people.

Many current approaches to parenting advocate for a strong focus on young people's strengths and achievements. These approaches are important in helping young people develop a sense of self-efficacy and self-esteem. However, when it comes to resilience, it is equally important that young people learn that they can and will cope when, not if, things do not go their way.

Therefore, key to the development of resilience, is the fact that young people cannot develop it if they do not have any exposure to adversity or challenge. Resiliency cannot be learned by avoiding difficult tasks, or by only ever experiencing success, or by doing things perfectly every time. Like the development of other life skills, resiliency cannot be taught in a classroom or learnt from a book. It can only be developed through lived experience and practice in challenging situations, the thought of which can be just as daunting for parents as it is for some young people!

Resilient thinking

Resilient thinking in young people (and adults) is thinking that is balanced — it is in perspective and in context, and accurately recognises what individuals are able to control in their life (i.e., your thinking and your actions) and what you cannot (i.e., other people, life circumstances, biology). Resilient thinking is helpful for young people in learning to achieve their goals and tasks, and helpful in terms of how it allows the young person to feel about themselves and others.

Resilient thinking is often incompatible with perfectionism. Perfectionists often lack resiliency as they are unable to cope with failure, and attempt to remedy this by either doing things perfectly every time; and often if they can't, they won't attempt the task at all. The resilient thinker sees what the perfectionist sees as failure, as an opportunity to learn more or to do things better next time.

How can you teach resiliency?

Parents, rather than professionals, are in the best position to teach their children skills in resiliency, and to build resiliency. Ideally, you will be the best role model in showing your children how to deal with adversity. Your children will carefully observe, learn and mimic the ways that you deal with situations such as winning and losing, challenging situations, successes and failures. If you only show your children your successes, you run the risk of setting them unrealistic standards that they feel unable to live up to. They may inadvertently learn that losing is not okay and should be hidden and avoided at all costs. Remember, your children are much more likely to absorb the lessons they live and observe, rather than the ones you merely describe. That means you need to show them what to do rather than just telling them. Therefore, in teaching resiliency, it is just as important to show and teach a young person how to struggle, strive, and lose as it is to show them how to win and succeed.

To develop resiliency in your children you will need to provide them with repeated age-appropriate opportunities to succeed, fail, and be challenged. This might be as simple as ensuring that your children don't win every game they participate in. Remember, watching and allowing your children to struggle can be difficult (just as it is difficult to watch your baby be immunised!). However, just because it is difficult to watch, does not mean that it is not useful. While it may not be as enjoyable as watching them succeed, it teaches them a life skill that is just, if not more, important.

Ensuring that your children are well resourced — emotionally, cognitively and in terms of the people in their life, will also promote resiliency. Developing a strong connection to you, others and the community can provide additional resources and serve as a protective factor in helping children develop resiliency.

As a parent or carer, be supportive — be present and coach them through their experiences, their successes and their challenges. Allow them age-appropriate self-determination and self-expression.

In summary, the challenges for parents in raising resilient children who are able to adapt to change and challenge, are in finding the right balance between focusing on positives, building self-esteem and self-efficacy and teaching children how to fail and to view such experiences as an opportunity to develop in ways that were not previously possible without that experience.

Dr Vanessa Spiller

ENHANCING HAPPINESS AND WELLBEING

Happy people live longer and enjoy a greater quality of life. They are less likely to experience depression and, if they do, are likely to both manage it better and get on top of it quicker. They enjoy better quality relationships and more lasting relationships. They are less likely to experience anxiety, stress or anger. In other words, building greater levels of happiness in your life not only serves as a buffer against suffering psychological problems, but also helps you enjoy life more fully.

Of course, being happier within yourself, with others, and with life is not a guarantee of lifelong immunity against encountering psychological problems. We are human, and we all experience the full range of emotions that make us human, including grief, loss, trauma, depression, fears, anxiety and relationship issues. However, if we are happy, we are more resilient and better able to cope when such times inevitably occur. So how can we increase our happiness and wellbeing? How can we create greater happiness when we feel in the pits of despair? Basically the answer is simple, and following are 12 ways that research shows you can use to enhance greater happiness. They are simple but not magical. Applying them may take some effort and practice. If you work at them, then practise them some more, and some more ... you may enjoy each small step toward a happier life.

1. *Be Physically Active.* Research shows that physical exercise is as good, if not better, than medication, in helping to lift your mood. The good news is you don't need to be a super athlete. Just 5–10 minutes per working day of walking, cycling, jogging, swimming, or playing a team sport will help.

2. *Be Socially Outgoing.* The very happiest people have good positive relationships with friends, partners and family. Allocate uninterrupted quality time to those you care for. Actively listen to them, show your affection, and do fun things together.

3. *Be Flexible in Your Thinking.* People run into trouble when they consistently respond to life's challenges in the ways they always have done — such as by becoming depressed, getting anxious or being angry. When next faced with a challenge, think of other possible responses, do something different or experiment with a new option.

4. *Be Passionate.* When we are passionate about something we feel alive, vital, engaged. Our life feels fulfilling and fulfilled. So find the things that attract your interest and absorb you. What would you like to be doing more of in your life? What have you done for fun in the past? How can you do more of that now?

5. *Be Compassionate.* Helping others also helps ourselves. Because we are social beings, being caring, loving and compassionate is good for the person who is offered help, the person helping, and for the community as a whole. Look out for the ways you can give someone a hand, listen to someone in need, offer a genuine smile and engage in acts of random kindness.

6. *Be Focused.* Keeping a clear focus on what is important and avoiding the trivia is an essential wellbeing skill. Learning mindfulness, meditation or relaxation skills can help. Good books and CDs are available but, like learning to drive a car, it may be best to have an experienced person (a meditation teacher or mindfulness-based therapist) sit beside you and show you how.

7. *Be Positive.* Learn to focus on the positives rather than the negatives. One simple but effective way is to reflect on the things for which you are grateful. Keep a notepad beside your bed. Before going to sleep at night, jot down 3 to 5 things you have enjoyed, appreciated or could count as a blessing in your day. Reread the list first thing on awakening. Gradually expand it to 5 to 10 things.

8. *Be a Strength Spotter.* When we are aware of the things we do well and make use of those strengths in our day-to-day lives, life is more fulfilling. Begin by looking for the strengths, skills and qualities you see in other people, then make a list of the strengths you see in yourself. What are you good at? What do you do well? When do feel at your best? How can you do more of those things?

9. *Be a Problem Solver.* People with good problem-solving skills generally cope better with the challenges life inevitably throws our way. Rather than get caught up with the problems (what has happened or who has said what), first look for the solutions (what you would like to see as the solution or outcome) and second, how you might get there (what are the means or pathways you need to follow).

10. *Be a Sensory Seeker.* Our senses put us in contact with the world around us. When depressed or anxious, we become inwardly focused and shut off the pleasurable stimulation offered by our senses. Make a list of the pleasurable sensations you have experienced in the areas of sight, sound, smell, taste and touch. Give yourself the pleasure of doing some of those things daily.

11. *Be More Spiritual.* People with faith, beliefs and good value systems are among the happiest, as well as those who live the longest. This is not so much about being religious, or the particular religion a person may hold to, but perhaps more about being spiritual, thinking beyond the self, having a commitment to good values and engaging with like-minded people.

12 *Behave Happily.* Carefully observe the happy people you know, and start doing the things that they do. Who are the role-models of happiness in your life? What do they do to enhance their happiness? How can you think similar thoughts, experience similar emotions, or behave in similar ways? Practising what they do may lead to greater levels of happiness and well-being for you too.

George Burns

EMOTIONAL INTELLIGENCE

Max manages his emotions; his emotions don't control him. He is aware of how he is feeling at any given time, and can accurately describe those emotions at the right time, in the right way and to the right person. Max readily picks up on the emotional tone of his interactions with others, whether it is a social conversation, a business meeting, or a more intimate interaction, and can use this emotional information to foster genuine and authentic relationships. Max can make the connection between the way he thinks and the way he feels, and can use this information to facilitate positive outcomes for himself and others. In short, Max is emotionally intelligent.

Emotional Intelligence refers to our ability to use emotions and emotional information. Emotions are signals about what is important in our environment and how we respond to these emotions has important implications for how effectively we deal with the events we encounter in our lives. The intelligent use of emotions is critical to a number of very important human endeavors including communication, learning, wellbeing and social relationships.

Emotional Intelligence is comprised of a number of different facets:

1. *Emotional Self-Awareness* — being in tune with your emotional experiences and understanding how emotions influence your outward displays, behaviours and decision-making, and how your emotions influence and affect the people around you.

2. *Emotional Expression* — your ability to accurately describe your emotions to others and to be consistent with your verbal and non-verbal expression of emotions.

3. *Understanding Other's Emotions* — being able to perceive and understand other people's emotions and to accurately interpret other's emotions in a range of contexts.

4. *Emotional Reasoning* — to be able to incorporate emotional information in to problem solving and decision-making.

5. *Emotional Self-Management* — to be able to effectively manage emotions as they arise to maintain adaptive and appropriate mood states.

6. *Emotional Management of Others* — to be able to appropriately and effectively influence the moods and emotions of others.

7. *Emotional Self-Control* — to effectively control strong emotional states that you experience so as to remain productive and resilient.

The key to understanding and developing Emotional Intelligence is to understand the link between cognition (the way we think) and emotion (the way we feel). Emotions are subjective and arise as a result of our interpretations or appraisals of our environment. When we perceive a threat in our environment we feel *fear*; when we perceive an injustice in our environment we feel *angry*; when we perceive a loss in our environment we feel *sad*. Understanding the link between thinking and feeling can help us understand the source of our emotions and gives us a starting point for modifying our emotions if they are unpleasant or unhelpful.

Event → *Thought/Belief Perception* → *Emotional Consequence*

Say, for example, you receive a message from your boss to come to her office. You may think; *Why would she want to see me? — unless the rumours about job cuts are true!*, and this could lead you to feel quite anxious. However, as it turns out, it was only a minor matter that the boss wanted to discuss with you, and as a result you felt very relieved. To avoid such a roller-coaster approach, it is important to use your emotional response to an event to increase awareness of what you are saying to yourself and to realise that you can change the emotion by rethinking your belief or interpretation of the event. Rethinking your interpretation in this example may lead to the thought: *Oh well, no use worrying about it, I'll just go see what she wants.*

In order to enhance your Emotional Intelligence you need to be aware of precisely what you are feeling at any given time. It is important to find your own *emotional balance* so you can allow your emotions to help generate more positive outcomes.

Suggestions for developing Emotional Intelligence:

1. Keep a mood journal to monitor the emotions you experience, the events that triggered particular emotions and what you were thinking at the time.

2. Make time for personal reflection. Consider how your emotions impact on your outward displays and behaviours, your decision-making and the people around you.

3. Develop a tool-kit of emotional management strategies. The three basic approaches to managing emotions are: modify your environment; modify your perceptions; or master other skills.

- Modifying your environment might include taking a different route to work to avoid peak-hour traffic; taking a break from a stressful situation; or re-organising yourself with *to do* lists.

- Remember that our perceptions drive the emotions we feel. Modifying your perceptions of a situation can level your emotional reaction to it. Ask yourself: *Is this thought reasonable? Would my colleagues/family/friends agree or disagree with it?*

- Mastering other skills involves accepting that some things are the way they are; that we may not like or agree with it, but we can live with it. Skills that may help are breathing exercises, meditation and yoga.

4. Build your immunity. Get good rest and sleep. Reduce caffeine intake. Get regular exercise. Eat a balanced diet. Find your work–life balance. Do something for yourself every day. Invest time in the important people in your life. Practise positive and realistic self-talk.

The benefits of developing *Emotional Intelligence* are significant. People who demonstrate emotionally intelligent behaviours also engage in more productive coping strategies, are less susceptible to stress, demonstrate fewer problem behaviours (e.g., depression, anxiety, aggression), have enhanced wellbeing, have greater life satisfaction, form and maintain quality interpersonal relationships and are more likely to achieve their academic and career potential.

Summary

Developing Emotional Intelligence is not complicated, but it does require awareness, patience and practice. Being emotionally intelligent is not about being more emotional or less emotional. It's not the emotion that you experience that is important, but what you do with the emotion that counts.

Dr Karen Hansen and Barbara Lloyd

ENHANCING MOTIVATION IN YOUR CHILD

Motivation is important for students' enjoyment of school, achievement, educational aspirations, and future life pathways. *Motivation is the energy and drive to learn, work effectively, and achieve at schoolwork — and the thoughts and behaviours that reflect this energy and drive.* This last part is important to understanding motivation. First, it indicates that motivation happens in the head — it is what children think, believe, expect, and assume about school, schoolwork, teachers, and themselves. Second, it indicates that motivation is also what children do, such as their effort, planning, management, persistence and so on. Thus, to motivate children we need to look at what they think and what they do.

It is also vital that we give our children very specific motivational information, advice, encouragement, direction, and support. This is where the *Motivation and Engagement Wheel* (www.lifelongachievement.com) is useful. The Wheel separates motivation into three broad groups: *boosters, mufflers*, and *guzzlers* (or the *good, the bad, and the ugly* of motivation). Boosters increase motivation. Mufflers impede motivation — they hold children back from potential. Guzzlers reduce motivation. Boosters are: self-belief, valuing school, learning focus, planning, task management, and persistence. Mufflers are: anxiety, fear of failure, low control. Guzzlers are: self-sabotage and disengagement.

If your child is not motivated, your aim is to increase the boosters and reduce the mufflers and guzzlers. If your child is travelling well, your aim is to keep the high boosters high and keep the low mufflers and guzzlers low. Following are some tips for each part of the Motivation and Engagement Wheel:

Increasing boosters (the good):

Self-belief

- Challenge your child's negative thinking with some optimistic common-sense — for example, a poor result is not the end of the world; rather, it indicates what needs improvement next time.

- Encourage your child to recognise the many (small) ways they can succeed in a day and a week — for example, spending an extra 30 minutes reading can be a success and a basis for self-belief.

Valuing school

- Identify ways that school, school subjects, skills learnt at school, and even social connections are relevant to life and can help us in many ways — now and in the future.
- Look for opportunities to show your child that you value school — this includes attending school events through to being responsive to any academic issues that arise.

Learning focus

- Focus on the journey (e.g., effort, learning, skill development, improving from mistakes, understanding) more than the destination (e.g., marks, ranks, pecking orders).
- Increase the emphasis on personal bests (PBs) and reduce the focus on comparisons with others.

Persistence

- Encourage your child to set clear and achievable goals and to monitor his/her progress towards them — these help sustain motivation through a task.
- Talk to your child about effective help seeking — e.g., in a difficult task, identify what they do and do not know, and ask the teacher some sensible and focused questions to assist.

Planning

- Encourage your child to get it clear in his/her mind what the task is asking, dedicate some time thinking out how to do it, and outline the plan to do it.
- While doing the task, monitor progress against the plan.

Task management

- Look at how to do homework and study under helpful conditions — for example, turn off the television and remove other distractions, ensure sufficient light and space, and have appropriate materials for the task.
- Manage study and homework time better — for example, do not leave things too late into the night, prioritise important or large tasks in each study or homework session, and have a weekly and daily homework/study timetable.

Reducing mufflers (the bad):

Anxiety

- Identify an effective relaxation technique that works for your child — for example, exercise, meditation, yoga, and Tai Chi. This helps reduce general anxiety/arousal and develops your child's ability to quickly relax him/herself.

- Because much school anxiety revolves around test anxiety, get some common-sense resources with tips to help prepare for tests and exams.

Low sense of control

- Encourage your child to reduce their focus on things outside their control (e.g., good/bad luck, easy/tough marking).

- Encourage your child to focus on three things that are in their control: effort (how hard they work), strategy (the way they do that work), and attitude (what they think about that work and themselves).

Fear of failure

- Reduce your child's fear of failure by having them see that failure provides information about how to improve. Failure is not a reflection on them as a person.

- Make it clear to your child that if he or she does not do well after trying hard, this usually means they need to develop more effective study and school-work skills — that is, it is the quality rather than the quantity that needs some work. This is in their control. It does not mean that they are dumb.

Reducing guzzlers (the ugly):

Self-sabotage (e.g., procrastination)

- Encourage your child to see that effort is a determinant of improvement — trying hard does not reflect poorly on their ability or intelligence.

- Try to reduce the link between your child's worth and his or her achievement — thus, poor performance does not mean he/she is a bad or useless person — it simply reflects on the behaviours (often insufficient study) that led to that poor result.

Disengagement

(Many of the above strategies will also be needed to address the causes of disengagement).

- Connect and communicate with the school to develop a coherent school–home approach (also, ask what ways you can help the school help your child).

- Identify any skills that need attention immediately and in the medium to longer term for example, literacy, numeracy, handwriting.

- Connect with relevant professionals and practitioners if necessary (e.g., guidance personnel, psychologists, paediatricians, occupational therapists, tutors).

Every student can learn to improve, work more effectively, become more interested in schoolwork, and strive to achieve their potential. There are many straightforward strategies that parents and students can use to enhance motivation and to maintain motivational strengths.

Dr Andrew Martin

CREATIVITY TO GET THROUGH THE TOUGH STUFF

Of all the neuroscience research findings during the past decade, few have been as precious as those about creative intelligence. We now know how our creative brain works, that we are born with infinite amounts of creative intelligence, that it's natural for us to be creative, and that our individual creative brain profile is as unique as our DNA. We also have a clearer understanding of how our creative brain recognises, optimises and profiles our creativity powers, and how we can apply creative, problem-solving techniques to our everyday life.

Additionally, it's been discovered why almost two thirds of today's adults use only a minute proportion of the creativity they used as a child; and we can also dispel many of the creative myths, mysteries and misunderstandings that still negate a broader use of creativity throughout the world.

Are you consciously creative? Does being creative come naturally to you? Do you regularly experience the empowering satisfaction of using your own creativity to get through the rough stuff, or solve problems, or bring your dreams, goals or aspirations to reality? Or do you fit into the largest segment of research participants whose responses included: *I'm definitely not creative; I am bereft of creative powers; As a kid I was highly creative, but it dried up during my teens; I'm too shy or too scared to express my creativity because my school teachers and bosses failed to help me recognise my creativity, praise or reward my attempts to be creative;* or *I have no imagination because I never come up with new ideas.*

People often make these statements to colleagues, family and to themselves; however, none of them are probably valid. The reality is more people than not, sense that their creative powers just *evaporated* after childhood. The good news is they haven't, and our creative powers can be *reignited* and optimised at any time from our teens into our twilight years. To help you quickly reignite your creative powers, it will help you to know why such a small percentage of today's adults still use the creative powers they used as a child, and why so many of us wrongly believe that our childhood creative powers have evaporated, diminished or disappeared.

The answer is that for the first four or five years of our childhood, most of us are encouraged and often rewarded by our parents, relatives and friends for being creative and expressing our creative cleverness. However, from the moment we are placed in childcare or pre-school, we begin to be taught what to do, how to live, what is right and what is wrong.

We are trained to accept other people telling us what to do and to follow rules and systems without being told why. We are rarely invited or empowered to think for ourselves, or be creative, and often our efforts to think outside the square and dare to be different are met with considerable criticism and even punishment. Due to this social conditioning, our brain processes have become so restricted that when we do occasionally drift outside the box, it either doesn't work, or comes out so horribly our belief system receives further proof that we are not creative. And we just give up trying to be creative.

Creativity:

- The first step to recognising and reigniting your creativity is to remove the words *I am not creative* from your vocabulary. They no longer exist. Then ask yourself — *What kind of natural creative talent did I have as a kid? How can I reignite my creative powers? How can I create a better life?* Be honest with yourself and take a few minutes to think about it deeply. Then write down what comes up. Hold on tight to what you discover because this is precious. This is the key that will allow you to reignite and optimise your creative self.

- Understand that each successful creative project undergoes a specific wholebrain process beginning with emotion/desire (upper right brain — defining *what I want and when*). Step 2 is conceptual/imagination (lower right brain — *what I want it to look like, feel like, sound like*). Step 3 is rational/functional (lower left brain — *how it will work and how I can afford it*). Step 4 is practical/delivery (*upper left brain — how I construct/assemble the parts prior to my creation delivery*). And Step 5 is satisfaction/joy (limbic system — *the treasured ecstasy and elation I feel at having given life to my wonderful creation*). Within those parameters you can create any outcome you desire within your defined deadline.

- To commence each successful creative project, take a large sheet of paper and on the left-hand side define your desired outcome, goal, dream or aspiration in handwriting. On the far right-hand side write your deadline for which you want it to become reality. Then draw a straight line (critical pathway) between your desired outcome and deadline, and along that line write your conceptual, rational and practical *to do* milestones and notes. By doing this you will quickly learn to apply simple, practical and measurable steps in utilising your creative powers to solve problems, and even manage many of your creative challenges simultaneously.

- Try to pinpoint successful and satisfied people who are creative problem-solvers; who no longer just *make* things or *copy* what others have made. These people don't wait for things to happen and even in the face of adversity, they recognise their unique creative powers and apply them to define what they want, when they want it, why they want it, where they want it, how to conceptualise it; what it will look like, feel and sound like, how practical, viable and feasible it will be and how each creation will satisfy them.

- Immediately dispel the myth that creative geniuses are found only in traditional fields such as writing, theatre, art, dance, design, film, events, media, music or entertainment. Research clearly identifies today's creative hotshots are just as likely to be found in the trades, business, finance, sports, retail, hospitality, IT, mental health services, medicine, military, research, banking, home parenting, ecology, lifestyle, spirituality, health, science, law enforcement and personal relationships. They are creative because they are motivated to be creative and make more creative effort.

- Keep in mind that each of us is creatively stronger in some areas than others. Although our whole brain wants us to be creative, our creative intelligence is a process that we cannot reignite by sheer force. Initially it may seem slow, but eventually, through patient cultivation, it will become a natural way of being. It's only after you complete each creative project that you'll realise that the experience of being able to explore countless unexplored parts of your brain is as empowering, intoxicating and satisfying as anything you'll experience in your life.

- Encourage your educators and bosses to introduce employee creative training programs that will help identity your personal creative intelligence profile, and recognise and reward your creative performance learning, project management and self-expression.

- Just coming up with ideas does not mean that we are creative. Anyone can come up with ideas, but if these ideas are not relevant, meaningful and intelligent to our desired outcome and deadline, then these ideas have zero value. Practice coming up with relevant ideas.

- The lack of creativity in our lives can make us feel empty, so our creative time is now! Believe that your creative powers can solve almost any problem. Deep down we all crave to be considered creative, so the more creative we try to be, the more naturally creative we'll become.

- Never forget that everyone has the creative intelligence and cognitive skills to become creative director of their own destiny. The more creative you think you are the more creative you'll become. Being creative will also allow you to touch your mind and heart and discover what you really stand for. And above all, your creativity will help you create a fulfilling life.

Embrace your creativity and be free to be whatever you want to be!

Lloyd Bond

ASSERTIVENESS

When you are faced with a communication problem with someone, you have various ways to react. You may choose to react in a *passive* way, where you say and do nothing. Unfortunately, this response may cause you to internalise your hurt, and increase your feelings of anxiety. If you decide to react *aggressively* you may make the situation worse, and even destroy the relationship with the person you are having difficulties with. The next option is the most effective, that is, to react in an *assertive* way. When using assertiveness you demonstrate respect for the other person, as well as towards yourself.

What is assertiveness?

Assertiveness demonstrates two concepts. It's not just being honest and respectful when you communicate with someone else, but is also linked to your own self-respect and beliefs about yourself. If you tolerate disrespectful or abusive behaviour, you are not being respectful towards yourself.

How can I develop assertiveness skills?

First, write a list of assertive-building skills you would like to achieve. In your list, aim for about 10 or more skills. For example, you might write: "changing an appointment time, reducing the amount of times you say *sorry* during the day, saying *no* to others, expressing an opposing opinion, speaking up during a meeting at work". All these are assertive-building tasks, and some are easier to achieve than others.

Assertiveness list

Once you have written your list, put them in order, starting from the easiest to achieve, to the hardest. Now work your way through each task, starting at the easiest task. You need to also reward yourself when you have completed a task. Work your way down your list, increasing the degree of difficulty. With each small victory your self-worth will grow, your self-respect will increase, and boundaries will be defined and reinforced. Set a reasonable timeframe in which to achieve your tasks.

Assertiveness program

During the first month, reduce the amount of times you say *sorry* to people. In the second month, say *no* to unreasonable requests at work. And in the third month speak up at a meeting at work, by saying one or two sentences.

Continue practising these tasks until you achieve the skills, rewarding yourself as you go. You will be amazed at how you will develop these skills. Most people fail to develop assertiveness skills because they try and do it all at once, or attempt the hardest task first. Don't start working on your hardest task. If you attempt a difficult task initially, you may find yourself failing, and this may discourage you from continuing.

Broken record technique

When you say *no* to a respectful person who has healthy boundaries they will usually accept your refusal or limit-setting. However, some people won't accept your refusal, and will exert pressure on you to give in and change your *no* to a *yes*. They will induce guilt feelings that distract and distress you, leading you to back down and agreeing to their demands. You need to be prepared, and to use a technique called the broken record technique. The broken record technique is a very useful and powerful tool. Once you have mastered it, you will find yourself feeling more confident and less likely to be manipulated by guilt.

Let's have a look at how it works — You take a short sentence and repeat it until the other person hears what you are saying, or you both reach an agreement. You must continue repeating the sentence. It's also helpful to change a few words around so it doesn't sound too parrot-like. If someone asked you to babysit for them tonight, and you want to be assertive and decline, use the broken record technique. What you might say is:

- *No, I am not available to help with babysitting tonight.* (Repeat, if they try to pressure you.)

- *No, I can't help you tonight.* (Repeat this if necessary, and don't justify or answer any *why* questions they may resort to.)

- *No, I'm not free to help you tonight.*

If you want to add an acknowledgment of their situation to soften your reply, you have the option of saying something like, *I can see it is a problem for you to find a babysitter at short notice, but I am unable to help you.* At this point refrain from saying *I'm sorry.* It is not your fault. When using this technique it keeps you on track, and greatly reduces the likelihood of you giving long explanations. Just make your statement, and keep repeating it. If the person asks you why you can't help with the babysitting tonight don't answer the *why* question. Just repeat the broken record sentence. Don't answer any *why* questions, as these questions are designed to elicit an excuse that they can argue against to entice you to give in. Remember you *do not* have to justify yourself.

Body language

Assertiveness is not only about words, it is also about your body language. Practise looking the person in the eye, don't avoid eye contact, but don't stare either. Avoid crossing your arms or slouching, stand up straight. This demonstrates confidence and firmness. Practising in front of a mirror is helpful, or with one of your friends.

Anne Evans-Murray

MANAGING FINANCIAL CHALLENGES

Financial challenges can occur to anyone. Money issues affect people from all walks of life: some people don't earn enough, many spend more money than they make, and others don't know what to do with the money they have.

There are two aspects to managing finances: *emotional* and *practical*. Often the emotional side of money is overlooked, therefore making the practical side of money, such as budgeting and saving, harder to achieve.

The important keys to being in control of your finances on an emotional level are belief and commitment. Many people create a budget to get on track, but unless there is belief that they can change their habits and a commit to creating a better financial position, all the budgets in the world may not help.

Belief will come once you have an understanding of your current relationship with money. When you can see the events that shaped your money personality, it will become clear to you as to what needs to change. Once you know what needs to change, your attitude towards money will transform and you will start to believe that you can make the changes required.

Often our attitude towards money is formed while we are growing up. Sometimes events in our lives as adults will tarnish the way we think about money. Once you have explored the reasons why your finances are not in order, you can start to create a new attitude and belief about money and the way you will treat it.

So, before you do that budget, perhaps you could ask yourself the following emotional money questions:

- What do I recall from my childhood about money?
- Was money a positive experience or a negative one?
- What are the positive and negative things I learned from my parents and society about money?
- Are there people in my life now who influence the way I treat my money?
- Have those experiences in the past influenced the way I manage my money as an adult?

- What can change immediately about the way I manage my money?

You cannot change your past ... but you can change your opinion of it

The questions above will give you a good idea of how your money habits and attitudes have formed. If your experience was perhaps a negative one, don't despair. This has presented you with a great opportunity for learning lessons and making changes. In order to change these habits, you now need to create a commitment to do so.

Commitment means being prepared to take the time necessary to create change. With any great achievement in life, there must be commitment. Sometimes we are not ready for the change, and it is important to recognise this for what it is and admit to ourselves that perhaps this is not the time. To ascertain if you are ready to commit to change, ask yourself these questions to determine your level of commitment:

- Am I able to invest time in myself?
- Am I willing to take time consistently to do the work required?
- Am I willing to take responsibility for myself?
- Am I able to examine my life honestly?
- Am I willing to change habits that are limiting me?

On the practical side of money there are some important points to take action on:

Become a conscious spender — being aware of where your money goes is the most important aspect of financial management. This means being conscious about your everyday purchases. Write down your purchases in a spending journal, or at least keep the receipts of your purchases and make 10 minutes at the end of each day to compile these.

Know your triggers — Spending money is often about being, not buying. We spend money to get a feeling. If you find yourself with the urge to splurge, think about why you are experiencing that feeling. Are you buying things to fill a void? If you suddenly find yourself wandering aimlessly around a shopping mall — ask yourself; *What was I feeling before I arrived here?* Perhaps it was boredom, loneliness, or unhappiness, and if so, is there something else you can do to counteract that feeling, other than shopping? Perhaps going for a walk, or calling to chat with a special friend.

Pay plan — Even if you don't do a budget, try doing a plan of your pay every single payday. Set yourself 20 minutes the night before your pay comes in to write down your income plus any money in the bank. Work out all of your expenses until the next payday. The two most important things about this process is that you must write it down (not just do it in your head), and make sure that you put every expense you can think of (even include things like coffee, lunches, phone recharge).

Pre-pay bills — It is far easier to find a small amount every payday than a large amount every three months. Try to pre-pay your bills directly into the bill. That way, when you receive the bill it will be paid for or even slightly in credit. If you can't do this with all your bills, just choose the ones that create a problem when they do come in. For example — car registration each year is approx $700. If you paid this each fortnightly pay, you would only have to pay approx $27 towards this … a much easier feat than finding $700!

Prioritise — If you have a number of debts, and many people do, it is vital to prioritise who you pay. This can be difficult when you are the one in the middle of emotional distress. The best tack is to get an outsider to assist you, preferably a financial counsellor, who can help prioritise and assist you to discuss your situation with your creditors.

Be informed — before deciding on a course of action to solve your money challenges, be sure to obtain an opinion from an impartial professional. A financial counsellor will help to explore all of the options available, and then assist you to execute the option most suitable for your and your situation.

Be accountable — top sportspeople and business people all have coaches. Find someone who is good with money to be your coach. Be accountable to that person for keeping on top of your finances. After doing this for a while it will become a habit and you will then do it for yourself.

Get help — don't be afraid to ask for help. There are great financial counselling organisations available throughout the country. Some of them are a free service to the public and do not have any affiliations with financial institutions or products. It is vital to obtain impartial and independent information if you are in financial distress. There are often answers that you might not have thought of or know about.

Take heart — it is worth remembering that you are not the only one experiencing financial difficulty. There are lots and lots of people who, at different stages in their lives, have discovered they were flat broke or not in control of their finances. Don't waste precious time regretting decisions you made to get here. The task now is to reposition yourself in order to achieve your goals in the future.

Cate Turton

CONFIDENCE AND SELF-ESTEEM

Being confident and having positive self-esteem makes life and dealing with life circumstances easier. People like to associate with confident, happy and successful people. If a person lacks confidence and has low self-esteem, what can they do to develop confidence and become optimistic and positive about themselves and what they do?

The following is a list of strategies and behaviours that will assist to develop confidence.

1. *What's in your name?* Write your name on a page and then write a positive word about you beginning with each of the letters e.g., PAUL = **P**ositive, **A**ccepting, **U**nderstanding, **L**ikeable.

2. *Finish the following with five different responses:* I am glad that I am me because …

3. *Self-Talk.* The positive and negative things we say to ourselves. What we say to ourselves influences our performance and behaviour. Touch each finger to your thumb (up and back) as fast as you can using both hands. While doing this say to yourself *I can't do this, I am hopeless at this, I've never been quick with my hands* and note your performance. Now say *I can do this, I am good at this, I have always been good with my hands* and note your performance. What you say to yourself affects you. We choose to think positively or not and need to practice positive self-talk. Some examples of positive self-talk are: *I am confident, I am a capable person, I can do this, I am calm and relaxed, Everything will be alright.*

4. *Dealing with killer statements.* Part of our confidence can be killed off by other people's negative comments. A way of dealing with negative killer statements is to use self-talk and to say the following to yourself: No matter what you do or say to me I remain a confident person.

5. *Responding to compliments.* There are three ways we can respond to positive statements made by others: A. Ignore it, believing that the person didn't really mean it; B. Say *Thank-you*; or C. Say *Thank-you* and turning the compliment into reinforcing positive self-talk. The last one is best. Example:

Compliment: Gee that is a nice outfit you are wearing. Response:; *Thank you* and say to yourself, Yes this is a nice outfit and I feel good in it.

6. *Confidence and self-esteem are linked to physical appearance self-concept.* (how good-looking we perceive we are and how much we like our appearance). Take pride in your appearance and make sure that you always look as good as you can. Accentuate your assets and dress down your blemishes. Dress confidently.

7. *Act confidently and be prepared.* Confidence breeds confidence. Say hello to at least three strangers every day for a week and observe what happens. Just say, *Good morning, how is your day looking?* And see what follows. A confident person is a prepared person. For example, if you have a job interview or need to have a difficult conversation with another person make sure you are prepared and have thought through how you would like things to progress. Have a trial with a friend and go over what you want to say.

8. *Children's self-esteem is closely aligned to their physical appearance.* Children are particularly susceptible and vulnerable to negative comments from siblings and their peer group, especially when the comments are focused on aspects of their physical appearance. For children and adolescents, parents should do all that they can to stop siblings saying negative things about physical appearance. When the negative statements come from peers, children should use the strategy described in 4 above.

Dr Paul Burnett

PROBLEM SOLVING AND DECISION MAKING

Problem solving and decision making are two of the most common and important things that an individual is required to do in modern day life. Your ability to successfully complete these skills (on a daily basis) is a huge determinant of how successful you will be in your life, and in the goals that you set for yourself. Below are a number of tips and techniques to aid you in effective problem solving and decision making within your life:

1. Remember to press the pause button, and to give yourself a time limit to obtain as much information as possible before making a decision. Aim to be somewhere in the middle on this continuum. Some people spend too much time gathering information, while others don't spend long enough gathering information.

2. When making a decision, realise that you will never have all the available information in front of you to make a definitive decision. Be comfortable with this fact. Remember not making a decision, is still making a decision. At this point in time (when you are in a position to make an informed decision), the important thing is that you make a decision, that is your own and not someone else's.

3. A lot of people dislike making decisions and prefer others to make decisions for them. Refrain from this behaviour as much as possible. There is a lot of growth to be had in making your own decisions. By all means, discuss different courses of action with other people, just make sure that you are the one making the decision in the end.

4. Use your intuition when problem solving and making decisions. Studies have found that we use our gut feeling to make effective decisions. We use reason and rationale later on to justify the decision that we have already made.

5. Don't rush into making a decision. If there is not a clear answer, then don't force one. Sometimes taking 24 hours or a weekend to make a decision is a useful idea. If an idea still makes sense at the start of the next day or week, then usually it is the correct option.

6. Develop a list of pros and cons when making a decision. Alternatively, identify what the key issues are that should be taken into consideration when making the decision.

7. Remember to play the devil's advocate or get someone to play this role for you. This usually involves thinking about all the things that could go wrong if a certain decision is reached.

8. Remember the Pareto principle; 80% of output is derived from 20% input. Remember not to overanalyse things. Identify the issues at hand and make a decision.

9. It is also important to think outside the box when analysing problems. It is sometimes referred to as changing your context. You can do this in a number of different ways. For example, change physical locations, or get a completely different perspective from someone who know. Remember to be creative.

10. Instead of focusing on the what, try focusing on the why. Why is this a problem for me? Instead of what needs to happen.

Mark Korduba

LIVING THE LIFE YOU WANT

This topic has been dealt with in numerous self-help books and textbooks and essentially comes down to identifying what you want in life (i. e., goals) and identifying how to reach them, along with living your life with gratitude and happiness. Below are a number of tips and techniques to help you to identify what you want in life, and how to generally improve your levels of gratitude and happiness:

1. Identify what your three or four most important values are in life. Values may include; importance of friends/family, being creative, career/finances, thinking outside the square or doing your own thing. Then it is up to you to live your life in accordance with these values.

2. Identify two or three important life areas that you want to focus on in the next 6–12 months. For example; work, family, friends, finances, career, romance, health and fitness. Remember that you can't focus on them all at once, so you need to prioritise.

3. Set three medium term goals, based around the life areas that you have identified above. Ensure your goals are SMARTER. (S)pecific, (M)easurable, (A)ttractive, (R)ealistic, (T)ime-framed, (E)cological, (R)eason. What are the specifics of the goal? How are you going to measure your achievement of the goal? How attractive is the goal? How realistic is the goal? By when do you want to achieve the goal? Who in your environment (e.g., friends/family) is going to help/hinder your progress towards the goal? Why do you want to achieve this goal? Remember to write the goals down and review them regularly.

4. Set weekly action plans that will help to propel you towards your goals.

5. Remember to review your progress regularly. Do this either weekly or monthly. You may find that you will need to adjust your goals or create new ones. This is ok and part of the process.

6. To improve your happiness, before going to bed at nighttime, think of three positive things that happened to you that day.

7. To improve motivation towards achieving your goals you may want to think about making your goals public. One way of doing this is to tell a few of your closest friends and family about your goal or to have a sponsor who you check in regularly with; someone who will keep you on track with your goals.

8. An important part of the process is renewal of your energies. Every 10–12 weeks it is recommended that you have a mental health day. This is a day which you devote to you. For example, you may want to go to a day spa, watch a movie, go to the beach. It is also very important that you take regular holidays. They should be taken every 15 weeks or so for at least 1 week.

9. Celebrate your wins. It is very important that you have milestones, which you celebrate on the path towards your longer-term goals. It is very important that you enjoy both the process as well as the outcome.

Mark Korduba

LAUGHTER

We all know that laughing makes us feel great and helps us connect with others. But did you know that laughter has a positive impact on physical, psychological and social health and wellbeing? We are all born with the ability to laugh. It's the in-built outward expression of happiness and joy. It crosses all language barriers, is found in all cultures, and is an important tool for early physical and emotional development.

The Greek philosopher Aristotle viewed laughter as a bodily exercise precious to health. Research suggests that laughter seems to reduce pain after surgery and indicates that when it comes to complimentary and preventative health and wellbeing, laughter has an ever increasing list of positive benefits. Seeking out positive experiences that make us laugh can do a lot for our physiology and helps us stay well. Even the anticipation of laughter has surprising and significant positive effects.

While researchers agree that laughter is important for good health, they also acknowledge that, given the proven benefits of laughter on physical, psychological and social health and wellbeing, and the fact that we all have the ability to laugh, laughter and laughing continue to remain much underutilised health and wellbeing strategies, and for all the reasons listed below, we all could add more laughter to our daily lives.

Physically, laughter:

- boosts the immune system.
- improves circulation.
- reduces the risk of heart disease and reduces blood pressure.
- provides a good work out for the heart and lungs.
- reduces pain.
- raises good cholesterol.
- provides a gentle aerobic work out.
- reduces the blood glucose levels of those with type 2 diabetes.

Socially, laughter:

- helps us bond with others.
- improves relationships.
- increases social tolerance.

Psychologically, laughter:

- reduces stress and anger.
- alleviates anxiety.
- relaxes the mind and body.
- helps us think more clearly and creatively.
- increases resilience and adds joy to our lives.

Do you laugh enough? Just 15 minutes of laughter per day helps maintain good health. The benefits gained from laughing continue long after the laughter has subsided so laughing in short busts, a minute here, two minutes there, is all that's needed.

Do you get your 15 minutes a day? If not, you may like to try the following tips:

Smile more: Not only does smiling make you feel happy, the more you smile, the more likely you are to laugh. As long as your smile includes the muscles around your eyes your brain can't tell if it's a fake or a real smile and will begin to produce the chemicals and proteins associated with happiness. So go ahead, wipe that smile ON your face.

Discover what makes you laugh: We all laugh at different things. Discover what works for you, it could be a funny movie, a particular type of comedy, a radio show, a good friend, the list is endless, and make sure you have more of it, or them, in your life.

Start a happy conversation: Instead of asking people how their day was, start your conversation by asking, what made you laugh today? When people ask you how your day has been make sure the first thing you tell them is something that made you smile or giggle.

Spend more time with people who make you laugh: Did you know that emotions are contagious? Spend less time with those who drain your energy and more time with people who make you smile and laugh.

Don't take yourself so seriously: Shirley McLean once said that a person who can laugh at themselves will never cease to be amused. Try to find the humour in all the things that happen during your day and allow them to make you laugh out loud, or at the very least raise a giggle.

Create a positive environment: The places where we spend our days have a huge impact on the way we feel. Be creative by adding a few things that make you laugh to your home and workplace.

Learn from the children: Rediscover your sense of childlike play, your inner child. Set aside a few minutes a day, or, depending on where you find your fun, a couple of hours each week, to do something that you really enjoy, something that makes you smile and laugh, and every now and then simply play like children. It really is a lot of fun!

Join a local laughter club: Research shows that you are more likely to laugh if you are with others who are laughing. Find out where your local laughter club meets and go along.

Be conscious of your laughter: Several times a day ask yourself, Have I laughed today? If the answer is no, put on a smile and allow yourself to giggle. You could simply stop, take a deep breath, hold if for a few seconds and then laugh the breath out. Just a short burst of laughter for laughter's sake can make the world of difference to the way your feel, the way you interact with others and to your general health and wellbeing.

Practice, practice, practice: The more you practice something, the easier it becomes. Practice smiling and laughing, when ever and where ever you can. Put on your biggest grin, giggle to yourself, smile and say hi to those you pass in the street. When you're out in public you might even like to try the laughter phone. Put your phone (or your fist if you don't have a mobile phone) to your ear, pretend that you're listening to the funniest thing you've ever heard and laugh out loud. Passersby will assume that you're laughing with someone else and you might be surprised by their happy reactions.

Remember that it only takes 15 minutes of laughter a day to have a positive impact on your health and wellbeing and every bit of laughter, real laughter, practice laughter, even fake laughter counts. You really can laugh your way to a healthier, happier you!

Bronwyn Roberts

PERFECTIONISM

What is perfectionism?

Perfection is being without fault or error. Perfectionism is the pursuit of perfection or high standards that are either unachievable, or unachievable on a regular basis. Perfectionists often base their value and worth on their ability to meet those standards. These standards are sometimes referred to as unrelenting standards because they are usually continual and rarely or briefly satisfied. Perfectionists commonly apply these standards to themselves, their performance, and to other people. Perfectionists may not necessarily be perfectionistic in all areas of their life.

Common signs of perfectionism:

- Setting standards that are consistently higher than others.
- Setting standards that are unachievable or rarely achievable.
- Setting standards or expectations that are inflexible even in the face of conflicting information e.g., I must get an A, even though only one person in the class will get an A.
- Deciding your worth based on achieving these standards.
- Difficulty finishing tasks as the product or performance is never good enough.
- Avoiding mistakes and hiding them when they occur.
- Procrastination or not starting things at all due to fear of not meeting standards.
- Having to do things the right way and seeing others as doing it the wrong way.
- Attempting to change other people to meet your expectations.

Problems with perfectionism

There is nothing inherently wrong with setting high standards. Having high standards becomes problematic however when they are not achievable or are only achievable at great cost and lead to a range of problems. Your productivity and sense of achievement are enhanced when you do things well. This is very different from having to do well to be worthwhile, good enough or adequate. The former brings satisfaction, but the latter often leads to temporary relief followed by a range of problems including:

- Regularly feeling anxious, stressed and under pressure.

- Feeling exhausted, out of control, and overwhelmed.

- Performance anxiety.

- Not having enough free time.

- Not starting things due to fear of failing or not doing well enough.

- Decreased productivity.

- Difficulties with other people.

- Low self-esteem.

- Fear of criticism.

- Vulnerability to depression.

- Anger or frustration toward others for not performing up to standard, resulting in isolation from others and relationship problems.

How does one become a perfectionist?

There is no single answer to this question. Some perfectionists only recall praise when they achieved highly, others received punishment if they didn't achieve high enough, and others observed their parents being perfectionistic. Regardless of how it developed, perfectionists have developed high expectations because of one or more of the following:

- They think this is what others expect of them and they will only obtain approval or affirmation of their worth if they comply.

- They think this is what others expect of them and failure to comply will lead to criticism, judgement or getting into trouble.

- They expect these standards of themself, to judge themself as good enough, adequate or worthwhile. This is often to compensate for their perception that they are not good enough, adequate or worthwhile.

But I know I can do better, I have done it before. This may be true but can you achieve to that level on a regular basis? Think for a moment of elite sports men and women. Most individuals or teams only reach their best once or a few times a year.

But I don't want to be a slacker or lazy. This is referred to as black and white thinking — I either aim high and do it right or I am slack, sloppy, lazy. Plenty of people are not perfectionists but still achieve highly, and perform important roles.

But shouldn't I aim to do everything just right? No one has the time, energy or talent to do everything just right or perfectly. When we try to do everything as perfectly as possible, devoting the same attention and energy on the inconsequential things as we do on the really important things, the result is practically nothing gets done and the really important things may not even be started. Does a surgeon have to cook their dinner perfectly, drive perfectly, talk perfectly, and iron their clothes perfectly or without error?

Basic tips for changing perfectionism:

- Accept your humanness as nothing is without flaw, and to err is human.

- Give yourself permission to make mistakes and view them as opportunities to learn.

- Accept that perfection is usually a matter of opinion, so how perfect a thing is depends a great deal on who is judging it. No matter how well we do anything there will always be someone who thinks it could have been done better or differently.

- Adjust your standards e.g., aim for 80-85% or for what is sustainable on a regular basis.

- Set goals and standards for yourself that lead to a sense of fulfilment and satisfaction rather than frustration, blame, and dissatisfaction.

- Learn to enjoy your experiences, rather than being preoccupied with the end result.

- Aim for your daily best rather than your absolute best i.e., doing your best on any given day is not the same as being at your absolute best that may only occur from time to time.

- Avoid the over usage of words such as "should" and "must".

- Recognise your worth is due to more than just your achievements.

- Avoid labels such as "worthless" and "inadequate".

- Accept people for who they are rather than trying to change them to what you expect them to be.

Ask yourself:

- Are my standards flexible, and are they achievable on a regular basis?

- Are my standards causing me problems and would my life improve if I lowered them even to small degree?

- If I aim for perfection, how do I know when I get there?

- Whoever said I had to be perfect?

- If you are still not convinced, weigh up the pros and cons of perfectionism, and the pros and cons of having more flexible standards.

- If the above sounds too hard, give yourself time to change and start with changes in one area of your life first.

Paul Rushton

HOME ORGANISATION — AVOIDING CLUTTER

Clutter seems to be part of everyday life. We live in a society where the acquisition of things is supposed to make us feel good, feel affluent and abundant, but its effect on us can be quite the opposite.

Clutter is an unnecessary excess of possessions in proportion to the amount of available storage space. Clutter does not necessarily mean untidy or dirty. Clutter can make us physically and emotionally sick! Four in ten people say they feel anxious, guilty or depressed when their home is cluttered and nearly 90% of homes have at least one cluttered room, and many of us are worried that our kids will inherit our clutter.

Clutter falls into four categories:

- *Emotional Clutter* — these are items with sentimental meaning but little financial value.

- *Just-In-Case clutter* — these are things with little or no sentimental value but are kept because they might come in handy one day.

- *Bargain Clutter* — these items are acquired on sale, from friends or family or for free which are discarded very reluctantly because they were so cheap.

- *Trend Clutter* — these are impulse purchases, often acquired recently, at a high price and that never end up being used.

Tips to Avoid Clutter:

- Make sure your belongings are equal to, or less than the space you have to store them.

- Ensure your environment is functional and suits your family, rather than just looking neat.

- Create rules so each member of your household is responsible for their own belongings.

- Don't hang onto items just for the sake of it; holding on to, too much stuff that might possibly be used in the future can prevent us from living in the present.

- If you have an item that evokes strong emotional feelings, are you truly honouring and cherishing this item? If it is sitting under a pile of clutter in a dusty box, what value are you really placing on it?

- Just because something was a gift you don't have to keep it. If it is a gift that is in good condition but simply doesn't suit your lifestyle, consider giving it to another family member (if it is a family treasure), or even sell it and buy something more meaningful.

- Avoid impulse purchases; don't take your credit card with you when going to the shops and take only enough money for the purchases you are required to make.

- When considering buying something because it is a bargain, ask yourself if you would still go ahead with the purchase if it were priced at full retail; do you really need it?

- If an item is broken or needs repair, ask yourself if it is really worth it, dollar wise, to have it repaired? If not, throw it away.

- Excess videos and DVDs? Are they still appropriate (say for children's videos), if not, give them to your local day care centre. If you have duplicates (i.e., the same film on both video and DVD) give one to charity.

- Excess toys should be pared down as you child out-grows them. Pass them to a day care centre, waiting room at your local doctor or church playgroup.

- Do not hold on to clothing in anticipation of a style revival. Whilst it may be similar, that shape, cut, colour and fabric will change.

- Hang your clothes up as soon as you get changed; throwing clothing on the floor adds to clutter and you've spent good money on your clothing so treat them with care.

- Put shoes into a basket either in the bedroom or by the front door.

- Photograph or scan all your children's artwork and save it to computer disk. The disk will outlast the original; use the images as a computer screen saver so you can still enjoy their creations.

- Encourage kids to pick up clutter; charge them 25c for each item left laying around out of place at the end of each day. As they get older the price should increase.

- Ask friends and family to create an experience for your child's birthday instead of so many gifts, for example, a day at rock climbing or at a fun park.

- Throw away all junk mail and don't even bring it into the house.

- It is unlikely that you need more stuff; avoid only buying something because it is on sale, not because you need it.

- Create a basic filing system for household documents; schedule a day/time to put them away each week e.g., Friday evening with a cool drink.

- Create a habit of using what you have; that applies to clothing, shoes, stationery, food, kitchen containers, gadgets, toys, and games.

- Clutter in your home attracts dust and dirt. Less clutter will create a healthier environment for you and your family.

Reducing or avoiding clutter, will reduce stress, improve your health and enable you to create a calm space for your family to flourish and enjoy life. As a family, we need to spend time with each other, not more stuff.

If you are overwhelmed by clutter and need further advice or hands-on assistance, you could seek the services of a Professional Organiser.

Adele Blair

CHRISTIAN SPIRITUALITY AND RELIGION

When I sat down to write this entry, Queensland was battling the great floods of 2011. When life becomes problematic, when we are menaced by forces of nature we cannot control or by circumstances in life we didn't choose, we find often ourselves face to face with spiritual and/or religious issues. The American writer and theologian Frederick Buechner observed: "we are more likely to live out of the depths of who we are than out of the shallows, when life becomes challenging".

We have little if any say over the cards we're dealt in life, but we have all the say in how we play them. In seeking to play the cards life deals us with integrity, we are in fact, whether we realise it or not, engaging the spiritual quest. It is difficult, when playing a scrappy hand, to avoid addressing questions like: Why isn't life fair? Is Shakespeare right, that life is full of sound and fury, signifying nothing? At such times we have a choice before us. We may turn outwards for guidance or sustenance to a faith community, with its familiar religious practices and beliefs. We may turn inwards to a spirituality, to a bigger, overarching story that helps make sense of the scrappy hand life has dealt us. Or we may turn to neither of these, finding ourselves instead seeking out someone to blame, stymied by ever-enlarging resentment or victimhood.

I've often heard people say: I'm not into religion, but I do have a spirituality. Others, describing themselves as regular church-goers, find their religious practice insufficient, silent or empty when they encounter tough times. There are also those who worship regularly and whose spirituality assists them not only to take up the hand they've been dealt, but to play that hand credibly and with satisfaction, where onlookers see only the cards of defeat and tragedy. Of such people Richard Rohr, the Franciscan priest, speaks: "suffering can take us to the edge of our inner resources where we have nothing to fall back on other than the arms of the living God".

Some people find that gathering with others around familiar prayers and church rituals strengthens their long-held belief that God never deserts us. Others, in simply telling the story of what has occurred to anyone who will listen, find an inner strength beyond their own. While religion can make space for the telling of such stories amid its more formal prayers and rituals, most Spiritualities welcome, encourage, even treasure this story-telling. But there's more to spirituality than telling our story to rapt attention. Robust Spiritualities take the further step of listening for the bigger stories we are implicitly telling when we narrate what's happening in our lives and around us. Robust Spiritualities seek out the stories we tell ourselves about the stories we tell. Beyond telling of visits to the doctor, of tests undertaken and of prognoses uttered, we implicitly or explicitly tell ourselves stories about what we've made of life, where life is leading, how God maybe at work in or absent from the hand we've been dealt.

We may even notice that our inner talk about what has happened may be self-defeating, incomplete or inadequate. While we may choose either spirituality or religious practices as our starting point for playing the hand life deals us, without each other, they are the sound of one hand clapping.

When we pursue spirituality isolated from religious practice with others, we may limit ourselves inadvertently to discovering what's best in ourselves. While the dictum know yourself is integral to most Spiritualities, it's only a short step away from self-absorption. Ron Rolheiser, a Roman Catholic priest, has helpfully commented that spirituality isn't a private search for what's highest in oneself but a communal search for the face of God. Religion offers the spiritual quest the benefit of what countless generations of believers have learned across the ages; words and images that help us understand and stand confidently under a benevolent reality larger than ourselves.

Religion can also alert us to spiritual dead-ends that we need not waste our time discovering for ourselves. On the other hand, when we pursue religion without spirituality, we're likely to endure, perhaps even champion, mere words and rituals that have been religiously attended to over our lives or across the centuries. Spirituality is the soul of religious practice. Religion is the memory of a robust spirituality. Together, they offer rigour and vitality in the on-going quest to make ultimate sense of the hand of cards life deals us. When people who have led what could be called a charmed life are dealt a joker, they often find religion lacking: why did God let this happen? Such times of disillusionment may, ironically, be occasions for letting go of what they've imagined God is like. When, as C S Lewis puts it, our religious faith collapses like a house of cards, it may be an occasion for letting go of an inadequate, caricatured image of what we have imagined God to be, and to meet, even in the face of tragedy, the living God.

Allow me to illustrate how spirituality and religion assist each other to play life's hand. I try to live out of a Catholic, Easter spirituality. This spirituality comes to life by participating in the rituals of the Easter season; kissing the cross on Good Friday, spending Holy Saturday listlessly even emptily; on

Easter day, lighting candles from the Easter candle, watching as adults and children are splashed with the water of Baptism and smeared with aromatic oils; hearing the story of Jesus' Ascension and celebrating Pentecost amid red Poinsettias. These are familiar prayers and rituals in which I have participated for a lifetime, practices that recall events in the life of Jesus. They are, equally, moments of connection for me as I seek to find the face of God amid the cards life has dealt me. If Good Friday marks Jesus' death, an Easter Spirituality identifies and names the range of losses, failures or regrets I have experienced either personally or communally. If Holy Saturday refers to the time Jesus spent in the tomb, it is, for an Easter spirituality, the time of sitting with the losses or the regrets, refusing to minimise their searing depth or pervading consequences, refusing to get over it too soon. Easter day celebrates God's power over loss, by raising Jesus from the dead, with the promise that we too will be raised up. We will not be irrevocably flattened by the loss or failure. The Ascension too is an important facet of an Easter spirituality. It reminds us that after an appropriate, perhaps seemingly endless time of grieving, we need not end up clinging onto what has been lost. There comes a time when it is necessary to let go, not to reject what has been lost, but to relate to it in a new way. Finally, and only after these prior steps, comes Pentecost, with its gift of the precise Spirit we need to live credibly the uninvited situation which now comprises our real life.

May this illustration of how an Easter spirituality enhances my religious practice (and vice versa) trigger for you a question; how, through starting with either spirituality or with religious practice, might you live with spirit whatever hand life deals you?

Rev Dr John Chalmers

SHEDDING GUILT AND SHAME

We can all relate to the metaphor of people being like icebergs — outsiders see about ten percent of who we are — and ninety percent remains hidden. What's in the ninety percent? Fears, secrets, vulnerability, insecurities, and significantly, guilt and shame.

Guilt is the feeling of regret, discomfort or embarrassment that emerges when we have done something wrong, made a mistake or believe our actions were not good, honest, authentic. Shame, a much deeper emotion is found within our personal identity: I am wrong, I am a mistake, and I am bad. Guilt can mobilise us toward doing better, making amends, trying harder, and correction.

Shame is often debilitating, immobilising and disempowering. Feeling guilty about not sending a friend a birthday greeting can motivate us to ring and apologise and invite the friend out for a make-up dinner. Feeling shame about gambling the rent money or having an extra-marital affair compels us to lie about our behaviour and either secretly try and fix it or minimise the unacceptable nature of the behaviour and continue doing it. Shame can also arise from the morally unacceptable behaviour of others, such as when abuse or domestic violence is present. Shame can be so immobilising it stops us from seeking help to address the origin of the feeling. Embarrassment and humiliation are close relatives of shame. A certain behaviour or event evokes some kind of thought associated with a negative view of self (*I'm damaged, I'm disgusting*) and this leads to the feeling of shame.

The link between behaviour or events, thoughts and feelings gives us a critical clue to the way in which we can shed feelings of guilt and shame. Broadly speaking, behaviour and events can be classified into four categories:

1. Significant and controllable (e.g., who we marry, the career we choose, what we say).

2. Insignificant and controllable (e.g., the colour socks we wear, what we watch on TV).

3. Insignificant and uncontrollable (e.g., whether your neighbour's cousin is vegetarian).

4. Significant and uncontrollable (e.g., violence against you, natural disasters, history).

Obviously, the most difficult for us to emotionally manage are the events in category four. It is vital that we recognise that if we cannot control an event or behaviour then expending emotional or physical energy on it is unhelpful at least and detrimental at worse. So, if we feel guilt or shame as a result of an event or action that falls into category four, then reminding ourselves of the futility of the feelings and working on acceptance of our inability to change the situation is the best way to shed the feelings. Acceptance might simply involve saying to yourself (over and over) something like, I accept that it happened and that I am powerless to change it now. I choose to nurture and focus on feelings of peace and resolution.

If the feelings of shame and guilt are underpinned by behaviour or actions that are controllable then we need to find a way to stop the behaviour. We may need support such as professional counselling, medical intervention or spiritual guidance. Feelings of guilt and shame will not dissipate if the underpinning behaviour continues.

Once the behaviour has moved from category 1 to category 4 (that is, it is now history), we must continually remind ourselves of the futility and possible unhelpfulness of holding on to the feeling of guilt or shame. Be prepared though, accepting past behaviour can be very difficult and sometimes needs to be accompanied by forgiving someone (or yourself) or making restitution (repaying debts, apologising, openly acknowledging mistakes in judgement).

You might also need to spend some time and effort rebuilding your self-esteem and reminding yourself of the positive steps you are now taking. All these processes take time, practice and effort. They invariably involve feelings of discomfort. Importantly, the discomfort of resolving feelings of shame and guilt is well worth it; the end result (being free of the burden of shame) is both liberating and deeply satisfying.

Again, if you are struggling on your journey of acceptance of history or changing underpinning behaviour, professional help can be of assistance.

Susan De Campo

MOVING HOUSE

Moving house is considered a significant stressor in most people's life. Unfortunately many of us have to move multiple times in our lives, and this can result in a lot of pressure over an extended period of time. The whole process of moving may take upwards of 12 months, depending upon whether you are buying or renting, and it is also quite expensive. The decision to move may be mediated by a number of factors, whether it is a change in life circumstances, relocating due to work or family commitments, or simply wishing for a change in environment. The costs associated with moving are sometimes prohibitive, and it is good to start planning ahead if you have the chance. This includes the process of packing, although it is often the case where sometimes it is necessary to pack within a short space of time. If you do have a little bit of breathing space, allow time to sort through your possessions.

If you are renting or selling, try also to clean as you go, it is scary how dirty your walls can get, especially if you have little children. There are agencies that include cleaning for rental bond refunds if you are very low on time. Also book your removalists to make sure you get the day that you want. If you are planning on moving yourself, make sure you book the truck and some friends.

Renting

If you are renting, as soon as possible is the time to start putting in applications. Unfortunately the rental market can be highly competitive, especially in the city and inner suburbs. Ensure that real estate agents know that you are moving and ask for their help in finding another property if you intend to stay in the area. They are often the first to know when houses are being listed and will place good tenants, because they are considered an asset. Also if you are planning a bigger move, get to know the real estate agents in the area and let them know that you are looking. Make sure you work out what you need and how much you can reasonably afford. Often people feel that they have no option but to rent a house that is beyond their means, simply because a lack of available rentals. Get all your paperwork together (e.g., bank statements, pay slips, utility bills) and photocopy a few copies of each for rental applications. Sometimes rental viewings can have many people looking at the same house so any little step that puts you ahead of the race is well worth it.

Buying

Buying a house is a big commitment for most people and depending on circumstances can be one of the most exciting, but also nerve-wracking, times in your life. Making one of the biggest financial commitments of your life means that people feel a lot of pressure to get things right. Once you find the perfect house after inspecting some not so good ones, you may want to secure the property before someone else does. This is not an unusual feeling, often you have looked at numerous properties that were too small, too big, no garden, too much garden, and so on. At this stage when you sign a contract to buy, there are two essential items that need to be included to protect yourself. Firstly consider making the contract conditional to a satisfactory (for the buyer) independent building and pest inspection, and also subject to bank-approved finance. This ensures that if finance falls through you are not obliged to buy the property, and also ensures that you are protected in case of termite infestation or structural problems that may not be initially noticeable.

Moving

If you are using a moving service, they will deliver packing supplies for you, so make sure you give yourself plenty of time to pack. Packing can start a month before you move, to relieve some of the pressure, work out what can be put away for a few months and what you use everyday. Things like books, extra sheets, decorations, spare china and other household items can all be packed securely ahead of time. Additionally always allow yourself extra time and take the time to sort through things and work out what you actually need. It is often the case that you may end up throwing things away when you have moved into your new house, and this is simply a case of wasted effort. It really is a simple equation, taking the time to sort through items prior to moving means that you have less to move; therefore making it easier. It may sound obvious but labelling or colour-coding boxes to indicate which rooms they are meant to go into also makes it easier. If possible, take a few days off from work to give yourself time to settle in and make the move that little bit easier.

Handy tip: use spare pillowcases, clothes, towels to pack breakables, this reduces waste (paper and bubble-wrap) and is perfect for ensuring items don't move around.

Unpacking

People generally move all in one day. If you plan to do this, pack a bag of things that you will need when you get to the new house. This generally includes changes of clothes, towels, medication, snacks, activity packs for the kids or the favourite toys for your pets. It is helpful to know where clean sheets are as well, as the bed is one of the first things that will need to be made.

After a full day of moving a house the last thing that you want to have to do is to unpack multiple boxes to get your essential items. In reality, for most people after a day of moving all you really want to do is have some take-out for dinner and collapse into bed; which is a highly recommended course of action considering the circumstances.

Susan Beattie

2

Couples Issues

COPING WITH A LONG-DISTANCE RELATIONSHIP

In recent years, as a result of the ease of travel and communication, modern society has witnessed an increase in long-distance relationships. Studies suggest that those in healthy, intimate relationships — long-distance or close proximity — have stronger immune systems and are healthier and happier than those who don't have quality relationships. As with all relationships, long-distance relationships, whether romantic, with family, workmates, or friends, all face challenges, require commitment, hard work and creative ways to keep them alive and healthy.

Following are some strategies for you to consider.

Stay positive

Research suggests that those who view their long-distance relationship as a positive experience stay together, whereas those who perceive it to be gloom and doom were more likely to end the relationship. Viewing your relationship as a positive experience and a time to grow individually will be of benefit to all. Catch yourself when you experience a negative thought and change it to a positive thought or image.

Establish trust and openness

Trust is an essential part of any relationship. Talk about your individual values and beliefs around trust, and then negotiate healthy boundaries that will work for you both. Romantic intimate relationships need to have clear discussions of expectations regarding exclusivity and fidelity. Sitting at home imagining that your loved one is out with someone else, or that your absent child is taking drugs or driving fast cars, is not going to be helpful for your personal wellbeing or your relationship. A lack of trust in any relationship will ultimately be a deal-breaker.

Staying connected — communication

Social networking sites enable instant communication with loved ones. Skype, facebook and instant messaging programs, like google chat and MSN, and video-sharing sites such as YouTube make it easy to stay in touch, share news, photos, and videos. These modes of communication not only keep you connected, but also inject some fun and light heartedness into the relationship.

Email and old-fashioned letter writing are also ways to maintain contact. Letter writing is quite personal — handwritten letters retain an air of intimacy unlike email. Included in these letters you can be little reminders of home such as clippings from local newspapers and other sentimental mementos. Sending or receiving small gifts (at times other than birthdays or anniversaries) are also a great way to show you are thinking of one another.

Other ways you can share activities at a distance can include: watching the same movie, or reading the same book and discussing them book club style; playing games online, sharing photos using Flickr and other websites that allow you to upload photos or videos to the same album.

Above all, it is important to schedule the times for communication. Discuss your needs for contact, establish a *how* (e.g., via Skype, phone, email, texting) and *when* (i.e., daily, weekly, monthly, randomly). Compromise when necessary, especially if dealing with differences in time zones. Alternate and take turns so that the responsibility for contact is shared.

Plan visits

With romantic relationships particularly, it is essential to schedule visits, be they weekends, holidays or longer vacations. Visit each other, meet somewhere central, or choose another location. While scheduling events may lack spontaneity, try to maximise your time together for novel experiences and building shared memories. It can be a stressful time given there has been little contact between visits, so take it slowly and let your time unfold naturally. When you are together, be realistic. Do not exert pressure on each other, or expect perfection.

Visiting family can also be stressful when it comes to expectations, especially during holidays like Christmas. You may feel stretched thin or overwhelmed by the demands of family members who want to see you, or plan how you'll spend your time without consulting you in advance. Since it is impossible to please everyone, schedule a lunch, dinner, or event that includes extended family and other friends you may not have time to see otherwise.

Flexibility, compromise, and managing conflict

Sometimes, even the best-laid plans don't come to fruition. Be prepared to work together by being flexible. Be ready to negotiate and compromise when the situation arises. Address fears and don't be afraid to discuss your worries. Get the hard stuff out on the table by being open and honest about your (separation) anxieties and any qualms you have. As conflict inevitably occurs, identify the real issues and don't let the tension simmer. Do wait for (or create) an appropriate time to address the matter. Blindsiding your friend or loved one with an unexpected issue is counterproductive and could lead to hurt and further difficulties. If feelings are hurt, don't play the blame game. You will feel so much better if you take ownership for your part in the conflict and let go of stubbornness. Being able to apologise and forgive is a gift we give to ourselves and each other.

Have a life

Maintain your own life and interests. Do not isolate yourself. Have other relationships outside the long-distance world. Focus on your own fun, interests, career, school, and other friends and family. Be social. Allow for personal growth and independence rather than dependence.

Distance hinders the day-to-day routine of a relationship with family, friends, and romantic partners. Long-distance relationships are certainly a challenge but not an insurmountable one. They require more care, thought, and planning, but they can be fulfilling and are worth the effort they will inevitably require.

Sandra Barletta and Jan Bond

GETTING MARRIED

Deciding to get married or establish a committed relationship is an exciting and important occasion. It provides the opportunity for a unique and wonderful form of intimacy. Prior to marriage, couples may often be in the honeymoon phase of the relationship and be reluctant to consider future challenges and problems. Despite this, they are generally emotionally strong during this period so it can actually be an ideal time to address potential differences and possible sources of conflicts.

Differences that can prove difficult to spot in the early days of the relationship can have the capacity to cause problems down the track. It can be useful to develop an understanding of your similarities, differences, hopes, expectations and assumptions about all aspects of your future life together.

Following are some topics couples will find useful to consider prior to marriage.

Communication Skills

Issues arise in all relationships and it is ideal for a couple to be able to effectively negotiate these using positive listening and positive speaking skills. Effective communication will allow both partners to speak their mind and feel they are being heard. It is especially important for both partners to be aware of their own strengths and weaknesses in communication.

Family of Origin Issues

Family of origin is one's earliest influence and so our family is where we first learn about relationships. In many ways each person brings his or her families to the marriage as well as themselves. It can be helpful to view diversity in families as neither good nor bad. Discomfort, rejection or criticism between a partner and the other's family of origin can strain the relationship. Understanding differences in family backgrounds and possible ways this could impact on the relationship can help a couple recognise future pitfalls. Being familiar with patterns in each person's family can enable the couple to implement strategies early and avoid perpetuating unhealthy behaviours. The challenge is striking a healthy balance with the marital relationship as the primary focus and appropriate bonding with families of origin.

Conflict Resolution

Conflict is inevitable in relationships. It is not the conflict itself that can prove catastrophic for relationships but, rather, how that conflict is managed. There are numerous ways to effectively de-escalate confronting situations. Strategies include developing your self-awareness and being aware of the part you play in provoking anger and frustration in your partner. Couples need to develop a way of resolving conflict and stick to that plan in times of difficulties.

Role Expectations

A clear and open discussion of both your own and your partner's expectations can improve mutual understanding and limit the chance of surprises after marriage. Some areas in which expectations of roles can be explored include finances, sex, intimacy, friends, interests, parenting/children, personality differences, and religion/spirituality.

Finances are a major source of conflict for many couples, so frequent open discussion of financial arrangements and concerns can prevent confusion and misunderstandings. Speaking openly about responsibilities, expectations of financial status and priorities, both as a couple and two individuals, can ensure both partners are happy with financial arrangements.

Sexual needs and intimacy are different for each of us and are often influenced by our religion, culture, family and society. Many couples feel a healthy sexual relationship can significantly bond the overall relationship. It can be a good idea to discuss these aspects of your relationship with your partner, letting them know of your sexual needs and desires, what you like in terms of intimacy and recognising what your partner likes.

Friends and interests can be both individual and shared and it is ideal if the couple develop a balance between the two. Shared friends and activities can strengthen the relationship whereas individual friends and activities enrich the relationship through bringing together diversity.

Parenting can both enrich a relationship but also, place demands on it. Understand each other's expectations and fears in terms of parenting. Practical decisions can hinge on issues such as: Do both partners wish to parent children? Who wishes to be the primary caregiver? Consider if you were to parent the children, what are each other's parenting styles?

Personality differences can be a great source of frustration and conflict as relationships grow and develop. It is ideal for couples to respect and accept each other's differences and also develop some effective and positive ways to deal with characteristics that they may find annoying or frustrating.

Spirituality and religion can be a key bonder for couples as it can be a shared source of hope, values and rituals, however differences in this area can be a great source of conflict and couples should consider how they would work around these differences.

Life Values and Goals

A person's core values define what is important and meaningful to them. Understanding each others core values and discussing personal and couple goals allows both individuals to develop a picture of their future together e.g., goals around children, careers and lifestyle.

In preparing for marriage, and throughout married life, couples need care and attention as relationships are dynamic and forever changing. Taking into account the unique differences, similarities and expectations in each of the above areas can help couples in determining their readiness for commitment, build a mutual understanding, and thus, a more solid foundation for a future together.

If you are struggling with some of these issues and believe it would be helpful for you and your partner to spend some time considering the topics mentioned, pre-marriage education courses and/or relationship counselling with a qualified professional will be helpful.

Samantha Robertson

GROWING INTO RELATIONSHIPS

Love is only the beginning of a relationship, and after the initial period of romance, magic and perception of perfection, there comes the hard work. If commitment is to be developed, and in order for a healthy relationship to progress, there needs to be understanding of the necessary skills to maintain a close connection. Otherwise, what will result is either an eventual breakup, or a long, lifeless, loveless relationship. The key is choosing to grow and stay creative with each other, regardless of what the future brings for example, children, financial struggles, issues of ageing.

Keeping things fresh

All relationships can grow stale over time. It may be inevitable. But attitude is crucial in ensuring that romance, sexuality, communication, individual needs, and parenting all receive deliberate nurturing. Relationships are like a garden. Without watering, feeding and tending, they will wither and die. It's simple. There are two individuals in a relationship and a third entity, the relationship itself, and that needs attention too.

Romance – time spent together regularly as a couple is vital. Both partners need to foster the element of surprise; stay spontaneous, think of unusual outings, bring flowers, plan romantic dinners, take holidays together, be best friends, and compliment each other regularly.

Sexuality – experiment, have fun, never take each other for granted, be spontaneous in and out of the bedroom, feel sexy yourself and then share it, never pressure your partner into having sex, never reject in an unkind way, stay faithful, and combine sexuality with emotion and spirituality.

Communication – a key component of a positive relationship is the ability to speak openly and honestly about needs, feelings, issues, grievances and anything else that is important to you. There has to be willingness on both sides for this free expression. Trust, a lack of fear, and the surrender of ego are all required. With good communication, difficulties can be resolved, but without it, even loving relationships can be overwhelmed.

Individual needs – no matter how much two people love each other, it's important not to become overly dependent on one another, and to still operate as individuals. This is the responsibility of each person but also to allow each other emotional and physical space, not to put too many demands on the other person and to foster separate interests, friends and activities whilst staying close. Healthy boundaries should be established from the start.

Parenting – once children are introduced into the mix, challenges for the relationship naturally increase, mainly in the areas of time pressures, finances, stress levels, emotional demands and intimacy. This is when a relationship can seriously falter. It's particularly important now that the couple make private time for each other, regardless of parenting requirements. Mothers must ensure that they don't neglect their partners after having a baby, and fathers need to be as supportive as possible. Co-parenting is vital so that children learn from the start not to play one parent off against the other. Specific skills are crucial and these should be gained from experts, as well as by common-sense and practice.

As a relationship and the partners age, boredom, resentment, and cynicism may develop. Each of us goes through many life-stages as the years pass — new jobs, new homes, children, menopause, mid-life crises, and retirement. Change is part of life and each transition brings inherent difficulties. A stable loving relationship is a great gift in the shifting tides of any lifetime but it requires work, compassion, love, tolerance and patience. With knowledge, especially knowledge of self, success is far more likely. Success is not just a relationship surviving, but really thriving and bringing joy.

Dr Charmaine Saunders

COMMUNICATION IN RELATIONSHIPS

Communication is a two-way street and the listener is just as active a participant as the speaker. We often forget this and come to believe that as long we are talking, we are getting our point across, and the listener automatically understands us. Nothing could be further from the truth. Poor communication is the single most common factor in relationship breakdown, and learning to communicate effectively, not just talk, is a vital skill in getting along with others; people we live with, work with, are related to, are friends with, or meet on the street.

Further complicating the process is that in the moment it takes for an utterance to leave a speaker's mouth and enter the listener's hearing, it is already translated into the listener's code, and that is why so much misunderstanding occurs between people. For example, you might ask a simple question which can be heard as an attack, you could pay a genuine compliment and be accused of being flattering, make an innocent comment and have it totally changed to something sinister in the mind of the listener. All this happens in seconds and is mostly unintentional. The best illustration of this process is the child's game of Chinese Whispers, where a chain of people repeat the same phrase or word over and over but the last person often finishes-up with a message that is completely different to the original word or phrase. This is often a fault of listening rather than speaking.

So, how do we help the people we love to listen better, and by doing that, improve our chances of being heard and understood?

General tips for better communication:

- Be a better listener yourself and always speak clearly and concisely.

- Make sure you have someone's attention before you start.

- Establish eye contact.

- Ask for confirmation that you've been heard.

- Approach every exchange in the same way; not one way for requests, one for criticism and one for general news.

- Minimise the chatter when you have nothing special to say, as people tend to tune out if you talk incessantly.

- Don't be too subtle, as hidden, or double meanings can easily get lost.

- Always communicate with love, even if you're angry, as verbal attacks simply put people on their guard or cause them to reciprocate with similar unhelpful emotion.

There are some basic requirements for effective communication that will help you achieve the desirable and important aim of being heard.

The most important requirements are:

Self-esteem — without a strong sense of self-worth, it will be difficult to find your own voice, let alone ensure people listen to it. Know that you have a right to speak up, that what you have to say is valid, and then speak without fear.

Empowerment — if you wait until someone asks for your opinion or allows you time to be listened to, it might never happen, so hold your own power and ask for these things and feel confident to offer your views.

Boundaries — have clear and firm limits that you are sure of and have outlined to others. Saying "no" is difficult but vital at times; not taking on issues and problems that belong to someone else; letting your family know you have individual needs that also merit priority.

Assertiveness — the rules of this most crucial life-skill are simple; speak softly but firmly; say it once; walk away after speaking or change the subject — don't stop to argue. Yelling is an ineffective way of trying to get your point across, and it's not good to be passive either (nor is it useful to give in all the time).

Assertiveness is the balance between the polarities of aggression and passivity. Let's look at a specific example — you are trying to get your partner to go out on a date with you. Nagging and shouting won't work because they feel justified to disobey when requests are presented negatively and sound like harsh criticism. An assertive approach might be something like — *To enable our relationship to grow, time together is important, and I'd like to go out with you on Friday*, without further additions or embellishments. If they sense it is important to you, because of your assertive manner, they might be more likely to oblige. Conversely, with someone close to you who's trying to get you to do something you really don't wish to do, a gentle but firm "no" with a brief explanation is the way to go.

In relationships there are three types of communication that are commonly used, to varying degrees of success: *complaint*, *request* and *news*.

Complaint — this form of communication needs to be avoided as the listener can easily turn-off from their partner, as they experience the complaint as criticism or contempt, all of which do nothing to build an interpersonal relationship.

Request — if you want to go to a certain place for a holiday or make a household purchase, state your case and offer your reasons and helpful information. Some people like to keep conversations simple — if they're given the facts clearly, they're more likely to consider your request seriously. Remember you are an equal partner in your relationship and therefore, have a 50% vote in all decisions.

News — do not to go on endlessly about a topic you know will bore your partner, for example, your boss's wife wore a new outfit to the office or a new recipe you've found. A good rule is not to tell news but to share news — ask about your partner's interests and their day, as well as talking about what you want to. Discussing daily events and news is an important way to learn about your partner's life, struggles and feelings.

As a general rule, do not repeat yourself, negotiate arrangements to the minutest detail or allow people to ignore you. After a request ask, *Do you know what I want?* After a criticism ask, *Do you understand my point of view?* Sometimes, it's also necessary to double-check with, *What did you get from what I said?* In this way, they realise you won't let things slide. Your time and energy are precious and you don't want to waste them on useless speech; make every word count. Be positive in your approach, expect to be heard, and you will be.

Ultimately, good communication is a matter of respect, honesty, caring, and mutual effort — the cornerstones of a good relationship.

Dr Charmaine Saunders

CONFLICT MANAGEMENT IN RELATIONSHIPS

All couples have conflict … that's a given. And contrary to popular belief, it's not actually a bad thing to argue at times. The problems occur when individuals don't know how to fight in a positive way. Very few of us were taught as children how to manage anger, so as adults we either repress it or express it inappropriately.

In looking at ways to disagree positively, we need to firstly understand the nature of anger. What is anger? Anger is usually classified as a negative emotion but it is, in fact, just energy and no different to any other. All emotion is good and part of the human experience. It only becomes negative when we hold onto it, try to suppress it and control it or, on the other hand, let it take us over. Every person has a dark side and when we accept it, we are free from its tyranny. When we judge and criticise our feelings, we give them far more power. Therefore, it's not about stopping or hiding anger. It's about accepting it and learning how to harness it in a way that is not destructive. We can begin this task by making a distinction between anger and temper. Anger is a feeling. Temper is the negative expression of that anger.

Anger in relationships

In relationships, anger is natural because the people closest to us are most likely to press our most sensitive buttons. But anger can be a pointer to resolution. It shows up differences, yes, but also can help us make things better. For without passion, there can only be indifference.

Let's by all means argue, let's disagree — it's okay. We just need to learn some skills of combat, such as good communication, listening ability, self-worth, generosity of spirit, stress management, mutual respect, resolving old baggage, acceptance and tolerance, honesty, and conflict resolution. Armed with these, we can indeed fight positively.

Misplaced anger

Often, when we feel anger, it is not caused by a present moment but rooted in the past. It can relate to another person, another time and another grievance. A common example occurs when a man is told off by his boss, goes home and yells at his wife or children. This outburst may have been triggered by a relatively small incident within the home but is actually caused by the stress of his outside life. Once we see this in our own behaviour, we can take a breath, stop, and express our frustration differently.

Conflict resolution

Instead of waiting for anger to erupt, possibly leading to a fight, the partners in a relationship should discuss disagreements and differences without emotion. Each person should bring their separate issues to the table, listen carefully to the other and then be prepared to brainstorm solutions. Compromise of course is essential. Once a strategy has been agreed, it needs a trial period, after which it can be reassessed. This may sound tedious but it prevents a build-up of resentment over time.

Releasing anger

Individually, we need to take responsibly for our own anger. If we allow it to bottle up, it will indeed run over and spill onto others. As with regular exercise, we should learn strategies of positive anger management so that it's part of our everyday life, not something we trot out when we are in a bind. Physical release is good as in playing sport, having enjoyable past-times, laughing, playing, talking out our concerns, practising positive thinking, being with nature, relaxing, stress management overall. Writing out our frustrations is very powerful because even the worst day, when viewed in a clear perspective, can be released when written down. Deep breathing, relaxation, swimming, yoga and Tai Chi, whatever works for you, are all useful.

After the battle

We can't leave this discussion without touching on how to cope with the aftermath if anger does spill over and there's an actual fight. I assume that I need not emphasise the need to completely avoid physical lashing out and verbal abuse. These have no place in positive fighting and healthy relationships. When tempers flare and they will sometimes, no matter how enlightened we are, it is essential that the positivity continues beyond the fight. Prolonged discussions in anger are to be avoided at all costs. When emotions accelerate, one or both people should call time-out. People are often unsure if they should walk out if they can see the fight is building into a nasty exchange. Typically it can be useful but not as a copping-out. Storming out is not the answer.

Calling a time-out has to have the promise to explore the quarrel the next day, when emotions have died down. A spirit of reconciliation and forgiveness is also essential as holding onto ill feelings, grudges and bad moods can prolong the quarrel and creates further resentment.

Positive fighting is an important aspect of human interaction in general, and close relationships in particular. It's a skill worth pursuing and practising. It is not about avoidance or glossing over problems, but rather a practical and healthy strategy for understanding our individual and relationship issues, then working them out together so as to reduce conflict and avoid the erosion of love and happiness.

Remember the main ingredients needed for this valuable life-skill: good communication, listening ability, self-worth, generosity of spirit/forgiveness, stress management, mutual respect, resolving old baggage, sense of humour, acceptance and tolerance, honesty, conflict resolution. Practise them well and often to stay close to your partner.

Dr Charmaine Saunders

COPING WITH INFERTILITY

Infertility is a growing concern among couples with about one in six couples under the age of 35 finding it difficult to conceive. These couples are healthy and have been trying to have a baby by having unprotected sex for about 12 months without success.

The medical reasons for infertility are evenly divided across three broad categories of male reproductive factors, female reproductive factors, and factors that cannot be explained. Regardless of the cause, the likelihood of conception decreases with age so it is wise not to wait too long before seeking help.

The first step is to make an appointment with your General Practitioner for a medical evaluation and, if a medical cause can be identified, you may be referred to an In Vitro Fertilisation (IVF) clinic. IVF clinics specialise in the treatment of infertility and have a team of specialists including doctors, scientists, nurses and counsellors to assist you.

In cases where couples are unable to conceive for reasons that cannot be medically explained, further options may be explored, including adoption.

Regardless of the reason for infertility, affected couples typically experience a range of normal emotions that trigger a number of self-directed questions:

Anger: Why is this happening to me?

Sadness: I feel deeply saddened — I don't know how to cope or what to do?

Denial: This can't be happening to me/us. We just need more time. It will happen.

Anxiety: What will my partner/husband/wife think of me if I am the one at fault?

Fear: Am I less of a man/woman because I can't have a baby? What can I/we say to our families and friends? What will they think of me/us?

Depression: Life doesn't have the same meaning for me any more. I don't want anybody to know about this. I feel as if I am being punished for something.

These types of thoughts and feelings are normal and can be dealt with by talking to someone about them. Help is readily available when you look for it.

You can talk to a close friend or family member, or contact a community agency for counselling services. If you want to remain anonymous there are several 24-hour telephone counselling services you can find on the Internet or in the telephone book. Alternatively, your General Practitioner may recommend a counsellor with whom you can discuss what you are going through.

Geraldine Coyne

SUCCESSFUL CHILDLESSNESS

Childlessness can be a choice that an individual or couple makes, or it can be a choice that is made for you, involuntarily. Those individuals or couples in the former group may choose not to have children for many reasons, these include: career aspirations, lifestyle choices, and concerns about genetics, such as family history of mental or physical illness, or bad childhood experiences.

Involuntary childlessness, those who have not chosen to be childless but have found themselves in this circumstance, can be individuals or couples unable to conceive a child due to fertility issues but also, those people who may be fertile but involuntarily childless, such as singles, gay and lesbian couples, out-of-phase couples, and step-parents in blended families.

Coping with involuntary childlessness can be one of the most challenging issues people face, particularly in the short term, and is something that can take some time to accept. In the long term the aim is to accept the reasons for your childlessness and learn to cope with circumstances that are different from your original plan. These feelings can be very similar to bereavement. Common feelings such as bitterness, sadness, anger, jealousy, hopelessness and failure are the beginning of the healing process and are a normal part of grieving. The grief may always be around to some extent, and although this can be difficult, it will become more bearable and easier to manage as time passes. You will discover other ways you can enjoy life and feel happy again.

If you have a partner, remember that their experience of grief may be different from yours. There is no set rule to follow in the grief process. Your partner may move at a different pace than you. Due to this shared experience you may find that you rely on your partner more at this time than you typically would. You may also find that there are some feelings and experiences you share but some that are entirely personal.

Others may also be grieving with you and for you — your parents, other family members and friends. Conversely, this grief may not always be acknowledged by others as much as other grief, as it is less visible and more difficult for people to understand. With other losses people may express their condolences, send flowers and cards, but this is typically not the case with childlessness.

Some people can speak more openly about how they are feeling while others can find it incredibly uncomfortable. If you feel able to, share your thoughts and feelings with someone whether this is a friend, family member or health professional. By being more open with those around you, you can avoid uncomfortable questions and set boundaries for others as to what you are willing to discuss. Remember those around you may want to be supportive but be uncertain how to show this. It can also be helpful to decide how you are going to answer some of the more common questions e.g., Do you have children? Sadly not. When will you start a family? Sadly it will only be the two of us.

Acknowledgment can involve a symbol, ritual or a personal way of acknowledging the loss. For example, planting a tree as a symbol of your loss or a day of remembrance. This is a way of honouring your experience and gradually moving forward. It can be worthwhile to select a day you can grieve so that you can focus the emotions in a particular time frame. During this time you have the opportunity to reflect and express some of the difficult emotions associated with your experience. This process allows you to let the emotions out and not bottle them up.

You may find that certain dates and/or events (e.g., Mother's Day, Father's Day, Birthdays, Anniversaries, Christmas) can trigger painful feelings, thoughts and memories and remind you of what might have been. It is a reminder that others have moved forward while you have stood still. This cannot be avoided but there are ways you can manage it. Consider being especially good to yourself at this time. For example, you may like to spoil yourself with a particular treat or outing, or take a day off work and do something special. Acknowledge that you might not feel good. Consider that you may not need to attend a child's birthday party, go to visit a newborn or attend a family function with lots of kids. You can still send a card, flowers or present to send your congratulations or, perhaps arrange a private visit when you feel ready. Do what you feel is easier on you, and best for you and your partner.

Acceptance of your situation can involve regaining a sense of self and what is meaningful to you. You may start to look for new purpose in life and develop new goals. Consider reasons you wanted to have children in the first place. Can you live by these life values in other ways? For example, having children can often be about nurturing, creating, passing on values, giving love, and receiving love. Is there another way you can nurture? Some people find they are surprised with how rewarding they ultimately find nurturing a garden or animal.

Sometimes nurturing can be met through relationships with other children, nieces, nephews, friends' kids, and other social environments. However, for some people, spending time with the children of other's can be too painful for now. While these relationships may never take the place of your own child, it can make life more meaningful and worthwhile. For others alternative parenting options such as adoption, fostering or surrogacy may be an attractive option.

If you are in a committed relationship now is the time to re-focus on that relationship. If infertility has been the reason for your childlessness, you may have spent a lot of time, energy and money on attempts to become pregnant, so while you can experience feelings of intense sadness and hopelessness there can also be a sense of relief that you no longer have to fear miscarriages, worry about tablets and injections, experience hormonal changes and frequent disappointment. As a couple you can plan again for your future, spend money on other endeavours, renegotiate the role of sex in your relationship and return to a time when sex was about pleasure and fun.

As time passes you may feel you can use unexpected flexibility to your benefit to explore other life options that would not have been open to you with children. Accept that there will be setbacks, good and bad days, and try to retain your sense of humour. Don't forget that this is a complex and difficult situation and have confidence that as the intensity of grief subsides happiness and enjoyment will return.

Samantha Robertson

RECOVERING AFTER AN AFFAIR

The discovery of an affair can have a devastating impact on your relationship. It is a violation of the very foundation of a marriage or committed relationship. It is an abuse of trust and an agreement between two partners, either assumed or stated, for emotional and sexual exclusivity.

Approximately 60% of husbands and 40% of wives admit to having had an extramarital affair. There are different kinds of infidelity and what is acceptable in one relationship may not be in another. Despite this, an affair usually involves sexual attraction, secrecy, deception and emotional intimacy. The type of affair may have different implications for the couple, that is, a long-term affair and a one-night stand may promote very different reactions. The former may take more time and be more disruptive to the satisfaction of a relationship.

Many people cannot imagine resuming a normal relationship after an affair has occurred, but many relationships and marriages do survive an affair. Many couples emerge with a stronger, more honest and intimate relationship but it takes a lot of work, time and patience from both partners. So if both partners have the goal of reconciliation and are willing to commit to this, the rewards can be great.

The initial discovery of an affair has both partners in the relationship experiencing intense emotions: shock, anger, resentment, rage, guilt, shame, sadness and remorse. It is not uncommon for emotions to vacillate, even many times throughout a day. For this reason, it can be a good idea to take time and space to digest the situation and process your emotions. It is often difficult to effectively discuss with your partner what has happened when emotions are heightened. Consider postponing such discussions until you can both talk without being angry and accusatory.

It is natural for the partner who has not had the affair to want to discuss what has happened. As such, a useful strategy can be to have an agreement about when, how often and what aspects of the affair will be discussed. This can avoid many hours engaged in conversation about the affair details in which conversations are often repeated over and over, and hurtful interactions reoccur.

Support from family, friends or a qualified professional can be helpful to offer comfort and provide an opportunity to discuss your feelings. Emotional support can be very comforting at this time but keep in mind that it is difficult for those close to you, like family and friends, to give objective or unbiased advice. Likewise, remember that if a relationship recovery is achieved, there will be many people who will know what has occurred, and as a couple you may wish for this to be avoided.

For the relationship to recover, firstly the affair must stop. For the relationship to be saved all communication and interaction must cease. In particular, continuation of emotional or sexual aspects of the affair undermines the trust and stability of the marital relationship. If it is difficult to stop all contact (e.g., same workplace) the unfaithful partner should set some strict boundaries around contact with the third party.

After ceasing contact the unfaithful partner may be experiencing withdrawal and may not be very remorseful. As such, be prepared for this recovery phase to not always begin with enthusiasm. The faithful partner can feel it's not their fault and both partners aren't ready to apologise. An apology at this point can make the step forward a lot easier and less painful.

Understanding the impact the affair has had on the relationship is a crucial step to recovery. After the initial shock the couple are more able to openly and constructively discuss what has happened setting the path for moving forward and recovery. This does not mean delving into all the details of the affair, rather it involves open discussion about what happened and the faithful partner having the opportunity to express how they are feeling and explain the impact this has had on them. It is vital at this time for the unfaithful partner to acknowledge and validate their partner's emotions and reassure their partner about their commitment to the relationship.

Trust has to be rebuilt and the unfaithful partner needs to accept and take responsibility for this. For some time, it can be helpful for the unfaithful partner to agree to some things that would not typically be present in their relationship to help their partner regain trust and feel secure and safe in the relationship. These may involve the unfaithful partner being very transparent about their whereabouts, emails and phone messages.

To heal it is vital that both partners develop an understanding of contributing factors to the affair. In this process both partners should be accountable for their role in the affair. If you have had the affair, it is important that you take responsibility for your actions. If you are the other partner, consider how you may have played a part. There may be many factors contributing to the unfaithful partner having the affair, some of which may include low self-esteem, acting on impulse, their needs not being met in the relationship, or a major life transition such as birth of a child.

Forgiveness on the part of the faithful partner is an important step in recovering and they will be looking to the partner who has had the affair for empathy and a sincere sorrow for the affair. This can take some time and the faithful partner tends to set the timetable in this regard. Often the person who has had the affair is anxious to put the past behind them and bury their guilt. Forgiveness and understanding takes time and it is crucial for each partner to have enough time to heal.

With time and understanding the couple can begin to restructure and rebuild the relationship. This is when the focus is not dwelling on the past but on strengthening the relationship, creating their desired relationship and eliminating the risk of a future affair. At this point the aim is for the couple to connect emotionally and develop some common goals and unified lifestyle.

For more information and support on recovering after an affair contact a qualified mental health professional to help guide you and your partner through this difficult time. It is worth the effort.

Samantha Robertson

3

Family and Parenting Issues

- Being a New Parent
- Building Attachment with Children
- Parent-Child Relationships
- Praising Your Child Appropriately
- Working Mothers
- Family Meetings
- Coping with a Child with a Disability
- Single Parenting
- Children of Divorce
- Sharing the Care of Children
- Step-Families
- Adult Children Returning Home
- Being a Grandparent
- Giving a Baby up for Adoption
- Adopting a Child

BEING A NEW PARENT

So now you have become a parent — *congratulations!*

The birth of a baby can be one of the most exciting and difficult things you will ever do. From the moment your baby is born, your life will never be the same again, you will learn something new each day that will enrich your life and make you feel all kinds of intense emotions. Some experiences with your baby will fill you with love, happiness, delight and amazement. At other times, you may feel anxious, frustrated, angry and even disappointed. All of these strong emotions are common and you may feel yourself going through them all in a single day. If you aim for the best possible emotional health during pregnancy and early parenthood, you'll get the most out of becoming a parent.

Some helpful tips to remember:

- Value your role as a parent — it is a very important job.

- Most parents find the first 6-8 weeks the hardest.

- Try to be realistic about what you expect of being a mother or a father.

- Mothers do not always fall in love with their baby right away (fathers too). It may take some time after the birth (especially if pregnancy, labor and birth did not go according to plan).

- Parenting is a skill you learn. With practice and time you will become more confident with your baby. Remember there is no right way to parent.

- Breastfeeding is also a learned skill. It will be easier for some mothers and babies than others. Remember that breastfeeding is a confidence game — the more you do it, the better you get.

- With all breastfeeding challenges there is always a solution. The right advice at the right time is very important. Talking with a Lactation Consultant or Child and Family Health Nurse is crucial.

- Babies do adapt to different ways of parenting, so it's okay if your partner does some things a little differently to you.

- Communicate and explore your differing feelings. Remember you are now shaping your own family culture; there will be some things you will include that your own parents did and there will be other things that you will most definitely not want to do with your own children.

- Don't expect your baby to just fit into your routine, you will need to work around your baby, especially in the early weeks.

- If motherhood is not what you expected, it is easy to blame yourself or believe motherhood is not for you. However, it is important to remember that no one is perfect. Motherhood is an enormously challenging job.

- There are many changes to adjust to and many parents will feel they are not coping at times. Not getting enough sleep is one of the biggest problems most new parents face. Try to rest or sleep when the baby is sleeping. This is especially important if you are exhausted, it is not the time to catch up on household chores. Remember, you don't have to have a perfect house. Babies do not know the difference between day and night at first. They will often sleep all day and be more alert, active and feed more at night. By 6–8 weeks they will turn this around and start to sleep longer at night. Some babies are easier to settle and comfort than others. It may not be that you are doing anything wrong. Every baby is different. If there are challenges with settling and comforting, seek advice from a Child and Family Health Nurse or a Lactation Consultant.

- Share the household jobs as much as possible, plan to have some extra support in the first few months and accept all reasonable offers of help.

- Mothers who are breastfeeding should remember to eat well, everything in moderation. Skipping meals can affect milk supply.

- Parenthood might also change your relationship with your partner — including your sexual relationship. You can both be physically and emotionally tired especially in the early months. Share your feelings and concerns with each other or someone you trust.

- Sometimes, women respond more quickly to their baby's cues than men. This doesn't mean she always knows what to do. Neither of you has all the answers — especially in the first few weeks. Be prepared to have a go!

- Give yourself time out every day and learn ways to relax. Plan some quality time together each week. Extend your family support systems and find someone you can trust and rely on who can baby-sit for you.

- Try not to spend all day in your pajamas. Getting showered and dressed can help you feel good.

- Get to know your local resources, like Child and Family Health Centers, Breastfeeding Association Groups and Playgroups.

- Have contact with family and friends who are supportive and positive. Try to avoid the people who are negative or critical.

- A little anxiety or worry is normal for parents. The trouble is too much distress and anxiety may affect your ability to cope. It is important to seek help — the earlier the better.

- Fathers, whatever their circumstances are, should remember to value their role. Be as involved as you can be, right from day one. Your baby and your partner need you in lots of different ways. Your time and help will contribute hugely to your relationships with both of them. Try to help care for your baby, take over some of the household chores, this will take some pressure off your partner, be prepared to jump in and have a go!

When parents are happy and content, they are in the best position to form strong, secure bonds that will ensure their baby continues to develop physically, mentally and emotionally.

Adrienne Wheatley

BUILDING ATTACHMENT WITH CHILDREN

Our first experiences with other people, within a family or another context, have a lasting impact on our lives. The way we are held, cared for, soothed, and our needs responded to in our development, effects biological changes within our brain and an associated sense of self in the world. The relational bond, or *attachment*, that we experience in the first few years of life with primary care givers profoundly influences how we see ourselves, others, the world, and how we cope and function in our lives.

Stages of Attachment

There are three distinct stages involved in developing a strong and positive attachment.

Newborn: Initial trust is established between baby and caregiver (0–6 weeks). This requires that the caregiver appropriately responds to the baby, most of the time (e.g., baby cries in distress and the caregiver responds by holding and soothing them). The baby will respond positively to these gestures and be soothed. Where this does not occur, the caregiver may employ different strategies, such as rocking, feeding, going for a walk in a pram. These types of interactions constitute a complex dance where caregiver and infant learn about each other and how to tune-in to each other. This dance needs to be led by the baby's needs and followed by the caregiver's responses.

Baby: Ongoing and reciprocal trust is developed within the relationship (6 weeks to 9–12 months). The caregiver and infant learn to read each other and respond appropriately. This strengthens the attachment bond. The caregiver becomes consistently attuned to the baby's signals, and the baby knows their caregiver will help them to manage their physiological and emotional needs. Paradoxically, this reciprocal process supports the baby to begin to establish her own ability to self-regulate, to recognise and manage her own physical, emotional, and psychological needs. This stage includes expressions of distress or anxiety when babies are separated from their primary caregivers.

Toddler: Autonomy and trust is developed (12 to 48 months). With a foundation of trust in the attachment bond, a toddler now begins to move away to explore their wider environment. At the same time they require their caregiver to remain close, as a safe haven to return to when they feel unsure, scared, over-excited, or hurt. The caregiver provides opportunities and encouragement to try new experiences, and also ensure safe boundaries for the child.

Attachment styles: Attachment styles refer to the relational expectations that may emerge for a child that are the result of the stability, availability and responsiveness of a primary care giver. These styles can be most simply divided into secure and insecure. Insecure attachment styles are a result of the less than optimal interactions between the caregiver and infant, and involve a decreased sense of trust in relation to self and others. The quality of our early relationships sets the stage for how we view ourselves, with a positive self-image or a negative self-image, and also how we come to view others as trustworthy or not. If a baby experiences responsive, nurturing and consistent care giving, they are more likely to have a secure attachment, which extends to expectations of others as also being trustworthy, caring and protective.

Samantha Walter

PARENT-CHILD RELATIONSHIPS

There is no doubt that parenting can be a demanding job. A job that takes us around the clock, one that sees us getting up to a sick child at 2 o'clock in the morning, or deciding on the right child-care or school, or when your teenager does not arrive home at their curfew and you stay up worrying about their whereabouts and racking your brains on an appropriate consequence for the behaviour. Couple all this with the fact that at birth your child does not arrive with a manual to prepare you for the highs and lows of being a parent.

During times of stress it can be easy to lose sight of the big picture of why we had children in the first place. However, despite the demanding nature of being a parent, the rewards far outweigh the sleepless nights, the grumbling sick child or the grunting teenager. The joys of watching children succeed at school, in sport, or in relationships is a truly beautiful thing. Developing a healthy relationship with your child requires time, energy and patience. It can sometimes feel like you are taking one step forward and two steps back, but don't give up, hang in there because there are things that parents can do to foster good parent-child relationships.

- *All children require love and affection.* But all children are different. Some prefer hugs rather than kisses, or words of encouragement rather than physical affection. Make time to find out how your child likes to receive affection. Observe how they give affection as this may be different to how they receive it. Also, as children grow, the ways in which they prefer to receive and give affection may change, therefore respond accordingly.

- *Provide quality time.* How you spend time with your child counts. Children love having parents' sole attention. Brief and frequent interactions with your child can work wonders for your relationship. For example, if you have a spare 5 or 10 minutes, ask your child how they would like to spend the time with you. Turn off your phone and give them your full attention.

- *Validate children's emotions.* For children to become emotionally resilient they need to be able to regulate their emotions. This begins with parents acknowledging the way children feel. For example, let's say your child wanted to go to the park but it is raining outside. Your child becomes upset and starts to cry, try responding with something along the lines of; I can see that you are upset because you are crying, I know you wanted to go to the park, but we cannot go as it is raining outside. Once you calm down you can pick a game to play with mummy.

- *Listen non-judgmentally.* Model good listening. Try not to interrupt children as they tell stories or explain a situation. Be aware of our body language and tone of voice as these convey powerful messages to children.

- *Be consistent.* One of the greatest factors in helping children feeling safe and secure is to be consistent. When children can predict from one day to the next that their behaviour is going to get a certain response, they are more likely to feel secure in exploring their environment. However, if one day you ignore their behaviour and the next day you reprimand them, they are likely to feel unsettled and unsure of how to respond which can diminish confidence and resiliency.

- *Separate the behaviour from the child.* Children have great memories for the things we have done or said. If you arc upset at your child for pushing their sister over, for example, instead of saying something like, look at what you have done you naughty boy, try responding with, Johnny, I do not like that behaviour, pushing your sister over hurt her and now she is sad, apologize for hurting her.

- *Remember that sometimes the things that provoke us the most about our children's behaviour are the things that we most dislike about ourselves.* For example, if you get frustrated at your child because they argue often, or seem to want to have the last say, think about how you engage in conversations; do you argue often? Do you always have to be right and feel the need to have the last say?

- *Encourage problem solving.* When children come across difficult situations encourage them to find solutions to their problem. Ask such questions as, what did you try? What has worked in the past? Who else could help?

- *Find time to laugh together each day.* Laughter is the glue that helps families stick together and helps them get through the tough times.

- *Praise your child often.* There many things children do on a day-to-day basis that we can praise them for. For example, when they try something new or persevere when things get hard, when they pick up their toys or do things without being asked. For every 1 negative interaction, we usually require approximately 5 positive interactions to counteract that negative one!

- *All relationships take time, energy and patience.* Take small steps each day getting to know your child. Find out what interests them. If you discover that you don't share a common interest, that is ok, but still make time talk or partake in this activity with your child as it is very important to them.

Remember you do not have to be perfect!

Emily Anderson

PRAISING YOUR CHILD APPROPRIATELY

Much of the research into the appropriate and effective use of praise and feedback has been conducted in the classroom but the findings apply to the home and workplace as well. The guidelines below summarise what has been learned about effective praise and feedback.

- Positive statements have a powerful impact and people like to know they have done well and their actions and achievements have been noted.

- Negative statements, put-downs and name-calling have a negative impact on people and should not be tolerated.

- Positive statements *must* be linked and related to a specific behaviour or performance. General praise that is not targeted or related to a specific behaviour or performance has little impact. You may like to use the three-phase praise process below:

    (a) use a simple praise statement,

    (b) personalise the praise by using the person's name, and then

    (c) describe what the person did to merit praise.

    For example, *Well done Rachel you did a great job helping with dishes* or *Fantastic job Tim you did a great job on that maths test.*

- Praise and feedback should mostly be given individually rather than publically. Interestingly only a third of children aged 8–13 years had a preference for public praise. Teachers and parents should monitor a child's reaction to feedback as nearly one in five children in this age range reported not wanting to be praised at all.

- There are two types of praise that can be given to children. Children can be praised for their hard work and effort (effort feedback) or the focus of the praise can be on their ability by noting that success comes because they are smart, clever and have good abilities (ability feedback). Children should be praised for both effort and ability where warranted and appropriate. Both types of feedback should be used despite having advantages and some limitations.

- Praise should be age appropriate. Younger children like to be praised for their ability, meaning that they find it rewarding to be noticed because they are smart and clever. As children get older they like be praised more for the effort and hard work that has led to their success.

- Children internalise what is said to them by means of self-talk. Teachers and parents should model and reinforce positive self-talk and self-reinforcement after praising a child by saying statements like: and if I were you I'd be saying, *Gee I am doing well at Maths*, to yourself.

- Teachers and parents should do all in their power to stop peers and particularly siblings from saying negative things about physical appearance to other students and brothers and sisters. Lots of negative statements by siblings and peers leads to high negative self-talk and low self-esteem in children.

- Avoid giving praise that is immediately followed by a negative comment or criticism. A critical comment wipes away the impact of the positive comment, example: *Vince, well done for making your bed — pity you don't do it every day* or *Sandra, you shared your doll so nicely with Debbie — what a pity you hit John with it yesterday.*

Remember, you can never praise too much! Children (and people) need praise each day. Your child will not be spoiled or big-headed if you give frequent, genuine praise that reflects the effort they've put into tasks as well as the outcomes they achieve.

Dr Paul Burnett

WORKING MOTHERS

Working mothers is a topic which seems to be inherently divisive. People may have polarising opinions, and mothers may encounter significant resistance when returning to work after a baby. Working mothers (particularly full-time ones) may face negative stereotyping as they may be seen as neglecting the traditional female roles and thus challenging an accepted social norm. Being a mother in the workplace can be seen negatively by peers, may result in increased pressure to perform, can be detrimental to career prospects, and can be something of an anomaly. Making the decision to return to work can often be a difficult one to make, irrespective of whether it was always the plan or is one mediated by changes in life circumstances.

Occasionally mothers encounter difficulty in obtaining a successful work-life balance. In most households, women still perform more of the household tasks, and in dual-income families, the expectations still rest with the woman to care for children. This stress can result in impaired functioning at both work and home. In addition, possibly the most difficult stressor that mothers have to cope with is guilt concerning whether they have made the right decision for themselves and their family, and whether they are neglecting their children. If this is a serious concern for you as a mother, monitor your children's behaviour closely.

Children tend to react to stress by externalising or internalising their emotions. Talk to your children about the change and be honest with them, check-in with them regularly to ensure that they are coping. One of the simplest ways of ensuring more quality time with children is to eat dinner with the whole family at least a few times a week, and read books to them before they go to bed. The reality is that children are resilient and often more adaptive than some give them credit for. Following are some practical tips to help you balance your busy life.

Ask for help

Unfortunately the chances that you are capable of performing feats of superhuman nature are relatively slim. Women often feel that asking for help means that people will think you are not coping, but in reality, this is a very important coping strategy.

Build social resources

Find a good childcare centre and stick with it; the best ones are those where staff have been there for a long period of time and they show genuine care for the children. Put your name on a waiting list if necessary, and try to settle the kids in before returning to work. If needed, use other parents to help for school drop-off and pickup (especially in an emergency), and babysitting, and reciprocate where possible.

Get organised

Cook meals on the weekend and freeze them. Get an organiser/diary, and assign tasks to all members of the family. Kids as young as two can often help out, for example, unpacking bags, putting their dirty clothes in the laundry. Making lunches the night before can help enormously, and freeze sandwiches and muffins so they can be used as needed.

Take a break

This is probably one of the hardest things to fit into the daily life of a working mother. Try to fit time into your day, even just 20 minutes, to read a book, go for a walk or take a long bath. This is your chance to refuel and recharge your batteries. Otherwise it is likely that you will burn out very quickly.

Get rid of time-intensive chores

Go shopping online for groceries as this saves time out of your week and also allows you budget and organize your food for the week.

Multitask

Try and find areas that you can cut back on or where you can multitask, for example, check your emails on the train or the bus, and think about the possibility of getting a cleaner even just once every other week to do the heavy duty cleaning.

Go easy on yourself

There will be days where your kids have breakfast cereal for dinner and days where you want to pull your hair out. Try not to be too critical of yourself. If anything, look at some strategies you may be able to put in place to ensure that in the future you don't have too many of these days. Try thinking about what you would say to a friend who is feeling guilty about these things. Be your own best friend and treat yourself like you would them.

Be clear with partners

If you have a partner or support person, make sure that you have a conversation about who will be performing what duties and be explicit so that there are no misunderstandings. The last thing you want is an argument at 5am about how you feel that the other partner is not pulling their weight, and find they actually feel like they have been going beyond the call of duty!

There are lots of online resources that may be of assistance. If you are really struggling to cope, think about scaling down your commitments, and talk to your boss about more flexible working hours. The best bosses will recognise your value as a staff member and want to retain you; use this to your advantage. You can only take on so much and ultimately the best thing for the family unit is going to be, at least in part, what is best for you.

Susan Beattie and Leigh la Roche

FAMILY MEETINGS

Family meetings are an increasingly popular way for the modern family to stay connected and well-functioning. Although family life can be busy, scheduling time together for meaningful communication, decision-making, problem-solving, and fun has many benefits that can ultimately save families time. Family meetings can also be used effectively by all types of families for any number of reasons.

Common uses of family meetings:

- Planning for upcoming events or activities.
- Clarifying family rules and expectations.
- Resolving conflicts.
- Establishing roles and routines.
- Organising chores.
- Co-ordinating schedules.
- Addressing issues and concerns.
- Celebrating successes.
- Sharing information and experiences.
- Spending positive time together.

Benefits for the family include:

- Strengthening family connectedness and a sense of belonging.
- Establishing a family environment of co-operation and shared understanding.
- Improving relationships between family members and reducing conflict.
- Providing opportunities for encouragement, support and praise.
- Diffusing tensions and preventing problems from festering.
- Fostering a feeling of family unity and harmony.

- Allowing family members to feel heard and valued.

- developing a shared sense of responsibility and ownership for family life.

Family meetings also provide an excellent opportunity to promote family values and attitudes. And to help children become responsible adults by developing their life skills in communication, problem-solving, negotiation, teamwork, conflict resolution, and self-discipline.

How to conduct a family meeting

Once you've decided that family meetings could benefit your family, you will need to establish some guidelines for conducting them. Here are some suggestions:

- Decide what the meetings will be called. Some families are happy with the term family meeting, while others prefer family time or get-togethers, for example.

- Establish a regular time and place to meet. At dinner time one regular night of the week is usually a good time for increasing attendance and facilitating family togetherness in a neutral location (dining table), whilst enjoying a special meal.

- Try to involve all family members via encouragement. Children as young as five years old can participate meaningfully in meetings and even initially resistant teenagers will generally come to value the process in time. Consider how you will deal with any resistance or non-attendance, but avoid making meetings mandatory.

- Although meetings are most effective if everyone is present, committed regularity is the key, so keep to the schedule regardless of who can or cannot attend.

- Some families prefer a structured or formal approach to meetings, while others prefer a more casual and flexible approach. Some families also like to open or close meetings with a ritual, such as lighting a candle or saying a prayer. Adopt whichever approach or rituals suits your family, but be consistent.

- Establish rules for the conduct of meetings such as allowing no interruptions or distractions, being respectful to one another and others' views, staying focused on the agenda items, sharing talking time, no yelling or swearing, and no personal attacks or gripe sessions. Keep firm boundaries for managing difficult behaviour.

- Parents need to model a positive approach towards meetings and a respectful attitude towards members' contributions.

- Set an agenda containing only a few items to help keep the meeting focused. Family meetings are ineffective in unifying the family if there is only a focus on problems, so limit the agenda to only one or two problems per meeting and ensure there is a balance in the amount of time devoted to solving problems and discussing positive or enjoyable topics, or participating in fun activities. Post the agenda in a prominent place and encourage all members to contribute items.

- It can be helpful to assign roles that are rotated each meeting, such as a chairperson, scribe, timekeeper and moderator. Although parents will need to take the lead to start with, everyone (including young children) should be encouraged to take turns at leading future meetings to foster their leadership skills and a sense of shared responsibility in family matters.

- Always begin meetings with compliments, praise or expressions of appreciation.

- The go around method is a good way of allowing each member the opportunity to contribute to discussions and to learn to listen to others. A talking stick may initially help signify whose turn it is to speak without being interrupted.

- Support all members in participating in meetings according to their age and ability.

- Avoid making an individual member's problems a topic for group discussion without their consent. This could prove embarrassing and is better dealt with privately. However, if an individual brings up a personal problem, such as being bullied, they can benefit from the support and problem-solving efforts of the whole family.

- Keep the focus of problem solving on finding solutions and not on assigning blame. Involve everyone in brainstorming possible solutions for discussion and try to reach a consensus on the best option to promote compromise and shared ownership. Also discuss what could be done differently in the future to prevent the problem recurring.

- If no agreement can be reached, parents may choose to make a decision until a consensus is reached at a later time.

- Although parents need to avoid controlling or dominating the meeting, or dictating solutions, they should veto areas that are not up for negotiation or suggestions that do not comply with established family rules and values.

- Keep meetings brief (approximately 20–30mins) and end them on time.

- Always conclude the meeting in a positive way and finish with an enjoyable activity such as a family game, jokes, a special dessert, or a positive story.

- Write down any decisions or agreements from the meeting, including details of who will do what and when, and what consequences will be applied if agreements are not followed through. Post the list in a prominent place for everyone's reference.

What if things go wrong?

Accept that problems may arise and that agreements may not be reached at every meeting. Families may need time to develop new skills or to think about what has been proposed. Existing family issues may also influence outcomes. Unresolved matters can be carried over to the next meeting for further discussion, but don't allow problems to continue to be discussed between meetings.

If the family cannot agree on important issues, it may be necessary to seek professional help (e.g., mediation). Consider that some individuals may benefit from debriefing with someone outside the family after a difficult meeting.

Diane Barber

COPING WITH A CHILD WITH A DISABILITY

To find out that your child has a disability can be devastating news for many. You may feel as though your life has come crashing down around you. All your hopes, dreams and lifelong plans are lost. You ask yourself a series of questions which all lead to — how will you cope?

Ten strategies to help

1. *Research your child's disability.* Knowledge is power. By understanding the disability you will feel empowered to cope with the challenges that lay ahead.

2. In order to receive government services and disability payments, if applicable, your paediatrician or GP will be required to complete the necessary paperwork. Make an appointment a soon as possible if this has not been done.

3. A child with a disability may have access to disability services in their state before they start school. Early intervention is critical and helps children get a start in life through physiotherapy, occupational therapy and speech therapy. You may have to get paperwork prepared by your GP or a specialist practitioner before seeing representatives from a disability service.

4. Get involved in, or have access to, a support group. There are specific organisations available which provide information and resources. Such as those focused on Autism, Down syndrome or Cerebral Palsy.

5. Ask your disability organisation, social worker, or paediatrician to put you in contact with a parent who shares similar challenges to you. This can prove invaluable, because friends and relatives may sometimes not fully understand the anxieties or challenges experienced when having a child with a disability. Whereas a parent in the same situation as you will understand. A problem shared is a problem halved. The same goes for your child's successes. A parent in the same situation will appreciate how much effort is involved when your child reaches a milestone.

6. Ask for help. Being a parent of a child with a disability can be physically and emotionally draining. Don't be embarrassed or ashamed to ask for help if you feel you need it. Respite services are available to parents who need a well-deserved break from their children. This benefits both the child and the parent.

7. Say "yes" if someone offers their assistance. Often family and friends wish they could help your situation and they can if you allow it. Picking up kids after school or doing a load of ironing can be a big help if you're feeling overwhelmed.

8. Don't be too hard on yourself and remember to nurture you as well as your child. A parent of a child with a disability needs to take time out for themselves. By having some down time you will recharge your batteries and be better equipped for ongoing challenges.

9. Have high expectations for your child. Aim for the stars but don't beat yourself up if you don't get there. Stimulation and setting achievable goals for your child will benefit them greatly. Their successes will be sweeter when they achieve their goals.

10. You are your child's best advocate. No one wants greater success for your child than you. Don't be afraid to challenge something that doesn't sound or feel right to you. Ask questions until you are satisfied or understand the answers.

Having a child with a disability has ongoing challenges and rewards. Take each day as it comes and appreciate the little things.

Maree McIntosh

SINGLE PARENTING

There are many parents in today's society who are doing it solo. Perhaps a partner has died, or left the family, or a man or women has decided to enter parenthood alone. Whatever the reason may be, parenting by oneself comes at a cost. There tends to be no one who can help you with those late nights of getting up to the kids, or organising them out the door for school, or having no one to back you up when it comes time for discipline. Couple this with the fact that you usually have to do all this on just one income. Children are expensive! And this can cause much stress and many sleepless nights.

Whatever your situation may be, there are things you can do to not only take care of your children's needs but also your own needs.

Find an appropriate role model for your children

If your children don't have regular contact with their other parent perhaps look to a neighbour, family friend, relative or local sports club for an appropriate role model to support their growth and development as a young man or young woman. Children need to see adults behaving appropriately so they can adopt such behaviours in their life. Developing appropriate relationships with teenagers or adults of the opposite sex may help to bring fulfilment in their life.

Resolve past hurts

If you find yourself parenting alone due to a family breakdown it is important that you find ways of dealing with the pain that the breakdown caused. Unresolved grief, pain and anger can have damaging effects on our relationships, especially with our children, the ones we love the most. If you need help visit your GP, or call a telephone helpline to speak with someone who can offer assistance.

Don't talk negatively about your ex-partner in front of children

It is important that children are not privy to conversations that could become heated between separated parents, as this can leave children questioning their sense of security. Try to talk positively about the child's other parent for their sake. If children hear you disrespecting another adult, this can in turn lead to children disrespect other adults in their lives.

Seek support

Be confident in reaching out to others and letting others reach out to you. Let's face it, doing it alone is tough. There will be times when you will need others to lend a helping hand, perhaps pick the kids up from school, or take them to appointments, or help clean the house! Find someone you trust with whom you can share your feelings. It is ok to feel overwhelmed but don't go it alone.

Take time out for you!

Of course this is the hardest of all the strategies. You might say, "yeah right, when I am going to find time to do that or how can I afford it!" Yes, all of the above is true, however, for your sanity it is important that you find time to do things you enjoy. Make it a priority to include one thing a week just for you. It could be something simple like watching a favourite TV program when the kids are asleep, or taking a bath, inviting a friend over, or going for a walk. Remember, if children observe parents taking care of themselves, they too will learn the importance of taking care of themselves. A happy mum or happy dad, generally equals happy children!

Check in with your child

Living without a mum and dad or just having one parent can be emotionally tough on kids. You shouldn't feel guilty about this, but rather make time to talk with your children about how they find being just the two of you, or having to go between houses. Be confident when talking with your child. Let them know you care about their feelings and that together you will find ways to manage the situation. Perhaps your child needs more regular phone contact with the other parent, maybe they are seeking quality time with you, but because you are stretched thin you don't have much time to spend with them. Whatever the reason, validate how your child feels even if you don't agree. Help them overcome unpleasant feelings by finding time to do things they enjoy. Perhaps suggest they draw their feelings or writing a story about their situation.

Set clear boundaries

All children need boundaries. They need to know that certain behaviours get a certain response. Set some clear household rules, usually less than five things, that would make home live more liveable. For example, *walk in the house, keep hands and feet to ourselves, use an inside voice, if you don't have anything nice to say, don't say anything at all!* Decide in advance what the rewards and consequences will be for each member who follows the rules. Examples of rewards could be an extra 20 minutes on the computer, a story at bedtime, or to go to the park on the weekend. Consequences can be things like loss of computer time, no bedtime story, cell phone gets taken away for the night, the TV gets turned off or going to be early.

Be consistent

As difficult as parenting can be at times, it is important that we try to be as consistent in our parenting practices as possible. Children tend to get apprehensive when things change frequently. Give children some advance warning when things like routines are likely to change. Try remaining as calm as possible when addressing children's behaviour. If you react negatively to behaviour this can escalate the situation, leaving everyone feeling upset and drained. Be prepared to walk away and come back and address the situation again when everyone is calm.

Emily Anderson

CHILDREN OF DIVORCE

Divorce is a common reality for adults and children. Currently almost half of first marriages end in divorce and a greater proportion of subsequent marriages end the same way. This means that there are inevitably thousands of children of divorce. Because of the clinical nature of statistics and ever-present media debates, it is easy to forget the struggle and pain represented by these figures. It has been suggested that about one third of the children of divorce will not experience significant adverse effects, while another third will have some short-term problems, with the remainder experiencing problems throughout their lifespan.

Divorce is not merely something that affects a husband and wife. The majority of divorces occur in families with children. Divorce is not a single event but a process of change that extends over a prolonged period of time. Divorce brings with it an extended period of psychological and social disequilibrium that adults and children often find exceedingly stressful. Divorce is only one in a series of transitions and reorganisations that follow separation and marital dissolution.

The following are some suggestions that may be helpful when supporting children of divorce. These recommendations are also useful shared with educators, who are increasingly dealing with children of divorce.

These ideas are not meant to be exhaustive, but are offered as starting points for discussion and intervention within a context of a caring relationship with children.

- Explain the divorce simply and openly.
- Avoid attributing blame and guilt for the divorce.
- Make it clear it is not the child who is being divorced.
- Eliminate competition for the child's love and attention.
- Let the child feel safe to express hurt and angry feelings.
- Assure the child that they are not responsible for the divorce.
- Give the child information about changes that may occur in their life.
- Encourage the child to talk about feelings, thoughts, and reactions.
- Be flexible with regard to daily arrangements.

- Encourage the child to keep in contact with friends and family.
- Be honest about the difficulties associated with readjustment.
- Help the child to problem-solve their difficulties.
- Support the child in the expression of their needs.
- Explain it is beyond their ability to reunite the parents.
- Reassure the child they will always be part of a family.
- Enhance trust via a positive relationship with the child.
- Develop self-esteem by setting challenging yet attainable tasks.
- Teach child positive self-talk techniques.
- Accept child's temperamental idiosyncrasies.
- Encourage the child to develop hobbies and interests.
- Encourage the child to reach out to others.
- Convey a sense of caring.
- Encourage and reward the child for helpfulness.
- Model a conviction that life makes sense.
- Structure experiences that challenge.
- Provide meaning and value to the child's life.

Divorced parents need to be clear, consistent and generous in offering love and affection to their children, while simultaneously setting firm boundaries and expectations. Parents need also draw clear boundaries for any new and ex-relationships. It is within these parameters that children can feel secure and develop greater optimism for the future. Children are likely to develop psychological hardiness if the demands upon them are moderate, if their parents support their efforts to perform new responsibilities, and if family members hold a positive view of divorce-related changes, given that children often like to maintain regular contact with both parents.

With children of divorce an escalating phenomenon, the resultant issues in homes and schools need to be addressed via quality interventions. As parents face the challenges on the home-front, well-planned and developmentally appropriate strategies should be focused on to help with any adjustment difficulties for the ever-increasing and potentially vulnerable population of the children of divorce. Professionals can aid you in this process too.

Dr John Barletta

SHARING THE CARE OF CHILDREN

A parent's separation is amongst one of the most stressful life events for both the children and adults. Fifty years of research has shown that it is not the divorce but the conflict between parents which causes the most damage. It is important to keep a focus. The two most important questions to ask before every decision is; *am I doing this for the children or out of my emotions?* and *what will my children think of this decision when they are adults?* By focussing on the future, and on logic, it minimises the conflict-based decisions.

When two parents live in the same home children can benefit from a maximum of attention (two parents present all the time). With a separation, the maximum is one parent half the time, so everyone misses out and children can only get a maximum of a quarter of what they had before.

There is a social myth often associated with Family Law that children must spend alternating weeks with each parent. This is not true. The laws say to consider equal responsibility and consider equal care, but if equal care is not practical or in a child's best interests, then both parents should have a reasonable and meaningful relationship. Therefore there are a range of options.

Research shows that a minimum of 35% parenting time is necessary to have strong relationship with one's children. That means an average of five days per fortnight is important. However, that can be made of half of the holidays and four days per fortnight. Many children cope better with a primary base and a second home, than being split across two homes. For many parents, being able to have a career and hands on time with children makes unequal shared care successful for children and their career.

Shared parenting research also shows that parents need similar styles, flexibility, live close (within 30 minutes), and communicate effectively for shared care to work. It is important to look at what the arrangement was before separation to see what children are used to (children do benefit if after separation they have more Dad time, if Dad worked long hours before separation).

Parents should consider what they do best. Some parents are academic, structured and routine. Others are sporting and active. If there is one of each, the first will do best with more school days, and second best with more weekend time and holidays.

Children need to have an easy-going temperament, not have developmental difficulties, and want the arrangement, for shared care to work. There are some children who simply do not suit long blocks away from a parent. Why else would we have expressions like "mummy's boy" or "daddy's girl".

Younger children (under three especially) need to have short frequent visits to both parents. Slightly older children will do better with regular times (one-or two-night blocks). Primary school-aged children do best with blocks up to five days, while older children may prefer alternating weeks. If parents want a 50% arrangement, younger children (ages four to ten) often do better on a 2, 2, 5, 5 plan (same two weekdays with each parent, while Friday, Saturday, and Sunday could alternate). Teens should have their views heard and considered however parents should be the final decision maker.

Lawyers are not necessarily the best people to work out the most appropriate arrangements for children. Their role is most often about gaining the best arrangements for the parent who they are representing. Similarly a general psychologist may not have specialist expertise in arrangements for children. Look around for special advice if you need help.

Dr Phil Watts

STEP-FAMILIES

How a family is defined in today's society certainly differs to that of past times when mum, dad and two children was the norm. Divorce rates were low and step- or blended families were a rare phenomena. Nowadays divorce rates are high, and parents are remarrying or living in defacto relationships which results in step-mums and dads, step-siblings, step-aunts and uncles, and even step-grandparents!

The blending of one or more families can certainly be a challenge, especially as each family comes with their own set of values, beliefs and ways of dealing with situations. Some parents feel guilty when their chid expresses sadness about not living with both parents, and at times can compensate or try making it up to their children. Parents may try to buy their child's love and affection, or shower their children with extra attention and gifts, or give in to their whims. Unfortunately, these responses are not particularly helpful.

Below are some suggestions to support step-families in becoming unified, and making their family unit work for them:

- *Spend time getting to know your step-children.* All children are different and depending on when you entered their life will depend on how much you know about them. Take time to find out what interests your step-children. Find time to engage them in conversations and activities they like, and remember that children are good at detecting our level of genuineness and authenticity, so be yourself!

- *Resolve past hurts.* Most of us have been wounded or hurt at some point in our lives, but what is important is whether or not we have resolved that hurt. Unresolved grief, pain and anger can have damaging effects on our relationships, especially with our partners and children, the ones we love the most. If you need help, visit your family doctor or call a telephone helpline to speak with someone who can offer professional assistance.

- *Back one another up.* Parenting your own children can be tough enough, but taking on the role of parenting another person's child — now that can be a challenge! However, if you both agree on some basic household rules and are supportive of each other, as well as encouraging respect for authority in

the home, when it comes time to enforce boundaries or implement consequences, things should go relatively smoothly. Remember that children feel
secure and know their limits when parents stand united.

- *Make time to check-in with each family member.* The process of blending
  families takes time, energy and a lot of patience! Make time to ask each
  family member how they are coping within the family. Hold family
  meetings. One suggestion is to provide a box for family members to post
  anonymous notes outlining the things they would like addressed at the
  family meeting. Anonymity reduces the likelihood of siblings picking on
  each other or someone being singled out.

- *Don't talk negatively about your ex-spouse in front of children.* It is important
  that children are not privy to conversations that could become heated
  between parents, as this can leave children questioning their sense of
  security. Try to talk positively about the child's other parent for their sake.
  If children hear you disrespecting another adult, this can in turn lead to
  children disrespecting other adults in their lives.

- *Agree on household rules, consequences and rewards.* It is important to establish
  a few household rules for all members to abide by (yes, even the adults!).
  Stick to less than five rules and decide in advance the rewards and consequences for following, or not following, household rules. Be consistent in
  enforcing consequences and rewards. Consequences can be such things as
  no television that night, no dessert, no computer time, or no pocket money
  if the behaviour continues. Rewards could be an extra story at bedtime, a
  trip to the park, a chance to earn extra money or 10 mins playtime with
  Mum or Dad.

- *Remember that transitioning takes time.* There is no manual on how to blend
  families, only a list of possible strategies to pick and choose from to support
  healthy family functioning from one day to the next. All good things take
  time. Blending families is a journey like any other and comes with its own
  highs and lows.

- *Validate the way your child feels.* It takes time for children to adjust to new
  surroundings, especially if they are not used to sharing you with someone
  else. It is common for children to experience an array of emotions ranging
  from anger, jealously, guilt, sadness and fear when faced with new situations. It is important to respect how your child feels about being part of a
  step-family. Provide lots of opportunities for children to express how they
  feel. Help them to regulate their emotions by problem solving with them.
  Provide prompts such as; how do you think we should handle this situation? Or what else can you do to calm down when you feel angry?

- *Some level of fighting is inevitable!* As humans we make mistakes. At times we will say the wrong thing, or look the wrong way, upsetting another person. Children are especially good at finding someone's buttons to push! Therefore, fighting amongst siblings, be it biological siblings or step-siblings, is not uncommon. Be confident in setting limits and boundaries. Be consistent at backing-up instructions with consequences. Remain calm and act promptly when fighting occurs.

- *Have fun.* Laughter really is the best medicine! It helps to break down all sorts of barriers. Make time to tell jokes, watch funny movies and to talk to one another.

- *Respect your partners' relationship with their own children.* There will be times when you may not agree with the method your partner takes in dealing with a particular situation with his/her own children. However, it is important that you respect the relationship he/she has with their children. If you have concerns talk with your partner, express how you feel to avoid unnecessary conflict where necessary.

Emily Anderson

ADULT CHILDREN RETURNING HOME

More and more adult children are returning to live with their parents. The reasons for this are varied, however it is likely to be because the adult child's personal circumstances have altered in a negative way for example, unemployment or retrenchment, relationship breakdown, or unplanned homelessness. Sometimes, the child will boomerang home to save money (i.e., for a house whilst studying) or they may return because it is easier — or so they think!

The reasons that underpin the return to the family home are important insofar as they might impact upon the rules and boundaries that the parents implement. If the adult child is distressed following a relationship breakdown, they will need emotional support and nurturance for a period of time. If they have returned home to have someone else feed them, do their laundry, and provide free accommodation whilst they save for an investment property, they need to be given a reality check around the responsibilities of adulthood and the extent to which parental generosity extends.

Unlike younger children where parents can, to varying degrees of success, set limits around expected behaviour and responsibilities in a fairly autocratic manner, the same dynamics do not apply with adult children who have their own ideas on how they ought to be able to behave. It's wonderful when all the adults are on the same page. It can be really unpleasant when the home-owners (the parents) have different expectations to the home-visitor (the adult child).

Here are some tips that might assist:

- Do not assume that everyone holds the same expectations around what the living arrangements will be. Who will do the cooking, cleaning, laundry, pay the bills, feed the pets? How will you divide the cost of living expenses; what about incidental or hidden expenses such as household insurance? What happens with visitors, entertaining, television, music, tidiness? What about personal space and privacy? How long will this arrangement last?

- Have a conversation that mentions all of the above (and anything else you can think of pertaining to co-habitation). The more areas that have been discussed and agreed upon, the less chance of conversations that include "but you never told me that".

• Revisit these topics as often as necessary. Keeping feelings of resentment to an absolute minimum, or non-existent, will avoid explosive arguments that could damage the relationship you have with your adult child.

• Set the conversations up to be as successful as possible. Go out for a drink or a meal and chat about how your child is going. Some people favour public conversations when there are touchy subjects to discuss. Ask if there has been a change of circumstances that has resulted in a shift in thinking on their part. Remind your child of the agreements that were previously reached if a conflict arises. Decide together how the situation can be rectified.

If agreed behaviours and boundaries cannot be reached independently, consider consulting a family therapist. It's not as scary as you might think and can result in a much more harmonious living arrangement for everyone.

Susan De Campo

BECOMING A GRANDPARENT

For generations, grandparents around the world have played a significant and valuable role in the family system. The role of grandparents has changed considerably in the past few decades, with many finding they are providing not only occasional child care but physical and emotional support for their grandchildren while the parents work, study and manage personal or health issues. Approximately 90% of grandparents report being satisfied with the relationship they share with their grandchildren. Attachment theorists suggest that, next to parents, grandparents can offer their grandchildren a warm, safe and stable environment when their parents are not available or during times of upheaval and stress.

Becoming a grandparent is a normal and a natural life transition, and for many, this will be a time of delight and celebration, while others may find themselves overwhelmed with a range of diverse emotions.

For some people, grand-parenting may come too early or too late. Others may struggle with the transition and the meaning of their role in their grandchild's life. Whatever your reaction to becoming a grandparent, its okay! If you find yourself struggling with your new role, talk to a trusted friend or health professional and consider the issues below:

- Remain mindful that you may experience a whole range of thoughts and feelings about becoming a grandparent for the first time. Some of these may include issues around ageing, your physical stamina, changes to your family of origin, your personal lifestyle, hobbies and interests. It is not uncommon for grandparents to worry about the new parents' financial and coping abilities, health issues, and the changes a new baby will bring to the family in general.

- Have a conversation with your adult child and their partner about your role in your grandchild's life. Ask them what will work best for them and then work together to create a healthy relationship for you all.

- In the early weeks, don't assume your son/daughter, their partner and new baby will be available to attend all family functions.

- Family of origin celebrations and traditions may also need to be discussed and renegotiated to consider the needs of the new family members.

- Respect the new parents' right to parent their way. Baby and child care has changed considerably over the generations and the new parents will have their own beliefs about how they will raise their children. Watching new parents struggle and make mistakes can be frustrating, but unless you are asked for advice, suggesting you know better can create insecurity and feelings of failure in new parents.

- Let them know they are doing a great job, even if it is different to the way you parented.

- Sometimes just being present to make a cup of tea, a meal or assist with daily chores while mum and dad tend their baby, can be of enormous value. You will still get lots of time to cuddle, love and nurture your grandchild as his/her parents become more confident in their new role.

- Create healthy boundaries for yourself and remember its okay to say no. It is important that you maintain your own health, lifestyle, relationships, work, hobbies, and interests.

The role you play in the lives of your grandchildren and the relationship you build with them will be reflected through future generations. You now have the opportunity to make a difference without the responsibilities of being the parent. Embrace the miracle of this new and precious life and cherish every moment!

Jan Bond

GIVING A BABY UP FOR ADOPTION

What is adoption?

Adoption is the process of legally placing a child with non-biological parents to rear as their own, whereby the biological parents give up all legal rights and obligations to the child. Adoption is a highly personal and complex process involving many emotions not only for the biological parents, adoptive parents and extended family members. Whilst adopting a child can be a joyous event, the decision for a biological parent to give their child up for adoption is typically a painful and extremely complex experience.

Common emotions

Placing your child up for adoption can involve particularly high levels of stress, guilt, fear, shame, doubt, anxiety, uncertainty and confusion. It is common for biological parents to experience feelings of grieving and loss after relinquishing their child.

Before making your decision you may want to explore the following:

- It is highly recommended that you talk through and fully explore all your options with your family, friends and professional supports.

- Contact your local social services to see what is available in the community that may be able to assist you through your current crisis prior to making such a life altering decision.

- It is crucial that you make the final decision without pressure from external parties as this can intensify psychological consequences of the adoption process and may harm your future mental health.

- Be completely honest with yourself and others about how this decision will impact upon your life.

- Carefully weigh up the pros and cons of adoption. Writing down the positives and negatives can be a good way to obtain a visual aide to ensure you are making a decision that is right for you.

- Some important questions to ask yourself may include: *Why do I want to give my child up for adoption and is it a good enough reason to cut all ties with my child? Will my child and I benefit from the adoption? Is this what I really want to do?*

- Make contact with others who have personal experience in the adoption process and ask lots of questions.

- If you decide to proceed, acknowledging the adoptive parents have gone through a long and arduous process in order to adopt your child may assist in reducing stress and anxiety.

- It may also be possible to negotiate to have contact with your child as they grow, such as photos, sending gifts or occasional phone calls.

- If this is not possible, then it is important to keep in mind that your child, at some time during their life, may attempt to contact you expecting answers. Be prepared and be honest.

Where to find guidance and support

Generally adoptions are processed by adoption services located in your local telephone book. You can also talk to your family GP, social worker, counsellor or adoption agency. Crisis phone lines are available and offer confidential counselling should you need it.

Sarah Sherrington

ADOPTING A CHILD

Adoption presents the child and adoptive parents with many challenges. Whilst it is individually rewarding, fulfilling and enriching, there are a series of stressors associated with the process, and challenges for both children and parents as time progresses. The process of adoption itself is demanding of parents and requires perhaps an uncomfortable degree of self-examination, external examination and may require a high degree of personal sacrifice.

Pre-adoption

Potential adoptive parents must undergo a thorough review process prior to being approved for adoption. The process involves criminal history checks, review of financial status and lifestyle, and views on parenting and strategies for child rearing. No other parent has this type of examination and it is threatening to be examined in this way. It is probably wise to remember that there is no one preferred lifestyle, or set of circumstances. The individual making the assessments has a duty to finding a safe and secure environment to place a child. In a sense every adoptive child has special needs so great care is taken in placing them. Keep in mind that the review process is not adversarial. Try to establish an open and honest relationship with the relevant department and the individual assessor.

Whilst the process is detailed the actual contact time spent with the assessors is low. Also it's not advisable to change your lifestyle or focus entirely on the adoption as the centrepiece of your life whilst waiting for adoption. Some people have been known to stop employment during the application process and set up a nursery years in advance of when a child may be available. Treat the waiting period as a protracted gestation period. Living with a nursery, and associated supply of baby goods for a protracted time whilst waiting for a child is likely to contribute to stress, and anxiety about the outcome.

Wait until allocation is confirmed. You will have plenty of time to prepare from that point. Adoption is expensive and caring for a child post-allocation is likely to be more expensive than you anticipate. Do all that you can to prepare for at least one year of diminished income if you usually rely on dual income. Financial stress is one of stressors of new parenthood that can be alleviated through planning.

Common stressors for adoptive parents

- *Review stress.* Being reviewed is likely to reveal fear, self-doubt, guilt, helplessness, frustration, numbness, shame, mood swings, anxiety, panic, emptiness, impatience, anger, relief, acceptance.

- *Health concerns.* It is most invasive to have an agency ask the question; Are you likely to succumb to illness when your child reaches maturity? Reframe the evaluation as a life insurance assessment.

- *Cognitive concerns.* Self doubt about your lack of knowledge about children may express itself. Ask the assessor if they can recommend a good book or two.

- *Behavioural and physical.* Crying, social withdrawal, sleep problems, restlessness, relationship stress.

Coping strategies

Maintain a balanced life. The adoption process is a long one and needs to be treated as a marathon not a sprint. Don't make radical changes to your lifestyle at the earliest stages of the adoption process. Use the adoption review process as a frame to identify what preparations you need to make, and when to make them. Use information nights and the communication channels presented through the adoption process to identify what issues are likely to impact on your particular circumstances. Talk to the person assessing your application about any concerns and ask them how others have dealt with any issues of concern in the past.

Dr Mark Bahr

Children and Adolescent Issues

CHILD PHYSICAL HEALTH AND STRESS

The health of infants and children is managed mainly by their parents and family. Child health nurses, GP, therapists and paediatricians may become involved if there are ongoing concerns with any aspect of a child's health. Children differ from adults in that their health also involves both their physical growth and undergoing changes in their developmental abilities (i.e., language, vision, hearing, fine motor, gross motor, cognitive and emotional).

Children exposed to psychological stress may manifest a range of physical symptoms and complaints that can be difficult to distinguish from real physical illness. These symptoms may also result in the child missing large amounts of school.

The basis of making a diagnosis of a psychological (or non-organic) illness is to be able to confidently exclude a physical cause for the child signs and symptoms, and to identify possible contributing psychological factors. This will usually involve an initial consultation with a GP who may later consider referral to other therapists or a paediatrician.

The conditions listed below can be present with significant symptoms which, at the end of the day, may turn out to have a psychological basis.

Enuresis (wetting)

Enuresis describes a lack of urinary control at an age where it would be expected. In most instances children achieve daytime control by three years of age and night-time control by four years. Diurnal enuresis refers to wetting during the day, nocturnal enuresis to wetting at night. Primary enuresis refers to the child who has never had bladder control, Secondary enuresis if a relapse has occurred, and psychogenic enuresis refers to instances when children will wet themselves when stressed. Common stressors include the birth of a new sibling, starting school or an episode of acute illness. It may be associated with major behavioural problems where children are negative and generally resistant about using the toilet. A detailed history enquiring into the pattern of wetting and whether there are any associated symptoms such as burning, frequency and abdominal pain, together with a urine-dipstick and culture will go partway to excluding organic causes (i.e., conditions related to a body organ).

Encopresis

Encopresis refers to the voluntary passage of a formed stool in an inappropriate place, for example in underwear or other place, for a child who is mature enough to have a normal bowel habit. If there is a non-organic cause, it may be indicative of a severe behavioural issue which may need intense psychology or child psychiatry management. It can be differentiated from soiling by the taking of a detailed history; investigations other than a stool culture and an abdominal x-ray are rarely necessary.

Headache

Headache is a relatively frequent symptom amongst school age children. Tension headaches are benign but can cause very significant distress by their frequency and intensity. They are more common in later childhood and are usually described as being band-like or constricting in nature. They occur more often towards the end of the day and do not interfere with sleep. They are often associated with stress and day-to-day issues in the child's life. Reassurance, simple analgesics such as Paracetamol or Ibuprofen, and the addressing of any stressors allow the headaches to become less frequent or resolve completely. More serious causes of headaches include migraine, meningitis and brain tumours. Headaches that are very severe and localised, interfere with sleep or are associated with vomiting may need to be investigated with either a CT scan (Computerised Tomography) or MRI scan (Magnetic Resonance Imaging).

Abdominal pain

Recurrent abdominal pain is experienced by 10–15% of children at some time during the school years. The majority of abdominal pains do not have an organic cause. Some are psychogenic and directly related to stresses within the family and at school. By taking a thorough history looking at the character, position, periodicity of the pain as well as any associated systemic, bowel or urinary symptoms will help in determining the need for investigations or imaging. Appendicitis, constipation, inflammatory bowel disease, coeliac disease and other organic causes of abdominal pain are usually confirmed with simple investigations.

Chest pain

Although many children will complain of chest pain, it is usually short-lived and benign. Much of the anxiety relates to the serious consequences of chest pain in adulthood. If the pains are persistent and severe then normal investigations including blood tests, chest x-ray and electrocardiogram (ECG) will provide reassurance as to the benign nature of the pains.

Developmental delay

A child's development is dependent on numerous factors including inherited disorders, intrauterine environment, birth history and postnatal input from those around them. A comprehensive history and examination will accurately assess any developmental concerns in relation to language, gross motor skills, fine motor skills, hearing, vision, and learning. Emotional abuse and neglect can present in an otherwise normal child as a delay in any or all of these areas. At times it is a regression of skills that is of most concern. The exclusion of organic factors and intensive input from therapists, day carers and social services may result in a dramatic improvement in the child's skills. If abuse and neglect occurred over a long period of time there may be some persisting learning, behavioural and emotional issues. If expected gains do not occur in the parental home, in significant cases, it may be necessary to consider options that are in the best interests of the child (e.g., foster care type arrangements).

As illustrated above, children can present with a multitude of symptoms that are not caused by an organic pathology. The symptoms are very real and must be managed sensitively with sympathy and kindness. It is important that significant illness is excluded and that both the child and parent are assured that there are no underlying concerns. Emotional and psychological causes should be explored and addressed accordingly. Ongoing monitoring of the child and their symptoms may be appropriate. This may involve the use of a symptom diary. During this time efforts should be made to encourage school attendance and other activities.

Dr David McMaster

SAFE SLEEPING FOR BABIES AND TODDLERS

Babies and toddlers spend a lot of their time sleeping. Some sleeping arrangements are not safe and can increase the risk of Sudden Infant Death Syndrome (SIDS) or cause serious sleeping accidents. There has been much research around ways to reduce the risks of SIDS and ways to create a safe sleeping environment for babies from birth. SIDS is the most common cause of death in babies between one month and one year of age. Most babies who die of SIDS are under six months of age and more babies die in the winter months than the summer months. Although extensive research has been conducted, it is still not clear what causes SIDS. From research to date, some risk factors have been identified and these form the basis of the SIDS and Kids Safe Sleeping Education Program. It is important that anyone caring for infants follows the guidelines, however, there is no guarantee that an infant may not die from SIDS.

Since the Reducing the Risks program was introduced in 1991, SIDS deaths have been reduced by 85%. The following tips will help parents of newborn babies and young children to create an environment that will ensure all measures have been taken for safe sleeping whether at home, a relative's place or in temporary accommodation.

Put baby on its back to sleep, from birth

Sleeping on the back reduces the risk of SIDS. The chance of babies dying from SIDS is greater if they sleep on their tummy or side. Sleeping a baby on its tummy (prone position) increases the risk of SIDS by 3 to 6 times. Sleeping a baby on its side doubles the risk of SIDS. Healthy babies placed on their backs to sleep are less likely to choke on vomit than babies sleeping on their tummies. Always sleep your baby on its back, from birth, unless your doctor tells you otherwise.

Sleep baby with face uncovered

Make sure that your baby's face and head remains uncovered during sleep as this decreases the risk. Unless instructed to, ensure that your baby is not wearing a hat, a bib or anything tied around its neck when being put to sleep.

Place baby's feet at the bottom of the cot

Placing your baby with feet at the bottom of the cot will ensure that the baby can't slip down under any blankets. Swaddle or wrap a newborn baby to reduce the amount of blankets used and to help baby settle. A light blanket or sheet can be placed over the baby and tucked in firmly. You may decide to use a safe baby sleeping bag instead of blankets. If using a safe baby sleeping bag ensure that the bag is not too large for the baby and that it fits well around the baby's torso.

Ensure that the baby's bedding has the following:

- A firm mattress that fits well into the cot structure to within 25mm (one inch) of sides and ends of the cot.

- The mattress base set in the lower position, the cot sides or end needs to be at least 500mm (20 inches) higher than the mattress.

- Spacing between the bars or panels in the cot sides and ends needs to be between 50 and 95mm (2–4 inches) — gaps wider than 95mm (4 inches) can trap a baby's head.

- Safety standards for household cots have a mandatory safety standard number. Check that your cot has a sticker that states that the cot complies with the standard.

- A mattress that is firm and has no soft edges or extra fabric surrounding or underneath the mattress for example, no lambswool underlay.

- Ensure that all the sheets are in tucked securely and firmly around the mattress.

- No quilts, bumpers, pillows (including U or V shaped pillows), doonas, duvets or soft toys in the cot.

- Bean bags, water beds and large cushions are not appropriate sleeping environments for babies.

Keep baby smoke-free before birth and after birth

Cigarette smoke harms babies before and after birth. Parents who smoke during pregnancy and after the baby's birth increase the risk of SIDS for their baby. In fact, if a mother smokes the risk of SIDS doubles, and if the father smokes too, the risk doubles again. Try not to let anyone smoke near your baby, in the house, in the car or anywhere else your baby spends time.

Sleeping in prams, strollers, car seats and portable-cots

If your baby is sleeping in a pram, stroller or car seat ensure that it has the safety harness done up. It can be fatal if the baby becomes entangled in the straps or loose restraints. Restraints will not be the safety measure they should be if they are not done up while using these types of baby equipment. If a baby is sleeping in a pram, ensure that the mattress is also firm fitting and that there are no extra blankets, pillows or soft fabrics that may be a potential risk. When using a portable cot only use the mattress that is approved for that type of cot, do not add any extra mattresses, pillows or fabrics. Make sure that all the safety latches are secure before placing the baby in the cot.

Dangling cords, strings, mobiles over cots or toddler beds

Place the cot away from any cords hanging from blinds, curtains or electrical appliances. These could cause entanglement or get caught around body parts. Keep mobiles out of reach and not directly over the baby's head.

Heaters and electrical appliances

Keep heaters, air conditioners and any electrical appliance away from the cot to avoid the risk of overheating or overcooling, burns or electrocution. Do not use electric blankets, hot water bottles or wheat bags for babies or young children. Any baby or toddler who becomes too hot or too cold is at risk of SIDS and SUDC (Sudden Unexpected Death of a Child).

Taking a baby into an adult bed may be unsafe if baby:

- gets caught under adult bedding or pillows,
- gets trapped between the wall and the bed,
- falls out of bed, or
- is rolled on by someone who sleeps very deeply or is affected by alcohol or drugs.

Feel comfortable asking your family doctor, pediatrician, specialist nurses, or other health professionals if you have any other questions or concerns regarding your baby's sleep.

Kelli-Ann Zakharoff

CHILD AND ADOLESCENT DEVELOPMENT

The journey from childhood to adolescence involves a series of multi-faceted transitions. In these developmental stages young people are typically expected to meet a number of developmentally appropriate milestones — emotionally, cognitively, socially, physically and sexually. However, while many of the typical developmental milestones are universal, shared across a range of cultures and countries, each individual's experience of these transitions will be quite different. And while all individuals will face these transitions, achievement of these milestones is not precise and the timing will vary from individual to individual. Some young people will manage the transitions of childhood and adolescence better than others, as will some parents! Although some young people will experience difficulties with some of these transitions (around 25%), many make these transitions successfully with the support of their families, peers and communities.

There are a number of factors that can impact on the achievement of developmental milestones. These include the following:

- Genetics.
- Temperament.
- Stresses and trauma.
- Family factors such as family structure, birth order, relationships.
- Culture.
- Peers.
- Environmental issues (e.g., pollution, poverty).

For these reasons, development is often not uniform. Factor issues such as those above may delay or push forward the achievement of certain milestones. Furthermore, it is not uncommon for young people to develop more quickly for one milestone than another. For example, they may experience puberty early but socially or academically be slower to develop. As a result, it is often not helpful to compare one child with another, even when they come from the same family.

While it is not possible to comprehensively describe development in each of the key areas in this contribution (many excellent books and websites are available on this topic), in general, child and adolescent development involves the ongoing acquisition of skills and abilities not previously achieved. The following summarises the key components for each area of development from childhood to adolescence.

Physical development

Physically, the transition from childhood to adolescence involves periods of intense growth, most notably at puberty. At this time young people, both boys and girls, experience increases in height, weight, muscle mass and body fat. Puberty is also associated with genital maturation and menstruation. Culturally, the experience of this transition may differ for boys and girls, depending on cultural ideals. For example, increases in height, weight and muscle mass may be welcomed by many boys but may not be experienced as positively by some girls, particularly those who have cultural aspirations of beauty that involve thinness.

Cognitive development

The developing cognitive abilities of young people during this time can be deceptive as we often expect a steady, linear increase in all cognitive abilities with increasing age. While this is true for some aspects of cognitive development, it is not true for all cognitive abilities. For example, during this period young people are able to acquire and apply increasing amounts of information, in increasingly complex, sophisticated and abstract ways. However, during adolescence the brain also goes through an intense period of brain specialisation and re-organisation. Although specific knowledge may increase, the ability to predict risk or to make decisions, especially in emotionally charged situations, does not increase at the same rate. This has obvious implications for the acquisition of certain life skills such as driving a car.

Emotional development

Young people also develop in the emotional realm. This includes the ability to be increasingly introspective while at the same time gaining a greater understanding of the impact they have on others. During this developmental period many young people seek an increasingly complex sense and understanding of themselves. They also often seek increasingly complex forms of self-expression. Young people's capacity to inhibit their emotional responses will generally increase, for example many adolescents will not cry in front of teachers or their parents, although there is considerable variability in the ability to do this.

Sexual development

Sexual development occurs across the lifespan but is particularly evident in adolescence at puberty. Young people typically become increasingly aware of themselves as sexual beings in this developmental period, and often require increasing amounts of privacy. Exploration of their sexuality and the quest for sexual identity (i.e., as heterosexual or gay) is common. Sexual exploration with others and the quest for romantic relationships is also important.

Social development

As young people develop a greater sense of self and seek increasing independence, separation from parents and increased identification with peers is common. Friendship groups often shift from being based predominately on geography (i.e., we are friends because we are in the same class) to being based on shared interests and values (i.e., we are friends because we both love basketball or independent music). Young people in these developmental periods may struggle between wanting to fit in with friends and establishing themselves as a unique.

Supporting your young person in transition

It is important to remember that young people will develop important life skills such as responsibility, primarily through practice. It is not enough to simply hope that young people will acquire a life skill (we wouldn't dream of doing this with driving!) or that they will absorb it by watching us. The development of these skills requires supervised practice with increased autonomy only occurring when a given task is consistently mastered. This is a different concept to just providing young people with increased responsibility simply because they are getting older.

The presence of mirror cells in the brains of young people as shown by research, is evidence that parents will be their most important teachers. They will learn by watching the people closest to them regarding what they do and how they do it, not just by what they say. Parents and carers require flexibility, information and to be prepared to walk the walk and lead by example. You may be required to resist preconceived notions of how and when normal development should happen.

How will I know if my young person is in trouble?

With so much variability in how young people develop across childhood and adolescence, how can you tell if something is not quite right? Looking for clusters of symptoms may be useful. If a young person is withdrawing from you, and their best friend, and from a well-established sports team, this may be more indicative of difficulties than any one of those things alone.

Also look for large departures from their usual or typical behaviour. For example, if your child is typically an extrovert and outgoing and they start to become extremely quiet and introverted this may be reason for concern. If you are unsure or concerned, it may be helpful to seek qualified assistance even if it just for yourself in the first instance. A telephone parenting helpline, school psychologist or guidance counsellor, or GP may be a helpful place to start.

Dr Vanessa Spiller

CHILD SAFETY AROUND THE HOME

An unexpected traumatic injury or illness that places a child in a hospital emergency unit can cause overwhelming distress and shock to a family. Unintentional injury is predictable and avoidable, yet motor vehicle incidents, burns and drowning in particular, remain some of the leading causes of death and hospitalisation amongst young children. Listed below are some tips on how to tackle the major safety issues for children.

Drowning

This can occur in swimming pools, bathtubs, ponds, buckets, dams, rivers, lakes, oceans, or tanks:

To avoid the danger of drowning, you should:

- Keep watch — supervise (never leave children alone near water).
- Fence your pool correctly (four-sided fences with a self-latching gate is best).
- Teach your child to swim (familiarise them with water safety).
- Learn resuscitation (CPR).

Scalds

This can occur with hot liquid, vapour or steam.

For young children, scalds are commonly associated with hot drinks; water being boiled for drinks, cooking, hot food (e.g., instant noodles) and most frequently hot tap water. The key factors in preventing scalds include keeping young children away from the kitchen when cooking and away from the bathroom. Keep all containers and appliances that contain hot liquid away from the edge of the bench, turn pot handles away from the front of the stove or bench. It has been proven that the best first aid for burns is to immediately apply running cold tap water to the burn for at least 20 minutes (do not use ice or ice water), and keep the child warm. This helps to reduce the pain and will assist scar healing in time.

General burn prevention

Install fire alarms, have a fire plan for the house, always supervise children around the BBQ and campfires. Having fire extinguishers and fire blankets in your home is highly recommended for the unexpected incidents that can occur, and keep hot irons and iron cords out of reach of children. Practice GET DOWN LOW AND GO GO GO, and STOP, DROP and ROLL.

Falls

These can occur on stairs, balconies, furniture, windows, bunk beds, or play-grounds.

To help prevent obvious falls always use gates for the top and bottom of stair-cases. Secure heavy pieces of furniture (e.g., bookshelves, stove, television). Always supervise children on nursery furniture and on play equipment. Never allow a child less than 6 years on the top of a bunk bed. Ensure windows, flyscreens and balconies are structurally sound and safe for children. Playgrounds should have a safe design and be maintained. Always use a 5-point harness to restrain a child in a stroller or high chair.

Car accidents

One of the major causes of child death and injury in car accidents is the child not being effectively restrained in an effective child car-seat restraint or seatbelt. Ensure children are restrained in age/weight appropriate child-hood car seats. Research shows that effective use of child restraints saves lives and decreases the severity of injury. Refer to you local government agency for more specific laws.

Low speed vehicle run-overs

These can occur in driveways, parking lots, streets, paddocks, or elsewhere.

Low Speed Vehicle run-overs most often involve young children from 0–5 years. This age group is most at risk due to their underdeveloped danger awareness and due to their stature; they are difficult to see behind any vehicle. Their small size leads to a higher risk of sustaining severe crush injuries to the head and chest, which are more likely to result in fatality.

To avoid these sort of accidents you should:

- Supervise your child whenever a vehicle is being moved in your driveway — hold them close,
- Use fences and self-closing gates to keep garages and driveways separate from play areas.

- Walk around your car before getting in to look for any potential problems, and keep children in mind when using your reversing mirrors, sensors and reversing cameras.

Pedestrian accidents

Older children (aged 5–13 years) are more likely to be struck by a vehicle on the street either walking to school or playing in local suburban streets. In these scenarios speed can make all the difference in outcome, unfortunately this is often out of our control, therefore it is essential to arm ourselves and our children to prevent any injury. As parents or carers always hold the child's hand near traffic, and set a good example — teach STOP, LOOK, LISTEN and THINK, practise walking near roads with your child explaining signs, rules, dangerous places and, if possible, near school utilise organised car pick up lines.

Kids in cars unsupervised

Unsupervised children in cars can be dangerous for a number of reasons. If a child is able to play in a car, this can result in the car being accidently knocked into motion and cause the child to be in an unrestrained car crash, or to fall out of the moving vehicle and be run-over. The other risk is the incident of a hot car; that is, the temperature inside the car begins to rise rapidly and airflow decreases, this can result in hyperthermia, dehydration, asphyxia and death. Never leave a child in or around a car unattended.

Bronwyn Griffin

CHILDHOOD ANXIETY

All children have various fears and worries that they experience throughout their development, and these can be expected at any given age. For example, we would expect that a two-year-old might be afraid of being separated from mum or dad, and a four-year-old might be scared of the dark. These fears are considered to be developmentally appropriate and will tend to fade over time, at times requiring some guidance and support. However, some children have fears that exceed typical levels, persist over time and interfere with day-to-day functioning. These worries could indicate the presence of an anxiety disorder, which is one of the most common mental health issues that can affect children, sometimes starting from a very young age.

Anxiety often triggers a fight or flight response in the presence of a perceived threat, which means that the body and brain will send out various signals (e.g., increased heart rate and muscle tension) to alert the individual that a danger is present and that it is time to take some action. This action is often avoidance, as individuals who feel anxious try to get rid of worrisome thoughts and feelings, and avoid situations that bring those kinds of thoughts and feelings their way. This is not always helpful, as when there is no real threat, avoidance behaviours can affect a child's confidence and inhibit him or her from living a meaningful life. Some children respond with the fight reaction, which can get them into trouble and also make it difficult for others to respond to the child in a supportive and empathic manner.

Types and signs of anxiety in children

There are many types of anxiety that children can experience, including separation anxiety, generalized anxiety, social phobia, panic disorder, specific phobias, obsessive-compulsive disorder, and post-traumatic stress disorder. Signs can vary dependent on the type, but there are similarities in that excessive worry and avoidance of particular situations are usually common. Children might have difficulty expressing their emotions adequately and therefore may display a variety of behaviours to do this, such as withdrawal, crying or aggression. Other behaviours that can be observed include school refusal, sleep problems and somatic complaints (e.g., sick tummy, headache).

Managing anxiety

Children can find it difficult to know how to manage anxiety effectively and often look to the adults in their lives to help them deal with these kinds of situations. The key to dealing with anxiety in childhood is for both children and their parents to learn skills for how to manage the worrisome thoughts, feelings and its associated behaviours so that families can put the anxiety to the side and pursue what matters to them most. It is impossible to eliminate anxiety, as everyone will experience it from time to time, but effective coping skills can be crucial in preventing the anxiety from taking over. Early intervention can lessen the severity of the disorder as well as decrease the likelihood of long-term problems, such as depression. Parents can help by teaching skills from a young age and model effective coping to their children. This means validating the child's feelings (e.g., *It's ok to get worried*), explaining how to cope appropriately (e.g., *Let's take a deep breath and use our words to say how we're feeling*) and model strategies in one's own anxiety-provoking situations (e.g., *Mum is feeling a bit stressed so I'm going to have a cup of tea to relax a bit*).

Anxiety management skills are being taught in many classrooms as the value in working preventatively has become more appreciated and widespread. However, specialist support should be sought if there are concerns that an anxiety disorder may be present. Contacting a psychologist with experience in child anxiety can be helpful.

Dr Mari Farry

CHILDREN AND ADOLESCENTS IN TRANSITION

Children and adolescents have to undergo a number of changes during their development, and while some adjustments are expected and can be prepared for (e.g., entering high school), others come completely out of the blue. Some kids have no problems adjusting to something different, and might even be excited by the prospect of a new adventure, while others can experience an array of fears about the unknown. Regardless of whether the change is planned or unplanned, parents can assist their children and teens with adapting smoothly and effectively by using a number of basic strategies. This includes the following.

Communicating the change or transition

Give advanced notice when possible. Children need some time to process information and to comprehend what is going to happen. This also means using simple and truthful explanations and allowing time for questions to be asked. Children's storybooks can be a great resource for discussing change with young kids, as there are books on any topic imaginable. It can also be useful to ask the child about what he or she thinks will happen, as it will allow the parent to see the viewpoint of the young person and clarify any misconceptions.

Validate their experience of the change

Change can create feelings of insecurity, anxiety, and lack of control, to name just a few. Encourage the young person to talk about how they are feeling and coping, and then empathise with their position. Their feelings are very real and whilst some fears may be unrealistic, children need to be able to trust the adults to help them feel secure again by feeling supported and listened to.

Establish a routine

Getting into routine helps young people with stability and predictability, as familiarity can assist with adjustments that have been made. This might mean re-establishing routines that were previously implemented or establishing new routines so the child can see what real life looks like.

Promote connectedness

A key factor to helping kids adjust to change is through their connections with others, as this allows them to access support as well as shift their focus to positive relationships. This includes relationships at home, so parents need to continue communicating and monitoring to maintain awareness of how the young person is adapting. It is also important for the child to feel connected at school, so if it is a new school this could mean visiting the school beforehand so that the child can have a tour of the school and meet some teachers. If the school has not changed, it could mean informing key school personnel that a significant change has taken place so that children can be monitored and supported adequately. Social connectedness is crucial for children and especially teens, and friends can be particularly helpful for smooth transitions. If a move has taken place where friends might have been lost, parents might consider helping the child become engaged in sport, clubs or co-curricular activities to help kids create a new social network. Children might need reassurance that they can still connect with loved ones that they leave behind, and it can be helpful to assist them with writing emails, sending photos and having telephone conversations.

Most importantly, change is a part of life so it is necessary for children and adolescents to learn how to cope with transitions. It might be necessary at times to consult with a counsellor or psychologist to assist with teaching coping skills to young people to enhance their ability to manage the new situation.

Dr Mari Farry

SHYNESS IN CHILDREN

Shyness is a term used to describe feelings of apprehension, lack of comfort or awkwardness in situations. Shyness can be part of a persons' personality, temperament, genetic makeup, or due to environmental factors, such as living with an anxious parent.

For some children shyness can be disabling and limit their potential by stopping them from taking risks, trying new things or socialising with peers. In some cases shyness can mask underlying psychological problems such as an anxiety disorder. If you are concerned that something other than shyness is at play in your child's life, make an appointment to talk with your family GP, school guidance counsellor or local community health centre.

On a good note, however, most children tend to grow out of being shy and go on to develop the confidence to face day-to-day challenges with relative ease. If you have a child who is shy, or you are shy yourself, try some of the following tips as they may be helpful in supporting you and/or your child to overcome shyness.

Model confident social behaviour

Children watch and observe everything! If you want to develop confidence in your child, demonstrate this by your actions. For example, when you enter a store look the shop attendant in the eyes and say in a confident voice something like: *Hello, how are you? I am looking for the children's clothing, can you please show me where the children's chapter is?* Explain to your child what behaviours you are displaying when you act confidently (i.e., using a brave voice and looking people in the eyes).

Provide opportunities for your child to practice being brave

Most shy children tend to avoid situations where they are the centre of attention and dislike being put on the spot! Help prepare your child for situations where they can take small steps towards feeling confident and brave. For example, when a child has to talk in front of his/her peers, or to talk to the shop attendant when purchasing items, or sitting with adults when visitors come over instead of avoiding conversations.

Teach children conflict resolution skills

Many children struggle to deal with conflict between peers, family members and so forth. However, conflict resolution is especially hard for shy or anxious children as they tend to become emotionally overwhelmed when conflict arises. Teach children to recognise their feelings. Do they become frightened, scared, angry or worried when conflict occurs? Teach children how to manage those uncomfortable feelings by doing things such as talking with an adult, counting to 10, breathing deeply, telling yourself: *It will be ok, I can handle this.* It is important that the child not run away from the situation but deal with the discomfort they feel. Confidence comes through perseverance, finding new strategies and challenging negative self-talk.

Find out what activities your child feels comfortable doing

When children feel shy in situations they are likely to see the world as a negative and scary place at times. To boost your child's confidence get the child involved in things they enjoy and that make them smile. We all need balance in our lives and doing things we enjoy helps us draw on our strengths during tough times.

Help your child to recognise and manage their feelings

Feelings are important because they help us survive in this life. They tell us when we may be in danger, they help us to interact with others, when to approach a person or perhaps when to stay away from someone, and they support self-growth and development. All feelings are okay as they are part of who we are. However, the important key is learning what to do when we feel a certain way. For example, if you notice your child is getting upset or distressed because you have asked them to try something new, acknowledge what you see: *I can see you are becoming upset, you are raising your voice and have tears welling in your eyes, it is ok to be scared, this is new, however, you need to boss back that scared feeling in your tummy and tell yourself you can do it and that you will be ok.*

Try not to criticise your child for being shy — separate them from their behaviour

It is easy to get frustrated when a shy child is reluctant to give things a go or to get out of the car at a children's party or won't leave your side when new people come over to the house. Sometimes parents get frustrated and say hurtful things such as: *don't be so silly; stop being a pain; there is nothing to be scared of.* Unfortunately, such comments only fuel anxiety and shyness. Try saying something along the lines of: *I know this is hard and I do love you, but let go of mummy's hand and sit down quietly please.* Be calm, loving yet firm.

Praise your child on their effort not the outcome

Children who are shy tend find doing things for the first time such as attending a new school or club or Sunday school, or having new visitors over to the house extremely difficult. Praise your child for their willingness to attempt something new or difficult, reward their effort, not the outcome. Make a big deal once they achieve their goal, it could be something as simple as putting their hand up in class to answer a question, or smiling at someone.

Encourage problem solving

Because shy children tend to also be emotionally sensitive they can find it hard to come up with ideas on the spot. To help them in difficult situations, encourage problem solving difficult situations in advance. For example, if you know your child is attending a birthday party and this experience tends to be rather unpleasant for all involved, find time to sit down and list ideas to help your child feel confident at the party. Help them list ideas of what to say if another child starts a conversation with them, or who they may feel comfortable playing with or asking for help whilst at the party. Get your child to put their plan into action and provide feedback on how it went.

Emily Anderson

ANGER MANAGEMENT IN ADOLESCENCE

Anger is a very common emotion and problem that a lot of adolescents and their parents have to face. The ages of 13–18 years is a time in an individual's life where there is great uncertainty and a time when a lot of changes are occurring; physically, intellectually and emotionally. Anger can often be directed towards the individual or outwardly towards others (e.g., parents, family, teachers and friends). Below are some strategies of how to deal with anger during adolescence, for both, yourself and your teenager.

- Anger outbursts are usually a result of a lot of built up resentment and frustration within the individual. It is very important to deal with anger as it arises through assertiveness.

- Refrain from consuming alcohol as a way of dealing with your anger. Alcohol will only increase the intensity, frequency and duration of your anger outbursts.

- As much as possible give your son or daughter their own space. As a parent this may be counter-intuitive but it is the best thing that you can do. When your children are ready to talk they will come to you and you will be able to have a productive conversation with them about their anger.

- When talking with others (e.g., son or daughter) about their anger determine in your mind whether they want to be heard or whether they would like some advice from you. A lot of fights occur when the adolescent wants to be heard and the parent attempts to give them advice.

- Regularly check in with other family members (e.g., during dinner). This is a great opportunity to raise any issues that have been on your mind in the short to medium term. It also provides others with an opportunity to raise any issues that have been annoying them. This activity is a great way to promote assertiveness within the family unit.

- When you do have an angry reaction to a given situation, acknowledge the feeling. If you feel that you are in control of the feeling, then to address the source of your anger (e.g., being assertive and having a conversation with the person at work, home). If you feel that you aren't in a position to deal your anger then and there, to remove yourself from the situation to calm down and make a mental note to come back later to deal with it.

- Ensure that your sleeping patterns aren't compromised. Try not to think about your anger towards another person before going to bed at night-time.

- Try not to replay the incident that is making you angry over and over in your head. This will make you angrier than need be. Identify that you are angry, and address your anger with the person as soon as humanly possible.

- Refrain from gossiping about the other person who has made you angry in the first place. It will not help you to deal with your anger and what you have been saying will probably get back to the person concerned, making it harder for you to talk with them about the issue.

- Minimise the consumption of high sugar or caffeine content drinks (e.g., cordial, soft-drink, coffee, energy drinks).

- Ensure that you engage in regular physical exercise. This will help to release pent-up anger and frustration.

Mark Korduba

CHILD BEHAVIOUR MANAGEMENT

The psychiatrist and educator Dr Rudolf Dreikurs wrote extensively about behaviour to help parents (and teachers) improve their relationships with children at home (and in school). His positive non-punishing concepts of democratic and respectful parenting, and classroom behaviour management, are the hallmarks of his beliefs about raising happy, independent, and responsible children. The basic concepts for positive parenting are:

- Children are social beings.
- All behaviours are goal-oriented.
- A child's primary goal is to belong and feel significant.
- A misbehaving child is a discouraged child.
- Social interest, responsibility, and a desire to contribute.
- A child is equal in value to an adult.
- Mistakes are opportunities to learn.
- Ensure a message of love gets through to your children.

An approach to understanding children

Every child has his or her own individual way of being in the world. There are some children who are quiet and passive, while others are more extrovert and active. Some children prefer quiet activities and others like boisterous ones. Observing and accepting a child's personality can help a parent to interact in ways that fit with the child's preferences and character. This knowledge only comes from spending quantity time with your child.

Why children misbehave

A child does not usually know exactly why they misbehave, rather they learn about the world by trial and error, and by observing role-models they have around them. As they behave they get feedback on what they do. If the desired result is produced by misbehavior, the behaviour may continue. As parents begin to learn how to understand a child's goals, it gives them clues on how to guide the child toward more positive behaviour. It must be remembered that a child has a desire to belong, and to find their place in their family and society. They continue behaviours that result in being socially included, and abandon behaviours that exclude them from others.

Four mistaken goals of misbehavior

Seeking undue Attention — All children desire and need attention, but children who need attention all the time will resort to behaviour to keep others busy with them or to get special treatment. Parents experiencing this misbehaviour will feel annoyed, irritated, worried, and guilty. The parent often responds by scolding or warnings but the child is only temporarily satisfied. The remedy is to ignore the misbehaviour, give the child attention (encouragement) when it is deserved but not being sought, and use logical consequences (rather than reward and punishment).

Seeking undue Power — For certain children a mistaken goal is to be the boss, that is, to be in charge. By this behaviour they are showing they are in control or that others can't make them do anything they don't want to do. Parents feel angry, challenged, threatened, defeated, provoked, and defeated, and will often get into a power struggle with the child. If the parent gives in, the child wins and stops the behaviour, until the next power struggle! The remedy is to avoid the power struggle, use appropriate humour, admit your own powerlessness, listen to the child, offer some choices, and negotiate reasonable limits (of time and action).

Seeking Revenge — These children believe that they have been hurt by others or that they don't have any power. They think the only way to belong is to get back at others. Parents are hurt (physically or emotionally), and feel disappointment, disbelief, disgusted and rejected by their own child. The remedy is do not show the child your anguish or retaliate, but rather be explicit about their good qualities that others like about them, and make some incremental progress toward using encouragement when appropriate.

Seeking to display Inadequacy — A child can just give up at times and display helplessness in their behaviours. They wish to be left alone and want few expectations to satisfy. Parents want to give up, enable, and over-help, they feel helpless to do anything useful. This form of behaviour may be shown selectively such as, only in certain tasks, like sport or homework. The remedy is to be clear about what you expect from the child, find activities in which they can be successful (with increasing difficulty), and reinforce the notion that not trying things means they will not know their potential. Encourage, encourage, encourage!

These four goals of misbehavior give parents clues to redirect their children to help them choose more positive ways to achieve the desire to belong. When we know that children are not consciously scheming to misbehave but that they have a mistaken goal, it reminds us to maintain a respectful and caring approach.

To identify the mistaken goal ask yourself:

1. When your child misbehaves how do you feel? (emotional response)

2. What do you most often do in response to the misbehavior?

3. What does your child do in response?

Helpful parenting beliefs

Remember that you cannot change anyone, only yourself. Improving your child's behaviour comes from changing your responses to their behaviours. Children have deeply held beliefs about if/how they belong, and it is from these perceptions that their feelings and actions flow. As a parent you also have feelings and thoughts, and as you get more aware of your emotions and values, and make changes to the way you respond, you will make a huge difference in influencing your child's positive behaviour choices.

A parent's role in shaping their child's behaviour is enormous. When you put in the thoughtful effort, the rewards for everyone will be satisfying and lifelong. Psychologically-balanced children are a delight to themselves and society.

Dr John Barletta

5

Health and Wellbeing Issues

COPING STYLES WHEN MANAGING HEALTH CONCERNS

As you deal with health issues and challenges in your life, considering how you alleviate your own psychological stress is critical to your wellbeing, quality of life, decision-making, and ultimate recovery. People use a variety of ways when attempting to cope with, or avoid, their difficulties. Some coping styles and strategies are clearly more helpful than others (e.g., using a fighting spirit is helpful and healthy; using alcohol is unhelpful and unhealthy).

To make sense of a health challenge in your life, it is useful to go through a process of reflection by answering these questions:

1. How much of a threat is this problem situation to you?
   (view of the diagnosis)
2. What can be done about it? Can I exert any control?
   (perceived control)
3. What is the likely outcome and how certain can I be about it?
   (view of your prognosis)

The way you actually response to your health concern will depend on how you answered the above three questions. For example, you could:

- Think the health issue can potentially be overcome.
- Deny that any threat even exists.
- Believe that what will be will be.
- See the threat as not being one that can be defeated.
- Worry incessantly about your health and outcome.

If the problem represents something that you can address, you will feel quite optimistic. If the concern is seen as a major difficulty that you can't have an impact on, you may feel somewhat helpless. In these cases, people see the situation as either being a challenge or a threat. The patterns of thoughts, feelings and behaviours associated with these appraisals represent the style of coping that you have naturally developed but are actually able to deliberately and intentionally change.

The Five Coping Styles

1. Fighting Spirit.

2. Avoidance or Denial.

3. Fatalism.

4. Helplessness and Hopelessness.

5. Anxious Preoccupation.

At the core of each coping style is a mindset that selects, filters, and interprets information about the problem. You will respond to the questions posted at the start of this chapter differently depending on your mindset, and your coping style will vary accordingly. For example, a person with a fighting spirit will attend to the more optimistic facts about what can be done, while a person with a helpless/hopeless view will ignore those facts and concentrate on any negative information available.

Fighting Spirit — *(Probably the most useful style to adopt)*

A person sees the problem as a challenge and has a positive attitude toward the outcome. They engage in various behaviours where they take an active role in their recovery and make an effort to live as normal a quality life as possible.

Diagnosis: seen as a challenge,

Control: individual exerts some control over the stress,

Prognosis: seen as optimistic.

Avoidance or Denial — *(Possibly has some usefulness at times)*

A person denies the impact of the challenge and behaves to minimise the impact of the problem.

Diagnosis: seen as minimal,

Control: issue of control is irrelevant,

Prognosis: seen as good.

Fatalism — *(Limited usefulness)*

Person has an attitude of passive acceptance and any active strategies towards fighting for themselves is absent.

Diagnosis: seen as a relatively minor threat,

Control: believes no control can be exerted over the situation,

Prognosis: sees the outcome of a lack of control must be accepted with tranquillity.

Helplessness and Hopelessness — *(Limited usefulness)*

A person is overwhelmed and strategies for fighting are absent, and there may also be a reduction in normal functioning.

Diagnosis: seen as a major threat or loss,

Control: believes no control can be exerted over the situation,

Prognosis: inevitable negative outcome is experienced as if it has already occurred.

Anxious Preoccupation — *(Limited usefulness)*

Anxiety is the predominant emotion in this coping style. The person is compulsively searching for reassurance, much time is spent worrying about the problem, and any hint of the challenge is immediately identified as a negative sign.

Diagnosis: represents a major threat,

Control : uncertainty for the possibility of exerting control over the situation,

Prognosis: uncertainty over the future.

As seen from the above explanations, when dealing with problems it is critical to become more aware of your own coping style (or combination of styles), appraise how useful it is going to be for you (and possibly others around you) to use, and make adjustments to your behaviour and thinking accordingly.

Although directly changing emotions and bodily feelings is very difficult, they will change as you actively choose to take more control over your own thoughts and actions. A positive psychological state has been shown to be helpful in selecting treatment options and recovering from a range of health challenges. So consider what you can do to activate a positive state for yourself, and seek help when necessary.

Dr John Barletta

SLEEPING SOUNDLY

Having a good night's sleep is critical for physical and mental wellness, yet many people struggle to get the quality and amount of sleep they need to maintain their wellbeing. Inadequate sleep is linked with problems such as apnoea, diabetes, heart disease, high blood pressure, obesity, alcohol and drug use, anxiety and depression. It also impacts our memory, concentration, driving, and work. A poor sleep cycle can start for a range of reasons, and might be maintained if deliberate efforts are not made to change the pattern. It may seem frustrating trying to resume a good sleep routine, but it is worth the effort for you and others around you. Here are many practical strategies for you to implement:

- Going to bed and rising at regular times, seven days a week, strengthens the circadian rhythm and leads to improved sleep and alertness. Getting up at the same time may even be more important than a set bedtime, because getting up is what resets your body clock.

- Correct use of light and dark reinforces your sleep schedule. Get as much natural light during the day as possible. Ensure your room is very dark at night (consider an eye mask).

- Although an excessively warm room disturbs sleep, there is no evidence an excessively cold room helps sleep. A quiet room (use earplugs if needed) with a temperature of about 15–20 degrees Celsius (i.e., 59–68 degrees Fahrenheit) is ideal.

- Hunger may disturb sleep, however do not eat a large meal just before going to bed. Avoid having dinner as the largest meal of the day. You may also need less sleep as you get older.

- Caffeine (i.e., tea, coffee, soft-drinks), alcohol, chocolate and spicy foods can interrupt sleep, increase reflux which disturbs sleep, and may result in heartburn-type symptoms.

- Alcohol may help tense people relax and therefore fall asleep more easily, but the ensuing sleep is then often interrupted. A light snack (e.g., brown bread and/or warm, full-cream milk) about 45 minutes before bedtime helps the onset of sleep.

- An occasional sleeping pill may be of some benefit, but chronic use is ineffective and over the long term could disturb the sleep cycle even further.

- People who feel frustrated because they cannot sleep should not try harder to fall asleep. Instead they should get out of bed after 30 minutes, do something boring until tired, then go back to bed. However, it is still important to still get up at the regular rising time.

- Keep the bedroom for sleeping and sex, not for watching TV or doing computer work.

- Watching the clock may increase the anxiety of sleeplessness and further disturb sleep. Put the clock on the floor so you can't see it. You will still be able to hear the morning alarm.

- A regular daily amount of exercise early in the day may be best, but some exercise in the late afternoon or early evening (i.e., two or three hours before bedtime) can also deepen sleep. Occasional exercise does not necessarily improve sleep and strenuous exercise just before bed may disturb sleep.

- The use of tobacco disturbs sleep due to the impact of nicotine and coughing.

- A poor mattress, pillow, sheets or bed frame can result in discomfort, tossing and turning.

- Some medications disturb sleep. Check with your doctor for possible sleep side effects.

- Stress is the enemy of quality sleep. Writing notes and plans for the next day, earlier in the evening, will clear your mind. Set aside worry time during the day if necessary.

- If you are concerned about an issue, as you go to bed, trust that your unconscious mind will find a solution by the time you wake in the morning.

- An hour before bedtime to relax helps the onset of sleep. Do a quiet, relaxing activity, such as stretching, listening to soothing music, taking a warm bath/shower or reading a book.

- Use relaxation techniques during the day, to help you fall asleep, and also if you wake during the night (e.g., mindfulness, meditation, deep breathing, visualisation, imagery).

- If you wake during the night and have difficulty returning to sleep, try counting backwards by 3, from 300. This boring task fatigues the brain and brings on sleep.

- Aim for eight hours of sleep each night. Avoid daytime napping or regularly sleeping-in.

- Dwelling a lot on your sleep patterns can contribute to sleep problems. Trust that your body will demand the sleep it needs, and ignore worrying thoughts about sleep loss.

When sleep is chronically disturbed, the cause needs to be explored. If these suggestions do not help after a few weeks, consult your GP who can refer you to a sleep physician or other medical specialist, health practitioner, or relaxation expert.

Dr John Barletta

EMOTIONAL CHALLENGES OF A MAJOR ILLNESS

We are all unique individuals who think, feel and act on situations in our lives in our own special way, and at our own healing pace. How we experience an illness, and how we choose to cope with it can be different for each person. Since we have all had a lifetime of coping with stress, it has been said that each one of us is our own best therapist, however there are times when our own wisdom feels challenged.

It is not easy to be told that you have a major illness. The impact of the diagnosis can be overwhelming and, for a while, coping with the practical and emotional issues that emerge can be very difficult indeed. Shock, disbelief, numbness and confusion are all common feelings that you and your loved ones might experience whilst seeking to understand the full extent of your illness.

As the reality sinks in, of what your illness and its treatment might mean to you, now and in the future, it is common to experience a range of emotions, some of which you might not be used to feeling or expressing. Fear, anger, grief, helplessness, relief, resentment, guilt and sadness are often felt. Knowing that these emotions are normal, and giving yourself permission to express them in whatever way you can, is an important part of your journey towards adjustment, acceptance and emotional wellbeing.

It is not unusual when you have been told that you have a major illness for your imagination to get the better of you, as you predict all sorts of negative and improbable outcomes for which you have no real evidence. Whilst acknowledging the seriousness of any problem can be realistic and helpful, catastrophic worrying only exacerbates the intensity of the way you feel and can cause you unnecessary anxiety and tension. It is important from the outset that you ensure that you obtain as much of the accurate information as possible about your illness and about the treatment choices that are available to you. An open and honest relationship with a caring doctor of your choice, is invaluable in helping you to take control of your worrying and in enabling you to make informed choices about your care.

Support and advice will be offered from family, friends and others. For some, accepting such support can be difficult, and might be contrary to your usual way of dealing with problems. Many well-intentioned people will want to tell you their own stories of illness and what you should do to cope. Remember that no two experiences of illness are the same, and no one person has all the answers on how you should best deal with it. Take what you feel you want from all that you hear and read, and never be forced into doing what you don't feel is right for you.

Talking to a trusted and caring person about your concerns and feelings can often help you to release your emotions and clarify your thinking. Some people choose not to talk in this way to those who are closest to them, fearing that they are burdening those who are already distressed. This silence — the not knowing what you are thinking and feeling — can be very distressing for the person who is trying to offer you care. Although this might be for the best of intentions, it can cut you off from a very valuable means of support. Sharing your feelings with a loved one might be painful and difficult, but it can often bring support and comfort to you both.

Such issues of emotional intimacy, as well as worries about sexual intimacy are common concerns with major illness. Couples best deal with this by communicating their worries and concerns with each other and working it out together. Make time for each other — time where you can focus on really listening to what the other person is thinking and feeling, without distractions, and without trying to rush the other into doing things your way. Time where you can cry on each other's shoulder (if that is your way), and where together, you can explore solutions and plan the future.

Maintaining a healthy lifestyle, eating a nutritious diet, and taking regular exercise and rest can assist you with your adjustment and recovery. Taking time out for fun and recreation can often give some welcome respite from illness thinking and helps re-energise you to better manage your stress and lift your mood.

To accept that illness has happened to you, in no way means that you have given up … quite the contrary. To accept that illness has happened enables you to turn your energies towards facing the reality of your situation. It empowers you to commit towards facing a present and a future where you can adjust to the challenges as they occur. It empowers you to adventure on, in order to live each day to the best quality you can, despite the illness.

Alan Hobman

WEIGHT MANAGEMENT AND OBESITY

Early humans evolved a genetic capacity to store fat, which helped them survive in times of famine. Since the Industrial Revolution, food has no longer been a scarce commodity most have to work hard to obtain. With the emergence of fast food and the supermarket society, food is easily accessible. Our genetic potential to store fat has been activated and obesity and chronic diseases have emerged. Since the 1980s, obesity has reached epidemic proportions globally, due to an overconsumption of food, aggravated by a sedentary lifestyle in an environment we now term obesogenic.

No single approach has been found to effectively treat obesity, and current research suggests that most people who lose weight, regain it within two years. To be successful with weight loss requires commitment, self-discipline, determination and persistence. Here are practical tips to help you achieve and maintain weight loss:

- Avoid fad diets. Most people go on diets to later go off them. The secret to weight loss is that there is no secret! The core of any weight loss strategy is to reduce your food intake and increase your levels of physical activity.

- Establish a regular eating plan and always eat breakfast. Being hungry can lead to over-eating.

- Avoid eating outside planned meal times. Preplanning reduces the likelihood of impulsive eating.

- Avoid buying energy dense foods that are easy to snack on like chocolate. Also reduce your intake of fast foods and convenience foods. Snacking and large portion sizes have been identified as major contributing factors to weight gain.

- Moderate your intake of nutrient dense drinks including juice, cordial, soft drink and alcohol. Drink more water.

- Eat in one place only, preferably at the table. Do not eat while watching TV, using your phone or computer, or reading. This limits opportunities to eat, reduces cues for eating, and helps you to be more aware of what you are eating.

- Eat slowly and mindfully, tasting and appreciating the food, and stop eating before you feel full. It can take your stomach up to 20 minutes to register it is full.

- Spend less time in sedentary activities such as watching TV and computer use, and develop leisure and social activities that require you to move more.

- Identify physical activities you enjoy and progressively increase the duration and intensity of the exercise as your fitness increases with the aim of being active for at least 150 minutes a week (e.g., 1/2 hour per day for 5 days in the week). For further health benefits, swap three of these sessions for twenty-minute high intensity sessions. Always get medical clearance and advice from an exercise specialist before proceeding.

- Identifying your barriers to weight loss and problem solving them is a key to weight loss success. Monitor the excuses you use to permit deviating from your healthy eating and exercise plan. If you are an emotional eater identify other activities or options that will help you more effectively address the issue.

- Motivation is never lost, it is disregarded, nor is it outside yourself. Attend to it daily to maintain weight loss focus.

- Consult a psychologist to address motivation, self-sabotage, emotional eating and any other issues you believe are a barrier to weight loss success.

- Consider regular follow-up with a weight management expert because outcomes are improved when you have ongoing support.

Anita Cochrane

PREGNANCY HEALTH

Pregnancy can be one of the most amazing experiences a woman will ever have; it is life changing. Here are a few pregnancy tips that may help you through what can be a wonderful time, and for some, a challenging time.

Eat wisely

- Healthy eating is the key to additional energy during pregnancy. Protein, vitamins and minerals required during pregnancy can easily be provided through a healthy diet, and supplements may not be necessary. Try to eat freshly prepared meals whenever possible.

- A weight gain of 9–13kgs is generally advisable. Dieting to lose weight during this time is not generally advised. If you were overweight at the beginning, then smaller weight gains are recommended.

The requirement for Vitamins, Minerals, Folic Acid and Iron

- The requirement for vitamins and minerals are increased during pregnancy. These can be found in whole grains, fruit and vegetables in your diet, and will easily meet these requirements. Unless recommended by your doctor, taking supplements is not necessary. Taking large doses of vitamins and minerals can be harmful to your baby.

- Folic acid (Folate) is essential for blood production. Tablets containing 0.4mg–0.5mg can be taken daily. Folate is recommended to be taken one month prior to and 3 months after conception. Folic acid is found in food in green leafy vegetables and liver — in salads, citrus fruits, broccoli, cauliflower, green beans, and brussel sprouts — although folic acid is lost during the cooking process.

- Extra iron can be obtained from food sources rather than iron tablets, which often cause unwanted side effects such as constipation. For iron, include some meat, poultry and fish daily (and add a food rich in vitamin C which helps your body absorb iron).

Constipation is common in pregnancy.

Having extra fibre in your diet will help relieve constipation. Fibre can be obtained from a wide variety of foods, especially whole-grain cereals and bread, legumes and plenty of fresh fruit and vegetables. Bran is a good source of fibre and can be made more palatable by adding it to gravies, casseroles, breakfast cereals, meat loaf or bean dishes. Drink plenty of fluids — at least 6-8 glasses per day. Laxatives should not be taken unless authorised by your doctor

Haemorrhoids

Haemorrhoids are protruding veins in the bottom. They can be painful, itchy or bleed.

- Avoid constipation, and rest with your feet up.

Morning sickness

Morning sickness can occur both in the morning and at night. Approximately 75% of women experience sickness of some kind during the first trimester (particularly 6–13 weeks). If this becomes a problem, talk to your doctor/midwife/or caregiver, as some remedies may be suitable for you. Bear in mind that while mild nausea is the norm, serious illness is not. If you are particularly unwell, are unable to keep food or water down, are not gaining weight, or are losing weight, speak to your health carer immediately.

Avoid alcohol, cigarettes and marijuana

- Avoid alcohol during your pregnancy. Those babies most at risk are babies exposed to mothers who binge or are heavy drinkers.

- Smoking during pregnancy increases the risk of small-for-dates babies and increases the risk of chest infections and illness in babies early years.

- Research now shows that marijuana may have harmful effects on the unborn baby, and should be avoided. The problem of passive smoking is applicable to marijuana as well as cigarettes.

Stretch marks

Stretch marks may appear on the thighs, breasts, and abdomen, especially during periods of rapid growth. The skin may sometimes feel dry and itchy – try rubbing in vegetable oil (not mineral oil) onto the skin. Avoid harsh soaps.

Exercise

Walking, swimming, low impact aerobics, stretching and dancing are good exercises during pregnancy. Consult a health professional for advice.

Varicose veins

Varicose veins may become a problem — mainly in the legs, occasionally in the vulva or in the form of haemorrhoids.

- Wear support stockings, put on first thing in the morning, can provide some relief.

- Elevating and resting your legs is helpful.

- Vitamin E (maximum dosage of 60IU/day) has shown to have some benefit.

Sleep

Sleep becomes increasingly more difficult as pregnancy progresses. Dreams increase in frequency, restlessness increases and emptying the bladder at night becomes a problem.

- Try using extra pillows to take the weight off the uterus.

- Raising your head on extra pillow will help avoid heartburn and indigestion.

- Try relaxation exercises or stretching before bed.

- Chamomile tea before bed may also help.

Emotions are very changeable

Some women find themselves withdrawn, introspective and irritable during this time — discuss your feeling with your partner. Some concerns may need to be addressed with your GP, obstetrician or a qualified health professional.

Sexuality

- There may be completely unexpected changes in sexuality during your pregnancy, with some women experiencing reduced libido and others increased libido.

- Tiredness and morning sickness can reduce your desire for sex and most women find their sexual needs change. It is quite safe to have intercourse up until the birth, providing it is comfortable and agreeable.

- It is important to discuss these feelings with your partner, so relationships problems don't arise.

- If there is a history of miscarriage, avoiding intercourse in the early months is advisable.

- Orgasm can cause strong contractions of the uterus, which some women find uncomfortable — this will not cause spontaneous labour unless this was about to happen. Intercourse can be used to induce labour when overdue and to avoid induction.

Implementing your birth plan

It may not be easy to have the birth experience you have planned. Caregivers and hospitals vary in their views and practices, and it is wise to work out your particular requirements early in the pregnancy, so you can take steps to find the services you will need in plenty of time.

Details of options in caregivers and birth practices are available via many sources. Find an experience that suits both you and your partner. Don't just rely on your friends' experience, ask around widely and decide on the option that suits you.

Find a hospital that not only focuses on birth, but focuses on lactation, safe breast feeding practices and follow up post-natal care. You may need a lactation consultation prior to birth — consult your local yellow pages for advise.

Finally, congratulations — enjoy this special time of your life!

Gaylene Hardwick

NUTRITION, DIET AND HEALTHY EATING

Eating a variety of healthy foods is vital to achieving a well-balanced diet, optimal nutrition and wellbeing. Diet is important in the prevention, incidence and prevalence of lifestyle diseases such as obesity, type 2 diabetes, high blood pressure, stroke, high cholesterol, constipation, diverticular disease and coronary artery disease.

The following combinations of food have been put forward as considerations on which to model diets by the National Health and Medical Research Council (NHMRC) committee that are drafting the new dietary guidelines for Australia. The food combinations put forward by the NHMRC are not dietary guidelines or recommendations at this stage, but parameters on what possible combinations of food will best meet recommended dietary intakes. The considerations are based on current research evidence for promoting optimal health and nutrition, and what is culturally acceptable and affordable. For more specific dietary advice consult a dietitian.

- Increase your fruit and vegetable intake.

- Eat at least 2 fruit serves daily (a serve is 150g) depending on energy needs.

- Eat a variety of vegetables (a serve is 75g) including starchy vegetables (e.g., potato, sweet potato, parsnip, sweet corn, peas), green and brassica vegetables (e.g., broccoli, cauliflower, cabbage, brussel sprouts, Chinese cabbage, bok choy, turnip, radish), orange vegetables (e.g., pumpkin, red capsicum, carrots, sweet potato), legumes (e.g., lima and kidney beans, lentils, soy beans, chickpeas, baked beans, tofu), and other vegetables (e.g., tomatoes, lettuce, celery). Eat at least 5 serves daily.

- Eat nuts and seeds (e.g., almonds, pistachios, walnuts, sesame and pumpkin seeds). They are high in energy so limit from once to twice daily, to twice a week, depending on your energy and protein requirements (a serve is 30g).

- Eat wholegrain cereals (e.g., wholegrain breads, cereals, rice, pastas, muffins and crisp-breads). Try to eat twice as many wholegrain food serves as refined cereal serves.

- Eat lean red meats (e.g., lamb, beef, pork, veal, pork, venison, kangaroo). People should not eat more than 455g of red meat per week, or 65g a day.

- Eat other meat and alternatives (e.g., poultry, fish, shellfish, eggs, legumes) to meet your protein intake from sources other than red meat.

- Eat a minimum of 2 to 2.5 serves of dairy foods (a serve is 250g) daily, a rich source of both protein and calcium. Choose lower fat options (e.g., <4% fat-reduced or skim milk and yoghurt) or medium fat options (e.g., 4 to 10% fat regular milk and yoghurts). If eating higher fat options such as cheese (e.g., >10% fat) limit it to 20g daily.

- Choose polyunsaturated and monounsaturated fats and oils (e.g., olive oil and polyunsaturated margarine). Around 0 to 2 serves a day (serve is 10g) is sufficient based on current research evidence.

Caution:

- Limit foods that have a low nutrient density and are higher in energy, saturated fat, or added sugars. Examples include soft drinks, alcohol, cakes, biscuits, confectionary and takeaway food like battered fish/chips and pizza.

- To avoid alcohol related heath issues it is recommended that healthy men and women drink no more than two standard drinks (100ml of wine or 30ml of spirits is one standard drink) per day.

Anita Cochrane

ADJUSTMENT TO INJURY

Personal injury and associated psychological injury is becoming more and more common in society and specifically in the workplace. The process of managing injuries and returning to your life, and work, can be quite complex and lengthy, often requiring the help of a number of different professionals (e.g., psychologists, occupational therapists, physiotherapists). Below are some tips and techniques of how you can manage your injury and return to life with relative ease.

- Accept that you are injured and that you are in the process of being reha-bilitated. A lot of people like to live under the illusion that they haven't been injured and have unrealistic expectations as to what they can achieve in the short to medium term.

- Try not to use your injury as an excuse not to do things in life. Definitely understand your limitations while being injured. But, instead of focusing on the 10% of things that you can't do, focus on the 90% of things that you are still able to do. Don't define yourself as the injured person. You are still the same person with the same capabilities and personality.

- Think of your rehabilitation as a full-time job. You may not be working at the moment, however, this doesn't mean that you can do nothing. For some people, you'll be paid by your insurance company, government or your employer while being injured. You'll have physical exercises to do, appoint-ments with medical specialists to attend. The time and effort that you put in will have a huge bearing on your recovery.

- As much as possible, try to focus on the here and now. Mindfulness training is a great way to achieve this outcome. During the adjustment to injury, it is very easy to think about the "what ifs" in the future, which you don't have a lot of control over. What you do have control over is what you can do now and how you react in the present moment. For more information on mind-fulness training, ask your medical or psychological professional.

- Remember to set short-term and medium-term treatment goals. This will ensure that you have realistic expectations. Also, remember to review your progress regularly and unemotionally for example, on the 1st Monday of every month.

- Keep yourself busy, without overworking yourself. Minimise unhelpful distractions (e.g., excessive TV, alcohol, drugs, junk food, web surfing).

- Keep an active social life. Often when people get injured at work, they tend to socially withdraw. Remember to keep in contact with work colleagues, friends and family. Be creative with how you socialise with people. If you can't physically see or speak with someone, the telephone or e-mail may be another good option.

- Be very mindful about the impact that your behaviour and mood is having on your immediate family members. It is very important to keep a positive outlook and remain calm to create a positive home environment.

- Be flexible and open to the possibility that you might not be able to go back to the exact same life you had before. You may need to change jobs. Whatever the challenge, you can do it.

Mark Korduba

USING MEDICINES SAFELY AND EFFECTIVELY

If you have been diagnosed with an illness and are receiving medical treatment, it is common to feel concerned about the physical, social and economic consequences of your condition. One way to improve your sense of wellbeing is to take an active role in decisions regarding your treatment. For many conditions, a wide range of options is available, so it's worth expressing your preferences to your health care provider. For example, you may be interested in managing pain without surgery or medicines. Did you know that physical therapists (physiotherapists) and psychologists might be able to help? Some conditions also respond well to lifestyle changes such as quitting smoking, reducing alcohol intake, eating better and exercising.

If you and your prescriber (e.g., doctor, physician's assistant, nurse, pharmacist, herbalist, or naturopath) decide that medicines are required, you may need to provide further information to ensure the most appropriate choice. Have you had bad reactions to any medicines in the past? Could you be pregnant? Are you breastfeeding? Do you smoke? Do you drink alcohol? Are you taking any other medicines?

Complementary medicines (such as evening primrose oil), over-the-counter medicines (such as cough mixture), supermarket drugs (e.g., painkillers), vitamins and supplements are all medicines. It's important to include these in your discussions as some medicines should not be taken together.

Medicines come in many different forms including tablets, capsules, syrups, patches, drops, inhalers, injections, pessaries and suppositories. If you have trouble with one form, ask your health care provider to prescribe or recommend another. If you have difficulty managing the packaging (e.g., bottles or blister packs that are difficult to open), ask if there are alternatives. If the medicine is unaffordable ask if there is a generic form or cheaper alternative and investigate whether your health insurance will cover any of the cost.

To get the best health outcome from your medicines, they need to be stored correctly (e.g., at the right temperature and disposed of when expired) and used only as prescribed. If you are unclear how to take your medicine correctly, check the label, read the package insert or ask your pharmacist. Generally the things to pay attention to are, the dose of the medicine (e.g., 2 tablets), the frequency (e.g., twice a day), the timing (e.g., morning and night), the duration (e.g., ongoing) and any other special instructions (e.g., take with meals).

When you first start taking a new medicine, or even if you have been taking medicine for a long time, you may forget doses. If you are unsure what to do regarding a missed dose, check the package insert or ask your pharmacist. If you have trouble remembering to take your medicines regularly, dose administration aids such as a dosette box (i.e., pill organiser or calender blister pack) that organises your medicines may help.

All medicines have benefits and risks. Side-effects can be common, infrequent or rare, and can be serious in nature or simply a minor irritation. When starting a new medicine, it is worth paying special attention to any side effects. The more medicines you take, and the older you are, the more likely it is that you will experience side effects or drug interactions. If the medication's side effects are serious or impacting your quality of life, talk to your prescriber or pharmacist. He or she may change the dose, the time you take the medicine, prescribe another medication to manage the side effect or switch to an alternative drug or treatment. You may have to be patient at the beginning as it can sometimes take a while to find a treatment that works well for you.

Some medicines require special monitoring such as blood tests or urine tests. If this applies to your situation, it is important that you keep up to date with visits to the pathology centre. The monitoring may be required to check your medicine is working or to check that it is not causing harm.

After taking your medicines for a while, you will most likely start to feel better. You may also wonder whether it's necessary to continue treatment. If you are thinking of stopping your medicine, it's important to discuss this decision with your prescriber. Some medicines can cause withdrawal symptoms and have to be reduced slowly. You may also have to weigh up the pros and cons of a return of your original symptoms if you stop treatment.

If you have had a recent visit to hospital, you may be discharged with different medications than you were taking previously. Sometimes there is confusion about whether to take the previous medications or not. If anything isn't clear, speak to your doctor or pharmacist. Each year there are many admissions to hospital for problems caused by medicines. In most cases these are avoidable.

There are many reliable sources of drug and medical information on the Internet that are targeted towards consumers. You may also find it helpful to access health information from organisations that specialise in your condition.

Jacqueline Bond and Dr Lisa Nissen

PHYSICAL ACTIVITY AND WELLBEING

Most people know that regular physical activity (or exercise) provides many benefits for physical health, and as such, is an important part of a healthy lifestyle. Physical activity is also an important part of a psychologically healthy lifestyle.

There are many scientific reasons to link physical activity and wellbeing:

- People who are physically active tend to have better wellbeing than those who are inactive. Similarly, people with poor wellbeing tend to be less active than those with good wellbeing.

- Feeling stressed, anxious or depressed can be an inevitable part of life, because of having to deal with life events, illness, relationships and other challenges. Not everyone needs or chooses to seek professional help for these difficulties. Physical activity is an important part of self-care in these situations, and can be a useful coping strategy. People who are physically active are more resilient than inactive people, and can more easily bounce back from hard times.

- Some physical health conditions (e.g., heart disease, diabetes, arthritis) can increase vulnerability to stress, anxiety and depression. Physical activity can help manage physical difficulties, and thereby reduce the risk of psychological difficulties.

- Many of the physical benefits of activity (e.g., physiological changes, changes in brain transmitters, reduced blood pressure, increased blood flow to the brain, increased oxygen use, improved musculoskeletal functioning, and endocrine responses) also provide psychological benefits.

- Physical activity can help manage some of the side effects (e.g., weight gain, lethargy) produced by various drug treatments.

- Physical activity can provide specific psychological benefits that improve wellbeing, such as personal time-out, improved self-image and self-esteem, opportunities for positive emotions, social interactions, and a sense of accomplishment.

- Specific types of physical activity, such as walking, are easily affordable, need few resources, can be done without supervision or professional advice, and can be done by almost everyone.

There are three different roles for physical activity in the context of wellbeing:

- *Physical activity can help maintain and improve wellbeing and resilience.* Physical activity can provide positive emotions, self-esteem, confidence, energy, stamina, satisfaction, a sense of mastery and control, social connections, quality of life and better sleep, as well as reduce fatigue, tension, stress, and negative emotions. People who do physical activity can also improve their levels of vitality and emotional and social wellbeing over time. People who stop doing physical activity can experience a significant decline in wellbeing over time.

- *Physical activity can prevent psychological difficulties.* Regular physical activity can limit the onset of depression, poor mental health, anxiety, stress and burnout over time.

- *Physical activity can be a useful adjunct to treatment for psychological difficulties.* Physical activity can be as effective as other treatments for mild to moderate levels of depression, anxiety and stress. For serious conditions such as schizophrenia, physical activity, in combination with other psychological/psychiatric treatment, can help reduce symptoms and manage some of the side effects of the drugs used.

What sort of physical activity should you do?

The best type of physical activity to do is one that you enjoy. Physical activity does not have to be vigorous, at the gym, or huff and puff exercise like jogging. You may enjoy other types of activity such as dancing, yoga, or bushwalking. Either moderate intensity or vigorous intensity activity can provide psychological benefits. Moderate intensity activity, such as brisk walking, is when you breathe more heavily than usual, but can still carry on a conversation. In some cases, even light intensity physical activity is helpful.

However, not everyone enjoys physical activity. If this is the case for you, then choose a physical activity that you can and will do. You might like to think about the style of activities that suit you e.g., scheduled sessions or flexible timing; individual or group versus team-based, supervised/led versus unsupervised, with people the same age and sex as you or not, competitive or social, varied versus routine, or needing skill and practice or not. The more convenient it is for you, the more likely you are to do it. You may use other strategies to help your commitment, such as listening to music, or going with a friend. Physical activity that is done as part of your leisure time may provide more wellbeing benefits than other types of activity for example, activity done at work, activities to get to and from places (e.g., walking, cycling), or house-work.

Physical activity that is done outdoors, sometimes called "green exercise" may provide more wellbeing benefits than activity done indoors. Outdoor activity, including gardening, can improve mood, revitalisation, energy, satisfaction, enjoyment, and reduce tension, anger and depression. These effects may be greater for women than for men.

How much physical activity should you do?

For physical health benefits, it is recommended that people do approximately 30 minutes of moderate activity on most days of the week. Similarly, psychological benefits can be obtained from 30-minute bouts of activity, and it may take 4–16 weeks to experience the benefits. People with depressive symptoms may benefit from doing bouts of 45–60 minutes, and it may take 10–16 weeks to experience improvement. People with anxiety symptoms may benefit from doing longer bouts of 60–90 minutes.

However, some activity is always better than none! Doing even an hour a week can provide psychological benefits, especially if you are currently physically inactive. If you are doing some physical activity, it is important to maintain this where physically possible, even if at a lower level, as stopping physical activity altogether can result in a decline in wellbeing.

Can physical activity create problems for wellbeing?

A very small number of people may have psychological difficulties with physical activity. People with eating disorders, such as anorexia, may overuse exercise as a method to lose weight. Exercise dependency is an obsessive behaviour where people do extreme levels and continue to exercise despite injury, illness, fatigue, or other personal demands. Elite athletes may overtrain beyond their capacity to recover and can stop making progress and loose strength and fitness. These situations would require professional assistance.

Dr Nicola Burton

HEALTH BENEFITS OF STRENGTH TRAINING

Why should I exercise? The real question is, why wouldn't you? If you knew what it did for your body and health, you would procrastinate no longer and get started tomorrow! People avoid exercising and use excuses such as *my back hurts, my knees give me pain, I don't have the time, I am to busy and I don't run*. In most cases, when obese people lose weight their knees are under less pressure to hold them up, and the pain disappears or reduces dramatically. For people who have knee problems, strengthening certain muscles helps get them back to a normal active life. Back problems are the most common issue faced in our sedentary lifestyle. If it's not lower back issues, its upper back or neck issues. All these problems are connected and can be fixed. You need to decide that you aren't going to give up seeking help until you get relief; you have to be committed. Lets review some of the things that exercise and strength training helps with.

Increase or maintain muscle mass

Did you know that muscle mass decreases in the body over time, and as we get older, the rate of loss becomes more rapid, then our energy levels fall as does our fitness level? Less muscle equals less strength, less support for good posture and reduced fat metabolism. Even if we do regular cardiovascular exercise such as swimming, running, walking and cycling, muscle will still waste away over time. Muscle wastage can be stopped, and even reversed, by doing continuous strength training. It could be said you are staying young by fitting strength training into your life 2 to 3 times per week.

Increase bone mineral density

This is particularly vital for women. Resistance training, specifically training for strength increases bone mineral density. Strength training places tension on the bones and muscles. With time and gradual overload, your body is forced to increase bone mineral density which is especially fantastic for women. Bone mineral density has been shown to be increased by up to 10% in as little as six months. High intensity weight training, using heavy weights, is by far the best form of training to increase bone mineral density and help reduce the risk of Osteoporosis (a disease causing bone degeneration and breakage) in women of all ages. Overloading muscles will make them stronger, so add strength training to your regime to reduce the risk of Osteoporosis, or slow the degeneration that has begun, to live longer and move better.

Promote faster fat burning and a leaner physique

One of the secrets to ongoing fat burning is strength training. Training with weights and growing stronger will increase your metabolic rate while increasing your lean muscle tissue. Your daily energy expenditure will also increase due to your higher metabolic rate. Remember for every 0.5kg of muscle you put on, you will burn off approximately an extra 50 to 100 calories every day! The more muscle means more fat burnt. Muscle is small, lean and hard; fat is soft, lumpy and twice as big as muscle at the same weight! Adding strength training to weekly workouts will get you in shape faster, helping you tone, tighten and terminate those flabby bits.

Increase metabolic rate

Over the course of your life, your metabolic rate slows down due to the loss of muscle. If you have put on some extra weight in the past 10 years and are struggling to lose it again, it is probably due to this fact. People who don't strength train will lose muscle tissue, move less and have a metabolism that slows down by approximately 2% per decade; some people who are very inactive may experience a loss as great as 0.5% per year. Heavy strength and resistance training programs have been shown to increase the resting metabolic rate. In turn, making you a lean, mean, fat burning machine! It makes sense to do strength training throughout your life. Age is no barrier to feeling energetic and looking fantastic.

Improve posture

Strong muscles will hold your posture in place. Think what our lives are like now. Most of us sit at a desk for long periods of time and have poor postural control, resulting in a large percentage of back, neck and shoulder issues. Strengthening all the right muscles that keep us upright and supports our bones and skeletal system avoids postural imbalances and reduces the risk of developing long-term joint, muscle pain and postural problems.

Increase functional strength

Strength training is also responsible for performance of functional everyday activities such as walking up and down stairs, lifting, sitting, playing with your kids. If you want to move better, make life easier and perform better, lift weights. Your body will adapt and make these activities easier, giving you additional energy to enjoy life.

Decrease risk of injury

Functional strength training will reduce your risk of injury and having a stronger body with stable joints will also allow you to recover faster from injury. Strong muscles significantly reduce the risk of injury from external and internal forces. Take, for example, football players all of whom carry large amounts of muscle for impact. These styles of impact sports require protection, and increasing the size of the large muscles in the body helps reduce the potential for injury, and helps support and protect the body. Strong muscles will also enhance the recovery of the body following injury, and strength training plays a vital role in the functional rehabilitation in and around joints.

Decrease blood pressure

Strength training will significantly reduce blood pressure, thereby reducing the chances of hypertension and the risk of coronary heart disease. On a regular basis alternating strength training with cardiovascular exercise, and a good stretching program, helps reduce blood pressure and reduces stress. However there are a number of things to consider when starting your new exercise program.

- Seek professional help. Plan your training with a GP and a health and fitness expert. Preferably people who have experience training people with high blood pressure.

- Build up slowly. Rome wasn't built in a day, so neither can your health be fixed in one almighty effort. Plan to progress over three to six months.

- When lifting weights, do not hold your breath. Breathe out during the most difficult part of the exercise. Holding your breath could lead to a peak in blood pressure.

- Always warm up and warm down. All to often people get injured or experience higher levels of discomfort the next day because they didn't warm-up and stretch during and after the session.

Decrease risk of Type 2 Diabetes

Type 2 Diabetes is directly related to weight and an increase in access to fast and convenient food has seen an increase in Type 2 Diabetes. There is, however, good news! Strength training promotes the increase of lean muscle mass, this in turn increases sugar uptake into the muscle cell, therefore reducing the incidence of diabetes. Getting stronger, leaner and losing weight may help you avoid this disease, or at the very least, reduce your risk of late onset Type 2 Diabetes.

Incorporating cardiovascular exercise and strength training can help reduce the risk of disease, increase your quality of life, and keep you young. There are so many benefits to a thoughtful exercise regime, only some of which have been addressed in this chapter. Given the amount of health issues in the world today, and the benefits exercise brings, people need to partake in regular exercise as a preventative approach to health. Don't wait for your doctor to tell you to change your life due to a health problem. Remember there are no quick fixes and no magic pills. Instead, what you get out of life is related to what you choose to change in your life.

Ammon Re Bradford and Tracey Bradford

RETURNING TO SPORT

Returning to sport or exercise after a long layoff can be exhilarating yet challenging, and special consideration should be taken to make it as smooth as possible. Personal trainers and fitness coaches help people gain strength, lose weight and feel better about themselves. It is great to see people who want to get back to their former sporting glory, and it is interesting how we hang onto our former days of sporting or exercise excellence, and get flashbacks of a passion buried in the past. So if you feel a need to satisfy that internal drive that keeps bringing you back to those feelings of sprinting to the goal-line, playing that five-setter, or pumping out a personal best on the bench press, then use some of the tips below to get you back on-track.

People often think they are ready to train hard but their body has changed over the years and/or their fitness level has dropped. Conversely, the body is raring to go but their mind and confidence level is low and holding them back. So if this is you, these tips will help you get started, make exercise a habit and avoid spending more time on the physiotherapist's bench than on the field.

- *Ease your way back into it!* This one is really important. All too often we see people go back to high intensity training or the sport they love, get injured and give up. If it's a sport you are returning to after a lengthy break, take your time by starting out at a grade or two lower than you were at before your break. Be mindful of your current capabilities, your skill level and most of all listen to your body.

- *Do some training in the lead up to the season.* If the off-season is for professional players to get stronger, fitter and recover, then you should too. Spend some time getting fitter and stronger and focus more on your flexibility.

- *Set realistic expectations.* If you have taken a break from sport, so has your body. During this break your body will have undergone some changes. Your fitness may not be as high, and your strength and flexibility has probably reduced. Going pro should be the last thing on your mind. Steady development will see you performing longer and getting more out of your season.

- *Medical clearance.* If it has been a long time between goals and trophies it may be necessary get a medical clearance from your doctor to return to training or sport. Knowing that everything is okay before you return is not only good for your body but a great confidence booster.

- *Deal with injuries immediately.* Seek medical attention if you are injured and take a step back if you need to. You can be part of the team in other ways. If you're in the gym use common sense and work on other parts of the body. For example if you have a sore shoulder, work your legs and other areas while you rehabilitate your injury. Continue with your training and don't stop altogether! All too often people give up because they hurt one part of their body. Doctors and other health professionals try and get you home and moving as quick as possible because it is better for the body than lying in a bed and not moving. Communicate with your coach or trainer to develop a plan that doesn't re-injure or keep inflaming an existing or previous injury.

- *Be patient.* Steady development and listening to your body is better than going flat out and injuring yourself. Be patient with the development of your strength and fitness, and if you are recovering from an injury, take your time and slowly return.

- *Get the right advice early.* This can't be emphasised enough. If you need help with strength get a strength coach or fitness coach. If it's a muscular skeletal injury consult a specialist in that area. Don't accept pain or injury long-term. Make the appointment and do something about it!

Follow these tips and you will find yourself back on-track enjoying exercise again in no time.

Ammon Re Bradford and Tracey Bradford

MANAGING MENOPAUSE

Menopause is the time when a woman's ovaries stop functioning and she is unable to conceive. The average age for menopause women in developed countries is 52, but this varies widely. Menopause before the age of 40 is called premature menopause and should be investigated and managed by your doctor.

A woman is called post-menopausal when she reaches 12 months after her last menstrual period. The lead up to this time may last several years and is called the perimenopause. The production of hormones by the ovaries in the peri-menopause slows and fluctuates which can cause changes to the menstrual cycle, such as changes in length of periods, heaviness of periods, or pre-dictability of bleeding. It is recommended that contraception is used until 12 months after the last menstrual period. Discuss with your doctor to decide on the most appropriate method for you.

Other physical and emotional symptoms which may occur during this time include:

- Hot flushes.
- Night sweats.
- Joint or muscle aches and pains.
- Crawling or itching under the skin.
- Headaches.
- Skin and hair dryness.
- Vaginal dryness.
- Reduced libido.
- Discomfort during intercourse.
- Tiredness.
- Insomnia.
- Forgetfulness.

- Irritability.
- Anxiety.
- Depression.

Not everyone experiences all these symptoms and about 20% of women will have no symptoms at all.

There are also serious health risks due to age and low hormone levels that become important to address for women at this time of life. These include:

- *Osteoporosis* — decreased bone mass leading to bone fragility and increased fracture risk
- *Cardiovascular disease* — increased risk of heart disease and strokes. Heart disease is the largest cause of death for women in developed countries
- *Prolapse* — weakness of the pelvic supports due to low Estrogen and weakening connective tissue
- *Life stressors* — e.g., ageing, children leaving home, elderly parents' needs.

There is quite a lot a woman can do for herself to minimise these symptoms and risks.

Maintain a healthy body weight

Being overweight is the biggest cause of chronic disease in many developed countries.

Healthy eating:

- Minimise caffeine.
- Minimise alcohol.
- Plenty of fibre.
- Plenty of water.
- Lots of fresh fruit and vegetables.
- Maintain a good calcium intake for bone health — around 1300mg per day. Dairy foods are the best source of calcium. Choose low-fat varieties.
- Avoid salty foods and take-away food — these can cause calcium to be lost from the body and also increase cardiovascular disease.
- Avoid carbonated drinks — these are acidic and contribute to osteoporosis.
- Maintain Vitamin D intake — average 10 minutes twice a day in sunshine (do this outside of peak UV risk hours).

Physical activity:

- Aim for at least 30 minutes of moderate to intense activity most days of the week.

- Regular weight-bearing exercise helps maintain bone mass.

- Exercise improves flexibility and coordination and this will reduce the risk of falls.

- Exercise reduces the severity of physical and emotional symptoms of the perimenopause.

- Make pelvic floor exercises a lifelong habit; see a specialised physiotherapist for training if you are in doubt about techniques.

- Cease smoking if you are a current smoker — cigarettes increase osteoporosis, cardiovascular disease and cancer risk.

Regular checkups

See your doctor for regular checks on blood pressure, cholesterol and pap smears. Have a mammogram every 2 years. Practice monthly breast self-examination.

Hormone therapy

Using hormone therapy can be very helpful to reduce symptoms of perimenopause. Like all medication, there are risks and benefits to its use and you should be guided by your doctor on your specific needs. There is no reliable evidence that natural or bio-identical hormone preparations are as effective or any safer than standard prescription hormones.

Dr Beverley Powell

MANAGING CHRONIC PAIN

Chronic pain is often not well understood, cared for, or treated. In fact, one might even say that chronic pain is the new depression. It holds the same stigma and discrimination that depression held (and still does hold) less than a decade ago, as being the most misunderstood, poorly treated and poorly managed illness. One in five people will suffer from chronic pain at some stage in their life, and chronic pain is the third most costly healthcare problem in many countries.

Chronic pain is the impetus for:

- Relationship breakdown.

- Job loss (and inability to find new employment).

- Financial hardship.

- Stress, grief and loss.

- Anxiety and depression issues.

- Addictions (to medication, alcohol, cigarettes, drugs, gaming, internet, sex).

Chronic pain alters everything about the person who suffers from it yet all too often, treatment focuses only on the pain and the injury, resulting in a pharmaceutical treatment (i.e., medication) that is sometimes far from optimal. Chronic pain needs to have a bio-psycho-social focus that takes into account all of the changes in mind and body of the person (internal) as well as the impact of the day-to-day life of the person (external).

Therefore, the best approach to managing chronic pain is a multi-focused Bio-Psycho-Social treatment plan developed by trained and experienced pain and injury specialists who may include a medical practitioner and a psychologist as well as other specialists.

An example of such a treatment plan and its benefits is presented below.

Biological focus

Nutrition. Avoid high sugar, fat, salt, and refined carbohydrates A healthy diet will help to keep weight down and the mind and body more able to cope with

Stresses. Supplements such as Magnesium, Omega-3, Zinc, Vitamin Bs may be helpful but always check for medication interactions before using.

Exercise. This is very important to overall health and weight management. Stretching should always be done before and after exercise to allow for flexibility of the muscles and can be used by itself to reduce tension. Walking improves movement and fitness, while resistance training helps to improve muscle tone and strength. A further benefit is that during exercise the 'feel good' hormone serotonin is released, aiding with stress and pain management.

Podiatry. Orthotics may be needed to improve imbalances in gait and general body biomechanics that may have occurred as a result of injury and to reduce further pain.

Physical Therapies. These may include physiotherapy, an exercise physiologist, massage therapy, osteopathy, and acupuncture, all of which can help with muscle imbalances. Periodic strapping and taping may be beneficial, as well as trigger point releasing, and targeted strengthening.

Blood Tests. Regular 3–6 months checks on hormone, sugar, and cholesterol levels as well as liver and kidney function, and ESR (Erythrocyte Sedimentation Rate) will ensure that stress, pain or medications have not negatively affected your body's biochemical balance and caused other issues.

Other Alternatives. Some non-medicinal approaches to pain management that may be helpful include topical gels, TENS (Transcutaneous Electrical Nerve Stimulation), exercise, and relaxation techniques.

Psychological focus

Pain can change a person's personality, communication style, social ability, stress tolerances, libido, and daily functioning which places stress on relationships and families. Pain intensifiers include grief and loss, stress, poor sleep/insomnia, fear of pain, anxiety, and depression. It is important to recognise these psychological stressors when managing your pain. Pain doesn't have to be in control. A professional pain and injury psychologist can counsel and train you, and your family, in ways to effectively manage pain and stressors so that control can be taken back and life can be lived again.

Social focus

A lack of connection and involvement with work, friends, hobbies, or sports when dealing with chronic pain can lead to frustration, grief, and anger. Such isolation from social activities is normal because the chronic pain sufferer does not want people to 'put up with them' or 'see them' like this. However you need to be involved in as many social things as possible even though you may only be able to go for 15 minutes or so at first. Building up tolerance to social events and allowing you to see that people still value you as a person rather than focusing purely on the pain and injury, is important.

Sometimes, people with significant and complex mental health conditions may suffer unexplained chronic pain. If this is the case then it is important to ensure that a full range of tests are carried out to determine what the issue is. Full blood tests, particularly for ESR levels, and similar tests that look for infection in the body, radiology scans, and a referral to medical and allied health professionals who specialise in pain management and mental health issues is recommended.

Kellee Waters

SOME FAQ FOR SEEING A THERAPIST

I hear my friends talk about seeing a therapist...to whom are they referring?

When people say they are consulting a therapist (or shrink) they mean they are seeing a University-trained mental health professional who is either a psychiatrist, psychologist, counsellor, psychotherapist, social worker, or even a mental health nurse. These people are well-educated in a range of psychological areas, are experienced in dealing with a variety of difficulties and types of people, and they are usually required by law to be registered/licensed by a government board and/or a professional association. Checking out the person online is easy, as most boards and associations have websites with practitioner lists, and therapists often have their own website. Most therapists will give you an Information and Consent Document (see Appendix at the end of this article) at the first session which outlines their qualifications, affiliations, experience, expertise, fees, and so on.

Are psychotherapy, counselling, and therapy different things?

No, not really. They are simply different terms used to describe the process whereby a therapist facilitates the development of self-exploration, insight and emotional awareness, as they work together with a client (or patient) toward an agreed goal. Remember that therapy is for individuals, couples, families, and groups, depending upon need and context.

What kind of therapy will be best for me or for the problem I have?

Therapists work in different ways. Some are very insight-oriented, while others are quite action-oriented. Some will be problem-focused, whilst other therapists become solution-focused reasonably quickly. Some therapists say very little preferring to listen and reflect, others are very interactive and analytical or educative. Whatever your therapist's personal style, theoretical approach or type of training, what is critical is that you are able to form a warm, close relationship with them, that you feel comfortable exploring the relevant issues in your life, and that you reach the outcomes you are after. A collaborative and harmonious relationship is more important than the specific type of therapy used. Whatever way you look at the process of therapy and styles of therapists, there are two things all therapies have in common; therapy helps you change how you think, feel or live; it also gives you hope. So it is hard to know what is best for you until you think about your preferences and try it.

How do I find a good therapist? And how much do sessions cost?

People often get recommendations when seeking a new restaurant or car mechanic. Finding a therapist should be no different. Ask the people you know for the name of any therapist they have seen or heard about. Particularly seek the advice of your family doctor as they will possibly be referring you to the therapist anyway, and hopefully they know you and the therapist fairly well. You can find names of therapists on websites of professional associations. This can be very useful as you can find someone who is close to your home or work, or who has expertise in your area of concern. Fees for sessions will vary depending upon profession, training, expertise, and location. The fee may range from about $100 to $200 per one-hour session. A psychiatrist's fee is usually more, given their medical training and the nature of their expertise (remember, they are the only therapists who prescribe medication). Often fees attract some rebate from private or public health funds, or sometimes employers have schemes whereby therapy can be assessed at no cost to the employee.

What should I do if I don't like the therapist I go to, or if they aren't helpful? What do I do if I have a complaint about a therapist?

Just in the same way you wouldn't return to a mechanic who doesn't listen to you or who isn't able to fix your car, you will probably end up leaving a therapist you think isn't interested in you and isn't helpful. First, be sure to attend a couple of sessions to enable the therapist to find how best to treat you and get a clear sense of what you are after. Next, discuss with them if you don't feel heard, or you don't like their style, and be up front about what you prefer and what it is that you want to work toward. Even therapists need reminders sometimes to stay on track! Then, if you continue to not get what you are after, find someone else to see. Just because one therapist wasn't helpful, does not mean you should give up on your desire for change. If you have significant concerns about the professionalism of your therapist, discuss this with them (if you feel comfortable enough), or contact their registration board and/or professional association if you think they have been unprofessional or unethical. These bodies will be able to guide you on whether or not you have cause for concern, and possible next steps.

I have talked to friends and talking it hasn't helped, so why would talking to a therapist, a stranger, help? How do I know I need to see a therapist and for how long will I see them?

Cultures have survived for a long time without therapy. For the most part, people solve their own challenges, and talk with friends, family and colleagues for help. These are the people you get friendly support and advice from, but sometimes that's not enough to overcome your challenges. Occasionally individuals and couples find their resources are low or the challenge is significant, and they need the support and guidance of a professional to help with important concerns. So they see a therapist who they know won't judge them and who has expertise to help. A therapist helps you clarify what is really going on and finds a way forward that friends and family haven't been able to. Also, people are able to talk to a therapist in a way they can't with the people they are close to, as the therapist doesn't have a vested interest. Most people need only a few sessions to achieve the relief, self-awareness and problem-solving they are after, while others require many sessions over an extended period of time. Ask your therapist how many sessions they think may be needed to sort through your issues.

Will a therapist tell me what to do?

Typically no. As they help you to understand your issues better, and you get to know more about how you operate, you will work out what it is that you want to do for yourself. Sometimes therapists will give you suggestions or tasks that will help you get back on track in a way that fits with the person that you are, or person you want to be. Sometimes a therapist will be very explicit about what needs to be done, usually only if you are in significant crisis or a high-risk situation. What is more common is that a therapist will want you to make your own decisions so that you have ownership of the plans and responsibility for outcomes. It should be noted that with some issues a therapist will teach you particular skills that will help you.

I am not sure how therapy starts ... what will the first session be like? I am a bit nervous.

It is normal to have some doubts and fears about the first session. You are about to share some fairly important personal information with your therapist, and they will be trying to get a good understanding about the type of person you are. Be open and honest about your issues. Know that the therapist is also a little anxious to do a good job so that they can be helpful, and that you return to therapy to continue the important work toward your goals. Remember, you are not crazy because you see a therapist, you simply need more or different help to what you or others can provide.

Is what I say to a therapist really private and confidential?

Yes (and No)! You should feel comfortable that whatever you are talking about with your therapist will go no further, just in the same way when you talk with your doctor, priest or best friend. Without being able to trust your therapist, the helping process would be compromised and it is their responsibility to create an atmosphere and relationship that makes you feel cared for and safe. The only time a therapist will breach confidentiality, and this rarely happens, is if it required by law (e.g., perhaps in cases of abuse, or if there is an order from a law court or an insurance requirement), if you or another person is at serious and imminent risk of harm, or if the therapist needs to report back to your referring doctor. Therapists are very good at keeping secrets and your personal stuff will generally stay only with them.

How can I get the most out of my therapy?

Lots of research has shown that therapy works in helping change people's lives, so you can relax in the knowledge that it is a proven process. Because therapy is expensive and time-consuming, you can maximize your time in therapy by being ready and committed to talk openly and frankly about your concerns. Trust and faith are central to the relationship and process. Take some risks to challenge yourself to look at new ideas and to do things differently between sessions. Your therapist might suggest books or courses as an adjunct, so be receptive as you would with your doctor. Develop a system of people around you who are supportive of you improving your life. Some people find keeping a journal helpful during the process of therapy as they reflect each day on what they are getting from the therapy, and what they are experiencing in their lives. Finally, be patient as you work hard to make changes; it may not be easy but it is possible and worth it!

What if I experience a crisis during the time I'm seeing a therapist?

If the crisis is life threatening then you should call an ambulance or the police immediately. You should let your therapist know what has happened after you are safe. There are support services for people with specific significant needs who experience a crisis between sessions. You can discuss these options with your therapist in session as the need arises.

What do you suggest if I want to take my child to a therapist?

I advise that the first appointment with the therapist should be with the parent/s only, without the child present. This helps the therapist do an intake to collate a comprehensive history and just as importantly allows the parent to get to know the therapist. As the parent, if you don't feel that the therapist is warm, compassionate, caring, professional, or competent, do not take your child to them. Find someone you feel comfortable with, someone who has experience working with young people, who can build rapport with a child or adolescent and who is comfortable working with this age group. Then I would say to the child;

> *I'm taking you to meet someone who is very nice and a good listener. Her name is Mary-Jane and she is a therapist. A therapist is someone who likes to help kids like you who are be feeling a bit sad, or angry or confused. If you want me to stay in the room with you when you meet Mary-Jane I will, until you feel ready to talk to her on your own. If you don't like Mary-Jane you don't have to*

go back — it's up to you. A therapist is someone you can talk to about how you are feeling and they help you start feeling better. Things you might do with Mary-Jane include chatting, doing art or craft, playing games, or playing with sand or clay. How does that sound? How would you feel about me taking you to meet Mary-Jane and then you can decide if you'd like to go back.

How is it that therapists themselves don't get affected by their patients' troubles and traumas?

Helping people through tough times can be difficult. What I enjoy about providing therapy is being able to use my curiosity about people's lives, seeing how they cope, connect with them, and watch as they grow and develop using their resources. Although the stories I hear are often quite distressing, and the therapeutic relationship can be intense, I know therapy is a time-limited relationship, that my role is to facilitate healing, and not to be unduly concerned for people's wellbeing. I know that people who have problems are still quite resilient and have lots of capacity for self-care. Outside of the therapy room my quality intimate relationships, diverse interests, and support from colleagues ensure that I stay in good shape personally and professionally, so I can continue to do the work that I enjoy without being significantly negatively impacted.

Dr John Barletta

Information and Consent Document

I am pleased you have selected me as your treating Clinical Psychologist. This document informs you about my background, to assist you to understand the nature of my therapy service, and to outline our professional relationship.

Qualifications and Experience

I hold a clinical Doctoral degree from The Ohio University, and have over 25 years experience in education, counselling and psychology in a variety of contexts with children, adolescents, adults, couples, families and groups in Australia, Italy, and the USA. I am Registered with the Psychology Board of Australia and I am a Member of the Australian Psychological Society. My practice is focused on Therapy, Mediation, Consultation, Training, Clinical Supervision, Assessment and Medico-Legal services.

Nature of Psychological Therapy

I see people as having the capacity to resolve their challenges through our consultations. Change occurs as you experience yourself as open and competent, and then more capable of finding solutions for more control and contentment. Most people need several sessions to achieve

continue next page

the self-awareness and problem-solving they seek, while some require many sessions over an extended period of time. As a patient you are in control and may end the professional relationship anytime. Sometimes exploring sensitive issues and the past can be distressing. If you become upset outside of sessions due to what is discussed, please raise this with me. Therapy is successful when you know yourself better and are able to face life's challenges without my support. Although sessions may be psychologically intimate and intense, remember we have a professional relationship not a personal one, and our face-to-face contact is limited to sessions. You are best served as our relationship remains professional and sessions concentrate on your concerns. You will, however, learn a little about me as we work together.

Referrals

If you require a referral to any other professional I will happily discuss this and help as much as possible. If at any time you are dissatisfied with my service please tell me.

Fees, Cancellation and Health Funds

The fee for therapy is $180 per hour-session and is due at each session. In the event you are unable to keep an appointment, notify me 24 hours in advance, otherwise you will be charged for the session. If you need a reduction in fee to continue with therapy, please feel comfortable discussing this with me. Most private health insurance funds cover some psychological services; contact yours to determine any rebate.

Records and Confidentiality

All of your communication becomes part of my clinical record. I will keep secure and confidential anything you say to me except where: (1) I receive your approval to tell someone else, or (2) Failure to disclose the information would place you or another person at serious and imminent risk, or (3) This is required or authorised by law. My aim is to safeguard your privacy within the constraints of the law. If you have been referred to me by a doctor I may collect information from, and disclose information to them to facilitate integrated treatment. If you are consulting any specialist or involved in a legal process, inform me as it may impact the treatment process and relationship. I do not electronically-record sessions and I do not grant you permission to record them, or any of our conversations, either.

If you are in significant need of support between sessions contact a 24-hr crisis agency, a hospital, or my consulting rooms.

If you have any questions about this document, please ask me at the beginning of your consultation. Ensure you retain this document for future reference.

Thank you.

Dr John Barletta

6

Ageing Issues

- Coping with an Empty Nest
- Planning for Retirement
- Positive Ageing
- Caring for Ageing Parents
- Coping with Dementia or Alzheimer's Disease
- Caring for a Person with Dementia or Alzheimer's Disease

COPING WITH AN EMPTY NEST

The term *empty nest* refers to the sense of loss, abandonment and grief that many parents' experience when their children move out of the family home. While it is often believed that women are more likely to be affected by this life transition, research suggests that men are also affected and may be unprepared for their emotional reaction. Often parents' lives revolve around their children and when the time comes for the child to leave home, the house feels empty and parents often feel alone and uncertain of their place in the world. For some parents, the transition is a time of intense sadness and grieving, while others embrace the opportunity to redefine their parental roles and relationships and celebrate a new-found freedom. Following are some practical strategies that you will find helpful:

- Anticipate and recognise that this is a healthy, normal, and necessary life transition.

- Acknowledge your feelings and give yourself permission to grieve.

- Don't compare yourself to others. You are individual and unique and so too will be your reaction to change.

- Be aware that children leaving home can put a strain on your relationship with your partner. Couples whose relationship has previously experienced difficulties may be more at risk. Help reduce this risk by planning ahead and creating opportunities for couple time.

- Avoid making major life changing decisions (e.g., moving house) until you have adjusted.

- Discuss your thoughts, feelings and plans for the future with your partner or a trusted friend.

- Keep yourself on track by establishing a routine and balance in your life.

- Catch yourself when you are thinking negatively and replace it with a healthier, more positive thoughts.

- Remember back to when you were busy with your young family and dreamt about all the things you had missed out on? Well now's the time to write a list of all those things and choose one that is achievable within the next few weeks.

- Take some time to reconnect with family and friends that you have not had time to catch up with while raising your family.

- Write a journal, create a scrapbook or photograph album.

- Reflect on coping strategies that have worked for you in the past.

- While you will always remain a parent to your child, it is now time to establish a new adult relationship and implement some healthy boundaries.

- Traditions and celebrations are an integral part of the family system. Now that your child is an independent adult, it is time to negotiate and make compromises around these occasions that will be acceptable to all.

- Maximise healthy foods, exercise and fresh water. Minimise caffeine, sugar, alcohol and cigarettes.

- Plan a special treat or outing every 1–2 weeks. You have earned it!

Rarely life's challenges happen in isolation and your child leaving home will most likely to coincide with other social and emotional life changes such as, family illness, menopause, death of a family member, or loss of employment. These events can intensify your feelings of loss and grief. If you find yourself struggling to adjust find support with a trusted friend, spiritual leader or health professional.

Jan Bond

PLANNING FOR RETIREMENT

With an extended life expectancy now a reality, especially for the baby boomer brigade, preparing for the non-income generating years is more critical than ever. This guide takes a holistic approach to the four key overlapping lenses through which to view your retirement planning. In order to get the best look ahead, try to engage the physical, social, spiritual and financial attributes of your preparation to achieve a suitable overview for developing the best individual strategy.

The underlying theme to this approach to your preparation is to maintain as much of the initiative as you can. Being proactive in such a critical area of your life needs to underpin the urgency with which you prepare. Consider the adage for those in work and approaching retirement: *Go when they want you to stay. Don't stay when they want you to go!*

Physical health and wellbeing

While physical health is mostly a product of genetics and lifestyle, the prospective retiree needs to consider the following issues:

- The greatest cause of ill health is linked to stress being perceived in the mind but felt in the body. Lack of a life-balance or prolonged anxiety is the root of much ill-health.

- Establishing a good rapport with a well regarded GP, younger than yourself, who is going to have an ongoing interest in your care.

- Regular check ups and attention to your own body symptoms and indices such as changing patterns of sleep, lumps or perhaps skin cancers.

- Developing an appropriate exercise routine that is challenging and yet interesting enough to keep you motivated. Thirty minutes of activity that raises the heart rate to a moderate level should become part of the daily routine.

- Appropriate attention to diet, minimisation of alcohol intake and cessation of smoking are essential to good physical health.

- Physical wellness is aided by emotional strength and resilience. Living with boundaries is a component of the richness of older age. Keeping positive and not sweating the small stuff has many advantageous spinoffs for physical and mental health.

Social skills

Relationships are a key element of the human condition. Ageing does not mean isolation. Who I am becoming is more important than how my current job title defines me. Retirees are not just ex-engineers or ex-nurses, they are people who are continuing to grow and change. It is the human being not the human doing that counts. As a consequence, preparing for retirement is a significant opportunity to consider the following tips:

- Developing friendship networks beyond the boundaries of current work colleagues with whom you are randomly associated. This may involve joining some new interest groups such as sporting or charitable clubs for which you have not previously made the time.

- Strengthening your key relationships in your marriage or with your partner needs significant attention. You probably married for richer and for poorer but probably not for a hot lunch together everyday! The diversity of your day brought about by going to your job needs to be replaced with new experiences that often need to be separate from those of your partner.

- Develop your healthy assertiveness skills in the new context of not having a job title or positional power.

- Optimistic resilience is a key attitude to enhance social contexts and retirement generally. Not being in control is linked to not being responsible for things anymore so there is great wisdom in trying to let go.

- The leadership skills you developed through your career are even more important going forward. So many clubs and organisations need the benefit of experienced leaders. Be enlivened by volunteering.

- Be prepared to develop your sense of altruism and community involvement. You will receive great satisfaction from helping others but also develop new social skills in unfamiliar contexts.

Enhancing your spirit

The spiritual lens of retirement planning is not limited to the sense of religion or faith practice. It may involve these elements but is centred in the human spirit as an individual. We speak of orchestras and sporting teams playing with spirit. This is about living the vital third of your life with spirit and enthusiasm not with defeatism and pessimism. The following tips for developing spirit deserve consideration:

- Develop a personal strategic plan. Where do I want to be in five, ten or fifteen years? What skills and talents do I need to be confident in reaching these goals? How and where will I develop them? When can I start?

- Life has taught you many lessons already. What are some of the key ones? How will I apply them in my new state?

- Daily meditation and relaxation exercises help many people to be better centred and balanced. How will I integrate these activities or ones that will similarly give me life into my new routine?

- Being time-rich was often something craved by working people trying to juggle career and family commitments. Now is the time to plan how you will relish this newfound richness.

- Reflect on how you will apply the wisdom that comes with ageing to your whole of life planning.

- Frequent travel or holidays are exciting but eventually become mere distractions. The human spirit is enlivened by people and quality relationships. Develop a reflective routine that focuses on these key elements so you are not sucked solely into the materialistic culture that can entangle some.

Financial preparation

This fourth lens is the one that often receives the most attention. While we know money can't buy happiness it can help us in many ways. Prudence and financial astuteness certainly enable elements of retirement to be less worrisome and more satisfying. However, living within boundaries is a realistic element of the human condition throughout the various cycles of life. The following tips are recommended to ensure maximisation of financial resources to support the physical, social and spiritual elements described above:

- Retain a competent financial adviser either through your retirement fund or independently.

- Read as widely as you can in financial journals and newspapers. There is significant advantage in developing your financial literacy as it helps to give you peace of mind and strengthens your ability to plan.

- Most retirement funds provide seminars on retirement planning and pension organisation. Make sure you attend as many as you can with your partner.

- Ensure domestic financial decisions are shared and both of you have retained an interest in household finances, budgeting and banking.

- Avoid the tragedy of the chaos that can result with the untimely passing of one partner by ensuring wills are up to date, the powers-of-attorney are current and that all assets and bank accounts are in joint names.

- Increase financial sustainability by accessing government welfare benefits and programs. You have paid taxes all your working life, now is the time to plan some return on that long-standing investment!

Dr Brendan McManus

POSITIVE AGEING

We live in an era of unprecedented ageing. Now, more than any time in history, people are living longer. This means that we don't really have any role models of how to live well into very old age. It may mean we have no examples, but it does mean that we can set the standard, pave the way so to speak, of how to age well. We can show younger generations that being old can be the best time of our life now, being fit and healthy, busy and engaged with life. And even those of us who do have illness or disability can still show others how to deal with it positively, how we can modify our lives and still embrace life. We can show younger generations that life is a gift to be used well, even when the gift is not perfect.

What do we mean by ageing well or positively? We probably mean that we want to have no or little disease of any kind, have good physical and mental health, and be actively engaged with life. Some may even say that they don't mind having the odd illness or ache and pain because it is part of normal ageing as long as they can still do what they want to do. And most of us also say we don't mind getting older as long as our minds stay clear and we are not a burden to our families or friends.

It seems that as we get older, we tend to choose those activities that give us pleasure and emotional satisfaction, and this involves staying connected with family, friends and the community we live in. We also probably tend to choose activities that give us pleasure over those that others suggest are good for our health but we don't necessarily enjoy, such as going to a social activity rather than going for a walk alone. There is nothing wrong with that, but as we get older, we may need to put some of these activities together to give us both exercise and pleasure.

If we would like to live long, and want to have good health and good quality of life in our older age we will need to work on it. None of us plan to live with disability or illness, but unfortunately if we do not plan to stay healthy and work on it, we will not age as well. There are a number of things we can do to age well, and here are a few ideas:

- We need to foster a positive and optimistic mindset in as healthy a body as we are able to have. Our attitude to ageing is one of the most important factors that will shape how we age. Celebrate your life. It is your story, and even with all the mistakes we all make, it is your unique story, worth celebrating and worth sharing. Make positive statements about getting older, seeing the benefits and positives, even when dealing with the negatives. An example: we live in a country with some of the best eye care in the world. Don't lament that you are developing cataracts, but be grateful that you live in a country where a simple operation can restore your sight. Imagine living in a country where becoming blind may mean not being able to find food!

- A sound mind needs a sound body. We need to pay attention to what we eat and drink: good food, plenty of fresh vegetables and fruit, not too much fat and sugar, plenty of water and not too much alcohol or sugary drinks.

- A sound body needs exercise. Walking is one of the best types of exercise as we get older, but we need to do it regularly. Walking improves stiffness and reduces pain in arthritis, helps to prevent osteoporosis and opens up the lungs and airways. Walking early in the morning in fresh air costs nothing and is good for body and soul. Late afternoon is also good, but it would be wise to avoid the midday sun. Wear good sturdy shoes to protect your feet, take a bottle of water with you, and perhaps a stick to ward off little yappy dogs. Ask your friends to join you or join a walking group in your local park.

- Have regular checkups with your doctor, including skin checks, a colonoscopy to detect bowel problems early, prostate checks if you are male; mammograms and pap smears if you are female; and any other checks as suggested by your medical history and/or your doctor.

- Keep your mind active and healthy. Learn new skills, meet new people, socialise with your friends and family, play music, cards, and games. Your mind needs to build new pathways all the time to help prevent dementia and cognitive impairment (forgetfulness) and it is the new learning that is the key.

- Stay in touch with friends and family and build social networks. Social connections seem to also improve physical health. Use the telephone, write letters and post cards or buy a computer, connect to the Internet and send emails. There are lots of opportunities for older adults to learn how to use computers, and computers are getting cheaper all the time. The Internet will open a whole new world.

- Do not ignore mental health issues. It is not a sign of weakness to become a bit depressed at times, and there are lots of different ways of dealing with it, from seeing a counsellor, to doing some kind of therapy, or taking medication. Your doctor will help you decide what is most appropriate.

- Be creative when you find you can no longer do what you used to do. Determine what is most important, and accommodate other things around it. If you love having your family around for a meal but cooking and cleaning is becoming difficult, make simpler meals and enlist their help with the cleaning. If you like gardening but it is getting too heavy, get someone in to help with the heavy work so you are not too tired to enjoy what you like to do. If you cannot clean the house or mow the lawn in one day without getting too tired or spending the next day in pain, break up the work into smaller bits and rest in between. Spend the time on what is important to you, not on what you think other people see as important.

- Be positive about using assistance. There is a large number of government assistance schemes designed to keep older adults functioning well and in their own homes. Use them positively. Do not see it as a shortcoming that you need help, but see it as a grateful society providing you with assistance so you can live well in your elite old age, and society can benefit from your presence and your wisdom.

- Spend time with children if you like them. They keep us young, and reward us with unconditional love when we pay attention to them. Older adults have more time and patience with young children, and playgroups, kindergartens and primary schools love older adults becoming involved, helping children with reading.

- Have a pet if you like animals. Pets reward us with unconditional love, and they can make us feel less lonely. They need us to feed and shelter them, giving us a reason to get up. Dogs can give us a reason to go walking. It seems that older adults with pets live longer and stay healthier. Even residential aged care facilities often have pets.

- Be grateful for life, and for what you have achieved throughout your life, mistakes and all. It has been a rich life, worth living.

Dr Jenneke Foottit

CARING FOR AGEING PARENTS

We live in a society that has changed dramatically from the one in which our parents grew up. People live longer and healthier, therefore we have a generation of older adults who now live longer than any generation before them. We are now, for the first time in history, dividing old age into groups of young-old (retirement to 75), old (76–85) and elite-old (over 85). This means that we now have situations where the adults who care for their parents are older themselves. It is becoming more common to find a person in their mid-fifties taking responsibility for his or her parents, and their parents (that is, the grandparents as well). At the same time we have a generation of young people who either have their children very young or much older, so that this family may have grandchildren in their care while their children work or study, as well as their ageing parents and grandparents. They may still be in full or part time work too. Current economic pressures on young people and older old adults on aged pensions will add more stress to this situation.

Given these facts, the middle generation will need to think very carefully about how they will manage what they see as their responsibilities — physically, emotionally and financially — for ageing parents and/or grandparents, while taking care of their own needs as well. The key to taking care of such diverse groups is open communication and planning. No one person can take on this kind of burden by themselves, therefore it is crucial to involve key people.

With this in mind, here are a few pointers to help:

- Older adults want to, and should, remain as independent as possible for as long as possible. The concept of dignity of risk suggests that older adults should be allowed a certain amount of risk of, for example, falling. It means we don't have to keep them safe from everything at all costs to the detriment of their dignity.

- Older adults need social contact and social connections to stay well. Encouraging membership of organisations of interest or communal hobbies and setting up mechanisms to manage transport will help them stay well and independent.

- If you suspect an older adult may have memory problems, address them early by involving their doctor and make sure you attend the appointment to clarify the problems you noticed for example (the person with memory problems will have forgotten that they have left the stove on, or got lost in the shopping centre). If they do get diagnosed with a dementing illness, find out what you can about it and start planning early.

- There are a large number of government and non-government organisations that provide a significant range of services to maintain older adults in their own home, from cleaning once a fortnight or so, to daily care activities. Find out what they are in your area, and use them as needed. Social workers at local hospitals are often good sources of information for this.

- Determine what support you are prepared to offer, in consultation with your own household, be it partner, children or a housemate. Discuss this with the older adult concerned too — you may have different ideas about what is needed. Do not offer help you do not want to provide — it will probably do all of you more harm than good in the long run. If you are prepared to take your older adult out for shopping or dinner, but not prepared to do their housework, say so and get services for that. Do not provide care for older adults from a perspective of guilt. Guilt is a destructive force that will make you resentful and rob you and others of enjoying your relationship. Only take on those care roles that you feel good about and can find some satisfaction and enjoyment in. Sometimes it is better to place an older adult in a residential aged care facility and visit them regularly, taking them out for outings, shopping, or dinner, than to try and take care of them at home and becoming so overwhelmed by the care burden that you cannot sustain it.

- Be prepared for changes in your role, sometimes predictable as the older adult becomes older and frailer, sometimes unpredictable as a stroke or heart attack can change the situation very rapidly.

- Tell key people, such as your employer, what your responsibilities are, and avail yourself of work-life balance options at work. You may be able to work a certain amount of flexi-time, or be able to take work home on occasion, to ease your care burden.

- Seek help early — do not wait until the burden of care overwhelms you. Talk to your doctor, or a social worker at the local hospital, depending on your needs. It is not a failure to need support with care giving.

- Work with your older adult to plan for the future when they may not be able to make their own decisions. Talk about powers of attorney for health care and for finances, advance health directives and end-of-life care issues. Find out whether they prefer burial to cremation, for example, and whether they have special wishes for a funeral. Help them to make an up-to-date will and sort out unfinished affairs as much as possible, but without pushing the older adult where they are not ready to go.

- Listen to the stories of the older adult and record significant facts and events — our memories are less reliable than we think. Go through photos and put names and dates on them where possible, allowing the older adult to reminisce. Perhaps grandchildren may be interested in this kind of project. They are often curious about the way our older adults lived *(What did you do if you did not have an Xbox, grandma?)*

- Take care of yourself, your own needs and your physical and emotional health. Care giving is long term and you need to look after yourself if you want to be able to sustain it.

- Enjoy the care giving. Our current older adults are fitter, more educated, healthier and more engaged with the community than ever before. They are also a first — the first as a generation to live so long. They, and us, are forging new ways — they will be teaching us how to live in the elite-old age. Enjoy the learning.

Dr Jenneke Foottit

COPING WITH DEMENTIA OR ALZHEIMER'S DISEASE

Dementia is an umbrella term for a number of disorders that have as their main characteristic the progressive, irreversible loss of memory. Such a diagnosis is a frightening prospect for most people and it is not unusual to become depressed for a while after receiving such a diagnosis. At the same time it is often a relief to have a definite answer for the problems that have lead a person to seek medical advice and it now becomes something specific one can deal with.

As there are a number of different forms of dementia, it is a good idea to get information about the type of dementia that has been diagnosed. It will shape the decisions to make and the care planning. An example is that people with the type of dementia called Alzheimer's Disease develop more and severe memory loss earlier than other types, and can also become apathetic. This can lead to a tendency to put off making decisions or planning because the person cannot be bothered.

Remember that dementia is a disorder, and that the person with dementia stays the same person they were before diagnosis. What changes is the ability to express who the person is and this is also influenced by the type of dementia and the amount of damage from the dementing process, personality and life experiences, the work the person has done, the learning done over time and physical health.

Here are some ideas to help deal with a diagnosis of dementia:

- Take time to adjust to the diagnosis. Getting a diagnosis of dementia is a shock and can leave a person feeling numb. It is not unusual to have a sense of despair in the beginning, but that will change as you get used to it, and begin to think about how to make the best of the situation.

- Take time to grieve. Knowing you have dementia will trigger a sense of loss about relationships and about plans and hopes for the future. This is a normal reaction, with a very real sense of loss. It is important to grieve these losses.

- Plan for a future with memory loss. Ignoring it won't make it go away, and will lead to significant problems for the people who will care for you when your memory becomes totally unreliable.

- Tell your story now — record it if you can — video or audio tapes or on DVD, writing it down, tell family members who are interested in history. Put your photographs together in a way that is logical for you and write names where you can, also other information you can remember. Other people will use that later to prompt your memories. Enlarge photos that are significant, particularly older ones, such as wedding photos. You will remember material from your younger days for longer than more recent events.

- Talk about your thoughts, feelings and opinions about subjects that matter — it will guide your loved ones in decision making when you can no longer do it.

- Make sure your loved ones know your preferences, even just in general, about end-of-life care (e.g., Do you believe people should be fed with a tube in their stomach when they cannot swallow and cannot talk, walk or care for themselves?). Include your thoughts on funerals, burial vs. cremation.

- Make sure you have a valid will.

- When you are ready, write an advance health directive, but don't wait too long — you will need to hold quite a bit of information in your short term memory for the doctor to decide you are still legally capable of making an advance health directive.

- Appoint powers of attorney for your health affairs and your financial affairs. They will make decisions for you when you will be no longer able to do so. Choose them carefully. They do not have to be family. You can appoint separate people to decide about your health decisions and your financial affairs, but make sure they get along — they may need to make some decisions jointly. You will need to consult a lawyer for this.

- Teach yourself routines for basic matters and stick to them without fail. They will guide some of your behaviour when you struggle to remember. For example: put a hook somewhere and always hang your keys there until it becomes such routine behaviour you don't think about it (like not thinking about the gears in a car you drive). That will lessen the risk of losing keys. Make a habit of always washing your dishes after you have eaten and then check your stove to make sure it is turned off. Do it in the same pattern each time. Write yourself reminder notes and put them where you can see them until your routine is automatic.

- Get a perpetual calendar (like a birthday calendar) and write all your significant dates in it — birthdays and anniversaries you want to remember.

Write full names, and year of birth to help you remember ages. If you can, put a photo of the person next to it.

- Talk to your friends and family about dementia. Educate them that you will always be you; you are only losing the ability to remember. They can help you by reminding you of your life story with them. Encourage them to visit you frequently — it helps with remembering. Teach them that while you might forget their names, you won't forget who they are, because you will remember that you had connections with them. The stronger the feelings and the more frequent the visits, the longer you will be able to remember. Warn your children that you may confuse them with other people, particularly a child that resembles a life partner. Tell them that you will still love them and that the spiritual connection with them does not depend on memory.

- You may not be ready to think about end-of-life care just yet, but at some stage you may need to let your family know your choices for when it may no longer be possible for you to live in your own place. Think about what you want for your care when you cannot care for yourself and do not recognise those who care for you. It may be necessary for them to place you in a facility that can help them care for you. It would be very helpful to them if you let them know you accept that it may be necessary, and tell them not to feel guilty about not being able to care for you on their own. Care in a facility is a type of shared care where the facility provides the physical care and the family provide for your emotional needs. You may not like the idea of residential care now, but as your memory deteriorates and your physical needs become greater, the family will need help with your care, and your permission will help them deal with the grief and guilt they will feel when they have to make that decision. You can discuss with them what kind of facility you think you would like, keeping in mind that your needs by then will be small — help with hygiene and food, and contact with people.

- Do not fear dementia. While it is frightening to think that one cannot remember, one of the advantages of dementia is the opportunity to live totally in the moment, and for a long time people with dementia can still lead enjoyable lives. Much depends on your attitude to it.

Dr Jenneke Foottit

CARING FOR A PERSON WITH DEMENTIA OR ALZHEIMER'S DISEASE

Dementia is an umbrella term that covers a number of diseases that all have one characteristic in common — progressive, irreversible memory loss. Knowing something about the type of dementia will help you understand why they don't always behave the way you expect. Most people with dementia fit into one of five main types: Alzheimer's disease, vascular dementia, fronto-temporal lobe dementia, Lewy body disease, and dementia as part of another disorder.

Alzheimer's disease (AD) is the most common form of dementia although many people have both Alzheimer's disease and vascular dementia. Alzheimer's disease is caused by amyloid plaques and neurofibrillary tangles in the brain and characterised by severe progressive memory loss and apathy. People with Alzheimer's disease tend to forget more and quicker than people with other types of dementia, and they lose interest in many aspects of their lives early. They are not depressed, they just cannot be bothered. That can put them at risk, for example, of ignoring pain because they are too apathetic to do something about what is causing the pain (like moving away from a heater).

Vascular dementia (VAD) causes brain damage across all areas of the brain because it is related to interruptions in the blood flow of the brain, similar to having little strokes. People with VAD forget progressively more, but their memory loss tends to fluctuate so that they may remember more on some days than on others. It is not possible to predict when they will remember better. Their deterioration tends to be more stepwise than slow and steady decline.

Fronto-temporal lobe dementia (FTL) is probably the most difficult form to deal with. People with this type of dementia present with personality changes first. They show a striking lack of insight into their disease or behaviour and become impulsive and disinhibited to the point where they would take their clothes off in public and not understand why that is unacceptable. They forget what is socially acceptable, like manners, become neglectful of hygiene and will go without washing or changing for days. People with FTL dementia also have language disorder where they lose their understanding of the meaning of words rather than forget the words. They talk to you expecting you to understand what they say because they know what they are saying, but it makes no sense, leading to frustration and anger. This can lead to angry outbursts, due to the lack of insight and self control as a result of the dementia.

Lewy body disease is a rapid and progressive dementia that presents as a movement disorder. Sufferers develop tremors, become stiff and walk with a slow, shuffling gait. They can have severe vivid hallucinations (seeing and hearing things that are not there) particularly at night, and it is almost impossible to convince them that the hallucinations are not real. Unfortunately they are also very sensitive to neuroleptics (medications that are often used to control hallucinations) and can suffer severe side effects on even low doses.

A number of people suffer dementia as a result of another disorder. These disorders are the main problem and the dementia is part of the disorder. Examples are Huntington's disease, a movement disorder where the person loses control of their muscles and the muscles move as if they have a mind of their own; and some forms of AIDS lead to dementia in the end stages.

When caring for a person with dementia, there are a few important points to remember:

- The person with dementia is still who he/she was before diagnosis. Dementia does not change who they are, just the way they respond. This is influenced by the type of dementia and the amount of damage they have but also by character and personality, life experiences, the work they have done, the learning they have been exposed to and their current physical health.

- In the early stages it is important to help the person remember with aids like calendars, reminder notes and alarms, but as the disease progresses the person needs to be allowed to feel safe without needing to remember. Then it becomes more important to join them where they are in their mind and world.

- Safety becomes a major concern for people with memory problems but there are many ways to deal with it, and many organisations that can help. Good starting points are your local doctor who knows you and your family and Alzheimer's associations. They also have good information on dementia.

- Caring for a person with dementia is very rewarding, but it can also be very hard work, particularly in the later stages. Take care of yourself and your own needs and health as well. Find out about respite care for your person with dementia, and start using it early, while they can still learn about new environments. This will make it easier for both of you when it becomes necessary to use other people to help you care for them. Teach your friends about dementia and invite them over frequently so they can become used to the changes in your person with dementia and the person can stay familiar with them. Don't refuse offers of help, and reassure people dementia is not contagious. If you find the care giving overwhelming, talk to someone — a doctor, social worker or counsellor, and do it early, before you burn out.

- Discuss options for care, advance health directives, and end-of-life choices early, while the person is still able to contribute. Put arrangements in place while the person still has capacity to make that decision. Communication is vital in the early stages, and may be a good idea to write things down so you can refer to it later. These topics are sensitive and both of you will need time to get used to the ideas, so take the time to work it through, but don't delay until memory problems make it legally impossible to establish guidelines.

- Take the time to grieve. You are losing a relationship, bit by bit, as the person forgets more and more. Allow yourself the opportunity to grieve.

- Celebrate your life and your relationship. Reminisce and write down important facts, stories and history. Gather photos and enjoy what they represent. Live in the moment. One of the joys of caring for a person with dementia is their ability to live totally in the moment (because they don't remember anything else). See how they enjoy an ice-cream like we did as children, join them. Find joy in the everyday to make the caring easier.

- The end stage of dementia can be very challenging. It is not unusual for the behaviour of the person to become difficult to manage, and in the final stages they will be unable to walk, talk, feed themselves, control bowel or bladder and will sleep poorly. It may be necessary to enlist the help of a care facility to help you care. See it not as a failure of providing care, and do not feel guilty — no-one can care for a totally dependent adult around the clock, by themselves. See it as an added help. The care facility will do the heavy physical work for which they are well equipped, while you do the emotional caring that they cannot do as well as you, because you have known the person much longer.

- Caring for a person with dementia is very rewarding and very challenging. Remind yourself often that you are doing the best you can and that is enough.

Dr Jenneke Foottit

Mental Health Issues

KEEPING YOUR BRAIN ACTIVE AND STIMULATED

Our brains allow us to think, work and to love. We experience the world, others and our own personality because of this amazing organ. Cognitive decline is something everyone fears; to lose our capacity for memory, learning and thinking robs us of the ability to participate in life. Worsening memory used to be considered a normal consequence of aging through the loss of neurons, reduced connectivity (dendritic connections between neurons) resulting in decreased brain function. The good news is that we now know this is not the case and not only do we make new neurons and dendritic connections, it is possible to reduce the rate or prevent cognitive decline. This is called neuroplasticity. The amount of neuroplasticity that occurs, the success of new neurons in grafting into existing neural tissue to repair neural function is governed by a number of factors. Even if factors are optimal there are limits to the capacity of the brain to rewire itself and repair damage. If there wasn't then we would not see many of the tragic diseases of ageing such as Alzheimer's disease and other neurological disorders such as loss of function created by stroke.

So how does neuroplasticity occur in relation to using our brains? This process is not well understood but mental stimulation, diet, exercise and some medications can influence this process. The likely explanation is that this activates certain genes in our neurons that in turn signal the release of brain-derived growth factors, proteins and other signaling factors. Neurotransmitters involved in memory and learning increase, neural connections strengthen, and/or new pathways are created and new neurons may be created and recruited into our neural networks. In fact, even the way we feel can affect the health of our brains. For example depressive illness is marked by a substantial reduction or cessation of neurogenesis, as is the under utilising of our brains, "use it or lose it". We understand this in relation to physical fitness for example, if we don't use our muscles they waste away, and this is equally true for our brains. The sooner we start lifestyle that keeps our brains active and stimulated, the more likely we are to protect our precious neurons, and preserve or enhance our mental function.

What can you do to optimally stimulate your brain?

- *Physical exercise.* Our brains like it when we do physical exercise. The proverb that a healthy body means a healthy mind is true. Sitting in front of a TV all day is not going to cut it for our brains, we need to get moving. Exercise, stimulates neural growth factors, the formation of new neurons and stimulates dendritic connections to grow between neurons. Of particular interest is that exercise appears to particularly benefit areas of the brain involved in memory and learning and mental health. All forms of exercise might be beneficial but aerobic exercise where the heart rate is raised appears best. While there is no conclusive proof in human research, high intensity exercise may be best when we are younger and moderate intensity aerobic type exercises from middle age onwards. Regular exercise has been shown to reduce the risk of cognitive decline and dementia in old age so might help protect against Alzheimer's disease, depression and anxiety disorders and improve recovery from addictions. Exercise certainly modifies risk factors for most health problems such as coronary heart disease, diabetes, hypertension, obesity and stress which are all factors that in the long term might be involved with cognitive decline.

- *Use your brain for what it was designed for, learning.* The effort we put into actively learning new knowledge often decreases as we get older. Consolidating knowledge and skills in our profession is not sufficient to keep our brain healthy, we must be challenging it to work hard, which means learning new things. Learning appears to stimulate neural growth factor, dendritic growth, neurogenesis and it ensures the uptake of new neurons into existing brain tissue. The actively learning brain has better quality connections and the storage of information and retrieval is better than under stimulated brains. The best kind of learning activities for our brains requires effort: puzzles, learning a language, complex games, taking courses in a new subject all are reasonable examples of the level of effort needed to get results.

- *Our social brains.* Our brains are wired to be social; they light up in remarkable ways in the presence of other people compared to being on our own. Social interaction is an important form of stimulation to keep our brains healthy. Simply talking to someone for a minimum of 10 minutes a day can improve performance on memory test scores compared to people instructed to have no social interaction. The more social interaction the better people perform on memory tests. A large population study of people aged over 65 demonstrated that those with at least 5 social connections for example, church groups, social groups, friendships, family or other social activity suffer less cognitive decline than those with fewer than 5 social connections. Social interaction also includes the quality of relationships and communication. Speaking to someone on the phone once a week is not the same as meaningful communication with someone on a day-to-day basis. Males are more likely to develop cognitive impairment before full dementia than females. This effect has been part explained by males tending to have fewer confiding relationships and they communicate less than women. In fact most males only speak a fraction of the number of words that females speak on a daily basis.

- *Get enough sleep.* Sleep appears to be very important for brain health and may allow optimal neurogenesis and dendritic growth or repair to occur. In animal models sleep deprivation reduces neurogenesis. Most of our new knowledge is processed, consolidated and stored into memory during sleep. Our memory center, the hippocampus, becomes very active during sleep. Dendritic connections between neurons strengthen and grow during sleep.

- *Manage your stress:* Constant stress is not good for our brains and triggers hormonal and metabolic changes. Cortisol, a stress hormone produced by the adrenal glands, is important for managing brief periods of stress by modifying metabolic response, however, chronically elevated levels suppress immune function, impair glucose control, damage arteries and become toxic to neural tissue. Some of the most disastrous effects of cortisol on the brain include atrophy of the hippocampus, which is our memory center, and killing neurons in various areas of the brain. The hippocampus is susceptible to stress as its neurons have a high number of cortisol receptors. Even the signal hormone for cortisol, corticotrophin releasing hormone, disrupts learning and memory. The net impact of high stress levels on memory is impairment and difficulties in new learning and memory, recall regardless of age. Therefore, assisting children and adolescents to manage their stress can enhance learning and academic performance. As people get older they may notice that stress has a greater impact on their mental function such as learning and memory. This can be to the point where they may not be able to concentrate and retain what they are trying to learn and/or they have trouble intentionally recalling facts or information. This means that even episodic and short-term stress can effect mental performance and negatively impact learning and memory. Avoiding stress altogether is not practical or even desirable, but managing stress to avoid the negative consequences is worth the effort.

Dr Matthew Bambling

BRAIN HEALTH

The proverb that you are what you eat is most true for our brains. The sad reality is that many people begin to show cognitive changes that are related to decline by the time they enter their 30s. The quality of food we ingest might significantly reduce our risk of age related negative neurological changes. While some say genes might predict conditions such as Alzheimer's disease, the reality is that genes only explain up to 30% of our chances of getting any disease. This means that up to 70% of our chance of getting a disease is explained by our lifestyle, health behaviour and living environment. Of course the relationship between genes and environment is oversimplified by this statistic, but the principle is that our nutritional and health behaviour environment is something we have a lot of control over is sound.

We slowly accumulate damage to our neurons and neural maintenance systems due to the wear and tear of brain metabolism over time. The older we get the more our brains are damaged because the brain is so metabolically active. Our brains burn energy like a coal at a power station, and in the same way generate large amounts of toxic by-products that must be disposed of by the body. The negative by-products of energy metabolism are oxidative reactions where atoms loose electrons in a chain reaction damaging cells, and glycation where glucose fuses with proteins in cells causing damage. Damage can affect gene expression and cause inflammation. The brain does not have the same ability to limit this damage as in other areas of the body because the blood-brain barrier restricts lots of potentially protective nutrients from reaching our precious neural tissue. The blood brain barrier consists of tightly packed cells to protect our brains from chemicals and pathogens in our blood. Even our own immune response in the brain can cause inflammation that can damage our neurons. Inflammation and brain tissue don't mix. Just think of all the damage done by a concussion and the consequences of brain swelling. Low level inflammation of neural tissue is thought to be a foundational pathogenic process in the development of Alzheimer's. Other reactions such as excitosis where neurons fire uncontrollably until they die is thought to be related to low levels of neural inflammation. Some proinflammatory chemicals in food that cause excitosis are certain preservatives, flavour enhances and artificial sweeteners. Higher levels of our own natural steroid hormones appear associated with better cognitive and memory function and better mood than low levels in older people. This might be another reason why exercise is important as it might stimulate these classes of hormones. Certain antioxidant nutrients that easily cross the blood-brain barrier appear very neuroprotective, reducing damage created by metabolism, waste products, excitotoxic reactions and modifying inflammatory reactions.

What can you do to keep your brain healthy?

- *Watch the sugar in your diet.* While we need adequate glucose for our brains to function well, more is not better, we simply need enough. If we eat too much sugar it creates much higher levels of glycation than normal and glucose that is not burnt up by our cells is converted to triglycerides (a form of blood fat). So does all this mean that skipping meals and snacking on sweets all day is a problem for our brain health? You bet it does! Our brain also needs a constant supply of amino acids as these are used as neurotransmitters and as building blocks for other neurotransmitters. Ensure enough protein in the diet, from plants, nuts, animal or dairy sources.

- *Get enough nutrients.* When our cells burn glucose or oxygen, this generates free radicals (an oxidation reaction) which damage the delicate lipid membranes and the micromachinery of our cells. Our body's antioxidant and antiglycation systems are easily overwhelmed by poor diet, stress and poor health behaviour; these systems also require nutrients to work properly. Some superfoods full of potent antioxidants that will protect your brain are blueberries, most other berries, grape seed extract, ginko biloba, curcumin which all contain phytochemicals that easily cross the blood-brain barrier and provide potent antioxidant and some antiglycation protection to neurons. Some of these, such as blueberries, appear to improve neurogenesis, neural connections and neuron function, while curcumin has potent anti-inflammatory effects. Likewise some vitamins such as E, the B group vitamin Choline, B12, folic acid, D3 and phosphatidyleserine (supports memory and neuroplasticity) and alpha lipoic acid (an antioxidant and antiglyication nutrient) is very neuroprotective and reduce inflammation and damage and stimulate important neurotransmitters involved with learning, memory and mood. Coenzyme Q10 is an antioxidant and supports energy metabolism. The newly available supplement pyrroloquinoline quinine is also very neuroprotective. Omega 3, typically sourced from fish oil, reduces inflammatory processes in the brain and protects it from toxic reactions and appears to support mood and memory. Acetyl-L-carnitine arginate is an example of a supplement which has been show to stimulate neural growth factor increasing the length and thickness of dendrites in the brain. There are many brain-friendly nutrients and it is worth learning about these and how to add them to your diet.

What about your mental health?

Some supplements appear promising in managing common mood problems. The natural compound S-Anenosyl-Methionine (SAMe) may be equally effective as prescribed medications for depression and it's a brain antioxidant as well. It may be useful for treatment-resistant depression, and when taken in addition to prescription medication, it has improved depression significantly for people who did not get good results on the standard prescribed drugs. SAMe is made from natural amino acids and supports neuron methylation which seems to regulate growth factors and neurotransmitters such as serotonin and dopamine which are involved with mood. Likewise Omega 3 supplements have been show to be helpful for some people with depression, learning problems and hyperactivity. However results for individuals may vary. St Johns' Wort has been shown to be useful for mild depression or low mood, however, may not be as effective as SAMe. L-Theanine, a natural amino acid, has been shown to be as effective as medication for treating anxiety in doses above 200mg per day with none of the side effects of tranquilisers; it even enhances concentration and memory. The herb Lemon Balm can improve the quality of sleep for most people between 20–40% with no sedative effect the next day. If you would like to try nutrients or supplements for mental health do not do this on your own as this is a specialised area. See a health care professional for advice and guidance on the best way to use these alternative nutritional approaches.

Dr Matthew Bambling

MENTAL ILLNESS AND MENTAL HEALTH

Mental illness or disorder refers to a group of conditions that affect the brain and interfere with a person's behaviour, mood, thought, perception, and/or judgement. One in five suffer from a mental illness each year and almost half the population experience a mental health disorder in their lifetime. Mental illness is particularly common in young people with at least one third of young people having experienced an episode of mental illness by the age of 25.

Mental health disorders include a list of conditions that have been selectively classified based on their range of symptoms and degrees of severity. The most common conditions are anxiety disorders, affecting one in seven each year. One in 16 people suffer from a mood disorder (i.e., depression or bipolar disorder) and one in 20 experience a substance use disorder. Other less common disorders include psychotic disorders such as Schizophrenia, eating disorders (e.g., Anorexia Nervosa) and personality disorders. Everyone experiences the symptoms defining some of these conditions at times. For example, everyone experiences excessive worry — a definitive feature of Generalised Anxiety Disorder. However, a mental health disorder is only present when these feelings become so overwhelming they impact on day-to-day activities such as workplace function, academic performance and/or social interaction. It is this feature of functional impairment that can make these conditions so disabling. Disability coupled with frequency and early onset has led the World Health Organisation to predict depression as the 4th most disabling illness by 2020.

Most mental health disorders can be treated effectively. Being mindful of genetic vulnerabilities, recognising early warning signs and symptoms, and seeking early treatment are all essential, as on most occasions the earlier the treatment starts, the better the outcome. If any of the symptoms develop it is important to seek help from a GP who can commence treatment or make a referral to a specialist who can continue or commence other treatments. Effective treatments include medication and/or psychological interventions such as promoting problem-solving skills, cognitive and behavioural therapies, and supportive therapies. For more severe conditions, or to avoid risk of suicide, hospitalisation may be necessary. Also, the use of electroconvulsive therapy (ECT or shock therapy) remains an important effective and well-tolerated treatment for certain severe or treatment-resistant illnesses.

Nonetheless, despite the effective treatments available for these conditions, they frequently are unrecognised and poorly managed, as only one third of people use health services for their mental illness.

Stigma remains a huge burden for people with mental illness in numerous communities and cultures. Stigma can generate misconceived stereotypes. This can then be associated with misunderstanding of a person's varied behaviour and can develop abuse, discrimination and social isolation. As a result, recovery is significantly assisted by understanding, compassion, and social support.

Remember, mental health disorders are extremely common and disabling. Mental health disorders are treatable; the earlier the treatment starts, the better. Stigma remains a huge obstacle. Empathy, understanding and support are fundamental to recovery.

Dr Matthew Hocking

DEPRESSION

Depression is a serious condition that is marked by a continual low mood, sadness, and physical symptoms such as low energy and poor concentration. Depression is twice as commonly diagnosed in females compared to males and up to 7% of the population suffers from depression at any one time, and everyone has a 20% chance of having at least one episode of depression over their lifetime. Depression can reoccur even after effective treatment. If a person has had one episode of depression they have a 50% chance of having a second episode, if they have a second episode they have a 70% chance of a third episode and if they have a third, the chance of more episodes is 90%.

Depression affects children, adolescents and adults. Depression typically is not a constant state and can improve over time and people may find themselves becoming depressed again after a period of remission. Depression is also the strongest predictor of suicide. This means if someone is depressed the suicide risk is automatically higher than a non-depressed person. If we think someone is depressed we should always ask them if they are feeling suicidal. There are some myths about suicide for example, if you talk about it, they might do it; if the person suddenly appears improved they are no longer at risk; or suicide attempts or suicide talk is just attention seeking. None of these are true and if people say these things they are still at risk. People rarely are successful the first attempt. Typically a successful suicide is preceded by two or more attempts. Talking to someone about suicide reduces the risk, however, it does not eliminate risk. Some people may be so suicidal that they need emergency assistance or specialist care.

Depression is not the same as dealing with loss and grief, or reacting to a crisis or life problems or major changes, although people may feel like they are depressed at these times. These are considered normal reactions signaling a period of psychological adaption to changes, which is referred to as adjustment. A person going through adjustment would be expected to make steady progress working through their thoughts and feelings and eventually return to normal mood. However, they can also get stuck in this process and in some cases adjustment might later turn into depression.

Causes of depression can be genetic (i.e., family history or predisposing genes); some health problems can also cause depression issues from our past such as abuse, trauma, rejection, learning negative beliefs about our self-worth and boundaries with others; and the current problems we are dealing with in our lives. We can see that all these things can provide stressors or triggers for depression. Our health or genes can create problems for us, we might be struggling with past hurts or traumas and negative beliefs about ourselves and the world or we are overwhelmed by problems in our lives.

There are some common symptoms to look for to identify if someone might be depressed:

- Has the person felt down or depressed for most days or most of the time for a minimum of two weeks?

- Have they lost pleasure in the activities that would normally make them happy?

If the person answers yes to at least one of these questions, and there has not been a previous loss or change in their life (adjustment) we want to know some more things. If they have answered no to both questions they are probably not depressed. Some more questions are:

- Has there been a change in appetite or body weight up or down?

- Are they experiencing trouble sleeping?

- Are they slowing down or becoming fidgety?

- Do they have low energy or tiredness nearly every day?

- Are they feeling guilty or not liking themselves?

- Do they have difficulty concentrating or making decisions?

- Is the way they feel causing them distress or affecting their role (e.g., employment, study, and relationships)?

- Do they think about hurting or killing themselves?

If a person answers "yes" to a minimum of five of the above questions they might be depressed. If a person is young they may have trouble understanding or answering these questions yet it is still possible to discuss what we can with them and consider whether their behaviour fits any of these symptoms. For example, children may have more behavioural problems, and adolescents more withdraw or acting out behaviours, which are as important to consider as well as anything they might say to us. The same approach might apply to people from different cultural backgrounds and/or where English is a second language.

The good news is that depression responds well to treatment such as counselling and medication. Cognitive therapy explores how our negative thoughts and beliefs reinforce our depressed feelings. If we learn to change our depressed thoughts we will no longer experience depressed mood. For example, if a person had an all or nothing belief or thought that they are failure as part of the series of thoughts that make them depressed, they can be taught to challenge and replace this thought. The first step is to be objective; how true is this really? Clearly a person is not a failure in every area of life and there are many successes. This rational-mind middle ground challenge to thinking counters the extreme distorted thinking of depression and often improves mood. Another common thought pattern in depressed people is to catastrophise which is to see the worst possible outcome in every situation. Once again using a rational-mind to challenge this — what is the evidence that our catastrophic prediction will come true, has it ever in the past, what is the more realistic outcome in this situation? — can improve mood.

Behavioural therapy explores the things that are worrying us or are going wrong, and these are typically real problems in our life and they can feel very overwhelming. However, if we set about working on these problems we will feel some control over our lives again. Underlying issues, another area treatment may focus on, things from our past that trouble us, or the need to understand ourselves and our reactions to others better. Does counselling really work? Yes. It has been show to work as well if not better than medication for most people. Research shows that counselling may improve areas of brain function similar to the way medication does. Medication can be very effective but there are also problems with side effects. For some people medication might be their preferred approach.

While you can do a lot to manage your own depression, or help others with depression, don't forget the risks. It is often better to get professional help from a therapist or GP than go it alone.

Dr Matthew Bambling

ANXIETY

Anxiety is a normal part of life. In fact we need anxiety to motivate us to do things and it can be a signal to adapt. It tells us something is wrong so we can do something to avoid consequences or protect ourselves, (getting off the road quickly if a car comes speeding along or getting an assignment done in time to avoid a fail grade). We may feel our physiology change, tension in our bodies, faster breathing and heart beat. The experience of crossing a busy road, or fear of failing, then become encoded in our brain as a part of a library of triggers that can then produce anxiety simply by thinking about them. This has a clear adaptive advantage as it helps keep us safe from danger. We learn what to avoid. Our anxious thoughts cause our brains to activate our sympathetic nervous system increasing stress hormones in our blood, which may increase blood pressure, heart rate, respiration, and clotting factors and alter our normal metabolism and hormone profile. This response is getting our bodies ready to either fight off a threat or to take flight to get away from a threat. In the short term, this is not a problem when we can reduce our anxiety back to normal levels. But in the long-term chronic anxiety keeps this fight-flight mechanism switched on, can affect our physical health, and increases our chance of major disease. In more extreme cases, the anxiety threat coding system in our brain will start to react to normal things that would not normally concern us in our environment as threats, and we will worry about things, avoid things, or develop rituals to try to control anxiety. This can lead to mental health difficulties. Anxiety disorders can affect children as well as adults. The rate of anxiety disorders has been reported as being 2–9% across the lifespan, with a lifetime chance of 10% of developing an anxiety disorder.

While the capacity to become anxious is part of our design as humans, anxiety disorders are not. Probable causes are:

- *Genetic* — there are higher rates for children with family members with anxiety disorders.

- *Family history* — abuse, trauma, learned fear behaviours, poor family coping skills, poor self-image and poor sense of personal control.

- *Current stressors* — major life problems or responsibilities, can contribute to anxiety.

The interaction of internal cues from our threat coding system and stressors in the environment is probably the most important in creating anxiety disorders.

The most common anxiety disorder is *Generalized Anxiety Disorder* (GAD) — worries and anxiety are present most of the time on most days for at least six months. The person might have difficulty controlling the worries, and the worries interfere with focusing on normal life roles and tasks, as well as feeling restless or tense, tired, poor concentration, irritable and having sleep problems. If you, or someone you know, would answer yes to having three or more of these symptoms, then there is a possible generalized anxiety problem.

Anxiety can represent itself as other disorders as well. For example *Obsessive Compulsive Disorder* (OCD), where for a period of at least a month, people are troubled by recurrent thoughts, impulses, images that they find worrying but can't get out of their minds (e.g., the idea that they are dirty, contaminated, or fear of harming or contaminating others). They can also be troubled by compulsive behaviours such as doing something repeatedly without being able to resist, such as washing or cleaning, counting or checking or arranging things over and over.

Anxiety disorders can also be expressed as *Phobias* such as fear of social situations where for at least a month a person has become fearful or embarrassed about being watched or being subject to attention such as speaking in public, eating in public with others, or being at social gatherings. They then worry continuously about these situations and may avoid social contact to reduce anxiety. *Specific Phobias* are the same except they focus on one thing, such as a fear of spiders or snakes, heights or enclosed spaces.

Panic Attacks are another class of anxiety disorder where people suddenly feel anxious, frightened, uncomfortable or shaky or dizzy in situations where most people would not feel this way. The attack typically peaks in around 10 minutes of starting and is unpredictable. Sometimes people think they have a physical health problem as a result of their symptoms.

Agoraphobia is a type of anxiety disorder where people feel very anxious or uneasy about places or situations where they might have panic like symptoms or even a panic attack e.g., being in crowd or on a bridge, at a busy shopping centre, travelling on a plane or train. The difference to panic attacks is that the person can endure these situations, if they must, even though they are very anxious or they more typically avoid the situations all together by not going out.

For such a debilitating disorder as anxiety, it is surprising how quickly psychological treatment can help most people. There are three levels of treatment.

- *Cognitive.* As our minds tell us how to feel and our bodies how to react, challenging the anxiety based thoughts can reduce our levels of anxiety. For example, I may worry about people making fun of me if I go to a party and tell myself that they will think I am a looser and don't belong there. This is catastrophic thinking where I am projecting a worst case scenario without any evidence. I can challenge this thinking; What is my evidence for this belief, is it possible that other people there will be just like me and hoping to make some friends? My negative belief can't be strongly maintained with counter positions. Cognitive interventions for anxiety are more sophisticated in psychological treatment than this example, but trying self-talk is powerful and can work well for some people and we all can do it.

- *Behavioural.* Because we experience so much physical arousal with anxiety we can learn to reduce it through behavioural techniques. For example, if I fear a situation I can gradually expose myself to the situation in small steps that I can manage. After repeated practice anxiety is often eliminated. This is called exposure and scientists think it works because of habituation; our nervous system gets used to the anxiety provoking situation and no longer reacts. The key is to do it in small manageable steps and don't give up as it can be hard work. Popular alternatives to exposure are relaxation training; anxiety is incompatible with a relaxation state and relaxation training is enjoyable to practice. Practice is critical in dealing with anxiety. Treatment feels like hard work, but the more we practice the better the result. While we can do some of these things ourselves, often a psychological therapist is required as they are trained in the required cognitive and behavioural techniques.

- *Medication.* The final approach to dealing with anxiety is medication. Medication can be very effective but there can be problems with tolerance, addiction and side effects depending on the type of drugs prescribed. For some people medication might be their preferred approach. Your GP can assist you with this option.

Dr Matthew Bambling

MANAGING THE CHALLENGE OF ASPERGER'S SYNDROME

The term Asperger's Syndrome was originally described in 1944 by Austrian Paediatrician Dr Hans Asperger. Asperger's Syndrome is a neuro-developmental disorder that forms part of the autism spectrum. Individuals with Asperger's Syndrome have difficulties with social/emotional reasoning, a narrow range of interests or a one-track mind, and often have motor skill and sensory problems. People with Asperger's Syndrome can experience discomfort in many social situations, increased levels of stress after social situations, and discomfort with certain sensory stimuli. They often have a different way of problem-solving, an obsessive approach to work and interests, and difficulties picking up on social cues. Difficulties with short-term memory, planning, taking the initiative and prioritising are commonly part of the condition.

Current estimates indicate that Asperger's Syndrome may occur in as many as 1 in 100 people. Asperger's Syndrome tends to be detected much more frequently in males than females with the sex ratio estimated at 4:1. However, this discrepancy may be inflated due to differences between the male and female presentation of Asperger's Syndrome, and the fact that the females with Asperger's Syndrome are often more difficult to detect. Research supports a genetic component to Asperger's Syndrome and while no specific gene has been identified as being responsible, the condition tends to run in families. The average age of diagnosis is approximately 7 years, but as more and more is discovered about the condition, the number of older individuals receiving a diagnosis is rising. People with Asperger's Syndrome are not immune to experiencing other mental health difficulties and a number of simultaneously occurring conditions are commonly seen. Rates of depression and anxiety are significantly higher amongst people on the autism spectrum than the neurotypical (i.e., non-Autistic Spectrum Disorder) population.

The best intervention for Asperger's Syndrome is knowledge and attitude. Knowledge means research into Asperger's Syndrome and understanding both the condition and how it relates to the individual. Attitude means having an attitude of optimism and discovery to understand the person with Asperger's Syndrome and his/her unique profile of abilities. It is about being open to making accommodations to the environment to assist the person to be able to adapt and to function the best he/she can within a social setting.

Asperger's Syndrome brings with it both gifts and challenges. Generally people with Asperger's Syndrome have average to high average intelligence so should be encouraged to use their intellect to work on better ways of managing their challenges. It is also possible for an individual with Asperger's Syndrome to have learning difficulties or an intellectual impairment. People with Asperger's Syndrome have a different way of thinking — they are not defective, just different. In fact, an ability to think about things differently can be very valuable.

Below are some ideas on how to manage and assist someone with Asperger's Syndrome to enable them to function well in their daily life. A psychologist with experience in this area will be able to provide more individualised strategies and advice.

Social skills and relationship development:

- Understanding the concept of friendship, identifying friendly and unfriendly behaviours, and the different levels of friendship.

- Understanding the importance of sharing, taking turns, compromise and how to cope with losing.

- Role playing to practice core skills and promote generalisation.

- Learning how to initiate and sustain play/interactions with others; work in groups.

- Understanding social hierarchy e.g., receiving instructions from a teacher or boss.

- Enhancing social communication, learning how to engage in reciprocal conversations, knowing when to pause, when to listen and being aware of the needs of the listener.

- Gaining teacher aid support in the playground and structured lunch times.

- Use of special resources such as Social Stories™ with younger children to understand socially and emotionally appropriate responses.

- Understanding the art of dating, choosing a suitable partner, progressing a relationship from friendship to intimacy, maintaining healthy relationships.

- Sexual education and appropriate behaviour.

- Managing small talk and office politics for adults.

Emotional management:

- Understanding of basic emotions (i.e., happiness, sadness, relaxation, worry, anger).

- Recognising facial expressions, different levels of emotions .

- Understanding how our bodies feel when experiencing certain emotions.

- Learning ways to expend physical energy associated with high levels of negative emotions and ways to calm down when experiencing low levels of negative emotions.

- Understanding individual triggers to stress and tools to assist in managing emotions.

- Understanding the relationship between thoughts, feelings and behaviours and how to modify unrealistic, unhelpful thoughts and attitudes.

A psychologist can assist by providing Cognitive Behaviour Therapy (CBT) to help with improving emotional awareness and management. CBT needs to be modified to focus for longer on basic emotions, using visuals in therapy, and avoiding metaphors.

Preference for predictability, routine, and sameness:

- Establish a routine.

- Use visual schedules for younger children, checklists for teenagers, digital organisers for adults.

- Provide advanced warning and preparation for change/transitions and how to cope with these.

- Use visual timers for children.

- Use rewards for following less motivating routines for example, getting ready in the morning.

Executive functioning:

- Provide extra assistance with planning for projects and assignments.

- Use colour coding for subjects and large wall planner to record assessments.

- Break activities or tasks into chunks and allow more frequent breaks.

Perspective taking:

- Use special resources such as Comic Strip Conversations.™

- Validate the individual's perspective but also provide your own and others' perspective.

Sensory issues:

- Obtain assistance from an Occupational Therapist who can provide an assessment and recommendations of the individual's sensory profile and strategies to assist with any problems.

- Provide sensory time or a quiet place to retreat to at school, home, or work.

- Help build self-esteem and self-identity.

- Focus on qualities and strengths, and record successes in a book for a permanent record.

- Use special interests to boost self-esteem.

- Provide enjoyable and responsible roles to the student.

- Build and maintain personal and social resiliency skills.

- Assist with understanding self-concept — explain the diagnosis positively.

Minds and Hearts

DEPRESSION AND ANXIETY AFTER CHILDBIRTH

Becoming a parent is a major life transition. Although it is a time of celebration and new beginning, it also brings with it significant changes and challenges. Many parents struggle to adjust to the changes, and some parents experience depression and/or anxiety at some point during the perinatal period. The perinatal period includes pregnancy and the first year following childbirth.

How common are depression and anxiety during the perinatal period?

Approximately 9% of women experience depression at any given time during pregnancy (also known as antenatal depression). Following childbirth, rates of depression are highest at 3-months post-birth, at which time around 13% of women experience depression (also known as postnatal depression). Anxiety is at least as common as depression during the perinatal period.

What are the symptoms of depression and anxiety?

Depression and anxiety can start at any time during the perinatal period and can come on suddenly or develop gradually. The symptoms are no different to depression and anxiety experienced at any other time in one's life. The symptoms of depression include:

- Feeling sad or unhappy most of the day.
- Loss of pleasure or interest in most activities most of the day.
- Significant weight loss or gain, or decrease or increase in appetite, unrelated to pregnancy.
- Difficulty sleeping or over-sleeping.
- Feeling restless or slowed down.
- Fatigue or loss of energy.
- Feelings of worthlessness or excessive or inappropriate guilt.
- Difficulties thinking, concentrating or making decisions.
- Recurrent thoughts of death or suicide.

These are symptoms commonly used to diagnose depression by health professionals. Not all symptoms are always present, but experiencing several of these symptoms (one of the other of the two first symptoms listed above) nearly every day for at least two weeks, may indicate depression. Women with fewer and milder symptoms may also benefit from help.

Anxiety often co-occurs with depression; however, some women experience only anxiety. Women may find themselves worrying excessively about the pregnancy, becoming a mother, how they will cope, their own or their baby's health and so on. They may be unable to relax, even with reassurance, and notice physical symptoms such as heart racing, dizziness, trembling, or sweating.

What causes depression and anxiety in the perinatal period?

There is no one definite cause of depression and anxiety during the perinatal period, however, a number of factors have been found to increase a woman's risk of developing postnatal depression. The most established risk factors include:

- Antenatal depression.

- Antenatal anxiety.

- Limited support (particularly from partner).

- Major life changes or events.

- History of depression.

- Low self-esteem.

Many of these are also risk factors for antenatal depression. In addition, other stressors, experiences and beliefs that may increase vulnerability to depression and anxiety during the perinatal period includes:

- Childhood history of abuse.

- Family history of depression.

- Unrealistic expectations about motherhood.

- History of miscarriage or termination.

- Viewing negative events in life as pervasive, permanent and yourself as the cause.

- Experiencing severe baby blues.

- Young maternal age.

- Having an unsettled baby.

- Complications in pregnancy or labour.

- Breastfeeding difficulties.

- Problems in couple relationship.

- High interpersonal sensitivity.

- Perfectionist and/or introvert personality.

Women may have many of the main risk factors and be coping well, or may not have any risk factors and yet be feeling down or anxious. Generally depression in the perinatal period is best understood as the result of a combination of risk factors that exceed personal resources at the time.

Who is affected by depression and anxiety?

Depression and anxiety in the perinatal period can have a negative impact not only on the woman but also on her baby. The symptoms of depression and anxiety can make it difficult to engage in joyful parenting and impact upon the interactions between mother and baby. Depression and anxiety can also put strain on the woman's relationship with her partner. Some partners may find they are having difficulty coping themselves and may need to seek help for their own emotional wellbeing.

Women may find it difficult to seek help for depression or anxiety during the perinatal period due to concerns about stigma, fear they will be perceived as inadequate as a mother or feelings of failure. They may have difficulty recognising symptoms or may be unaware of the treatments available.

Where can I get help?

While taking the first step to obtain help can be difficult, getting help early is of most benefit. The first step is to talk with someone about how you are feeling. This person may be your partner, a family member, friend, or a health professional (e.g., your doctor, midwife, or nurse). Investigate treatment options (or ask this support person to help you) and find what works for you.

Psychological therapy is effective for depression and anxiety, particularly Cognitive-Behavioural Therapy (CBT) and Interpersonal Psychotherapy. Given the effects of depression and anxiety on a woman's relationships with her baby and partner, mother-infant groups and/or couple therapy are also helpful for many women. Mother-infant groups aim to enhance the relationship between mother and baby. Couple therapy helps the couple recognise and better manage areas of difficulty in the relationship.

Medication is also effective for treating depression and anxiety, however, many women are concerned about taking medication during pregnancy and while breastfeeding because of the possible risk to the baby. This is an important consideration and should be discussed with a GP or psychiatrist who will weigh the risks and benefits to both mother and baby.

Information and support can also be obtained from self-help books, telephone support services and Internet resources. This can be helpful and sufficient for some women depending on the severity of their symptoms.

Tips to help you start on the road to recovery:

- Let someone know how you are feeling.

- Ask for and accept help from others.

- Nurture your relationships by spending quality time with your partner and making an effort to keep in touch with family and friends.

- Make time to play with your baby each day. It can be helpful to join a mother-infant playgroup.

- Make a little time each day to do something nice for yourself that you find enjoyable (e.g., reading a magazine or book, having a bath, going for a walk).

- Practice a relaxation technique such as deep breathing or progressive muscle relaxation.

- Look after yourself by exercising regularly, eating a nutritious diet, and getting enough sleep (this might mean napping when your baby does).

- Notice what you accomplish each day instead of focusing on what you have not done.

Try to be realistic in your expectations of yourself, your partner and your baby.

Dr Charlene Schembri and Dr Jeannette Milgrom

DELIBERATE SELF-HARM

Deliberate self-harm is when people intentionally injure themselves, without intent to die. Forms of self-harm are: cutting, burning, overdosing on medication or drugs, biting, scratching, overeating, hair pulling, scalding, and banging head against wall.

Common reasons why people self-harm:

There are many reasons why you may have self-harmed, or considered doing it:

- To punish yourself because you feel you are worthless and deserve to experience pain and suffering.

- You feel pressure to be part of a group who are self-harming (often teenagers).

- To experience a release of endorphins to get relief from a depressed state.

- As a cry for help to show people you need assistance. You may have difficulties expressing your distress in any other way.

- To feel physical pain as it distracts you from emotional pain.

A lot of people self-harm at some point during their life, and not because they are crazy, bad or a failure, but rather they are experiencing intense emotional distress. Self-harm is often an extreme reaction to feeling overwhelmed. You may notice thoughts or behaviours prior to self-harming — you feel depressed, angry, helpless, hopeless, worthless, anxious, confused or disconnected. Or you notice physical symptoms such as headaches, muscle tension, nausea, pacing, or shaking. Often people experience these symptoms in connection with memories of past trauma or feeling rejected or disappointed. Once it reaches the stage of self-harming, this is a sign your stress has progressed, perhaps beyond what you can manage yourself.

Pathway to recovery

It is important that you express your thoughts and feelings to someone you trust. This person can help you to think more clearly, and to decide what steps you need to take to improve. This person may be a friend or family member, or a professional such as a GP. If you notice that despite talking with others, you still don't feel any better, it is important that you receive more specialised treatment. Psychologists and psychiatrists can assist you with more specialised interventions. A number of effective treatments are available to help people to stop self-harming and to decrease the underlying distress e.g., Dialectical Behaviour Therapy (DBT), Cognitive Behaviour Therapy (CBT), or Schema Therapy. The way these therapies work is to help people change thinking patterns and behaviours to improve mood and wellbeing. Sometimes you may be additionally advised to take medication to reduce depression and/or anxiety.

Regardless of whether or not you see a professional, it may be worthwhile developing a safety plan. It is often useful to remind you of things you can do, and people who can help, when you feel distressed. Safety plans include such things as phone numbers of friends and family you can talk to, telephone helplines, and your local mental health service or hospital. They may also include things you can do to decrease stress, such as exercise, or relaxation strategies. You may want to discuss your safety plan with a friend or family member who can assist you in times of need.

Dr Angelo De Gioannis, Dr Katelyn Kerr and Andre Bauer

MANAGING SUICIDAL THOUGHTS AND URGES

You have suicidal thoughts if you wish for your own death. Suicidal thoughts can be passive (e.g., *I hope I die, I wish I would get hit by a car*) or active (e.g., *I am going to take an overdose tonight, I will go to the bridge and jump off*). Suicidal thoughts are usually an expression of a sense of hopelessness about the future. They often occur when people are depressed or anxious, or have experienced loss (e.g., loss of employment, death of someone you care about, separation from loved ones, financial problems).

When left untreated, suicidal thoughts may escalate into planning ways to end your life and even plan when and where to do it. In some cases people write suicide notes and make arrangements for their death, such as finalising their Last Will and Testament and giving away valued possessions. It is important to know that experiencing suicidal thoughts is not a sign of weakness, but a sign that you are feeling emotionally overwhelmed with your situation or life in general. In many instances, the presence of suicidal thoughts means you have a mental illness and that you are in need of help. Even though you may think your situation is hopeless, or that no one will be able to help, there is support and effective treatment available for you.

Common reasons why people think about or plan suicide

There are many reasons why you may have suicidal thoughts, and/or have the intention to end your life. These include:

- You feel hopeless and can't see any ways out of your problems.

- You may have a chronic medical condition that will not improve, or which causes significant pain and suffering.

- You may have a long-standing mental illness (depression, anxiety, eating disorders). Mentally ill people have a much higher rate of suicide than the rest of the population.

- It seems as though your circumstances are overwhelming.

- Separation from friends and family as this may lead to isolation and lone-liness. For example, you may not be able to see your friends, family, or children which leaves you feeling empty inside.

- To escape emotional pain.

- You feel as though there is nothing you can do to improve your life or your current situation, or you feel like you don't have any control.

- Being under the influence of drugs or alcohol can trigger suicidal thoughts.

- Trying to live up to unrealistic standards putting overwhelming levels of pressure on yourself.

There are many people who have suicidal thoughts at some stage during their lives. This is understandable, as everyone feels overwhelmed at some point due to the challenges that life throws at us. When people are in a crisis, suicide may seem to be the only option. This may lead to impulsive suicide attempts. In situations like this, the distress you are going through may affect your ability to think clearly; to think of other options to solve your problems; or to cope through this time until the distress passes. Therefore, it is important to seek help from someone you trust or a professional.

A pathway to recovery

If you have suicidal thoughts or you are considering acting on your suicidal thoughts, it is important that you seek help immediately. Other people can help you think more clearly about situations. This may be a friend, family member, your GP, or local hospital. Many hospitals will have a crisis phone number you can call and they can help you access support. There are also telephone help-lines that are available that have experienced staff who can help.

You may find beneficial seeing a psychologist, psychiatrist or mental health professional to help treat the underlying causes of suicidal thoughts and urges. There are a number of effective treatments to help you overcome your difficulties (e.g., loss, emotional pain, physical pain, or mental illness). The way these therapies work is to help people change their thinking patterns and behaviours to improve their mood and wellbeing. In some instances, you may be advised to take medication to reduce the symptoms of illness. These therapies can help you feel more hopeful about the future, and live a more meaningful and enjoyable life. The vast majority of people who have these experiences recover from the despairs of suicidal thoughts.

It is worthwhile to develop a safety plan so that you can keep yourself safe in times when you feel distressed. It is often useful to remind you of things you can do, and people who can help, when you feel distressed. Safety plans may include such things as phone numbers of friends and family you can talk to, helplines, your local mental health service. They may also include things you can do to decrease stress, such as exercise, or relaxation strategies. You may want to discuss your safety plan with a friend or family member who can assist you in times of need.

Dr Angelo De Gioannis, Dr Katelyn Kerr and Andre Bauer

EATING DISORDERS

Eating disorders are classified as a mental illness, not a choice, and are characterised when eating, exercise and body weight have become an unhealthy pre-occupation in a person's life. Generally eating disorders are most commonly experienced by adolescent females and young women, but also occur in males, people of all ages and across all socio-economic and cultural backgrounds. The most recognised eating disorders are Anorexia Nervosa and Bulimia Nervosa. There is no single cause for eating disorders; the variables include development issues, biological susceptibility, relationship and family factors, life events, and socio-cultural influences.

Bulimia Nervosa is characterized by a cycle of restraining food intake followed by a binging period, often resulting in feelings of guilt and low self-esteem which then triggers purging. As people with Bulimia Nervosa tend to be of average weight, it is often more difficult to detect compared to Anorexia Nervosa. Anorexia Nervosa is marked by the person's refusal to maintain a healthy body weight; although they continue to feel hunger they drastically limit food intake.

Signs and symptoms of eating disorders include:

- Rapid, dramatic weight loss.

- Amenorrhea (absence of 3 or more consecutive menstrual periods).

- Distorted body image (perceives themself to be overweight even at low weight).

- Intense fear of gaining weight or becoming overweight.

- Paler skin.

- Soft, fine hair (generally on face, arms and trunk).

- Sensitivity to cold (due to loss of insulating body fat, poor circulation).

- Frequent measuring of body weight.

- Obsession with calories, fat content, reading of nutritional information on food containers.

- Food related rituals (e.g., cutting food into small pieces, hiding or discarding food, weighing exact portions).

- Purging (use of laxatives, self-induced vomiting).

- Dental decay from induced vomiting.

- Recurrent episodes of binge eating.

- Frequent, excessive, strenuous exercise.

- Depression (may frequently be in a sad, lethargic state).

- Mood swings, irritability.

- Continued dieting despite being thin or dangerously underweight.

- Social isolation (avoiding friends and family, becoming withdrawn and secretive).

- Clothing (baggy, loose-fitting clothes to cover weight loss).

People with Anorexia often deny the seriousness of their weight loss and rarely see the need for treatment. On the other hand, people with Bulimia are more likely to be aware that their relationship with food is unhealthy but avoid treatment due to feelings of guilt and shame. First confronting someone that may be suffering from an eating disorder can be difficult as they may become very defensive and deny that they have a problem. Eating disorders are very complex but there are a variety of treatments available including Cognitive Behavioural Therapy (CBT), Nutritional Rehabilitation, The Mawdsley Method and Interpersonal Psychotherapy. In some cases hospitalisation may be required if the person has reached a dangerously low body weight. There are also numerous support groups that provide information and guidance.

Eating disorders also have marked effects on family and friends. Those caring for someone who has been diagnosed with an eating disorder benefit from seeking further information and support.

Top ten tips for family and friends when dealing with someone with a eating disorder:

1. Encourage the person you suspect to seek help from a well-trained health professional.

2. Gather information about the problem and about relevant treatment; this will increase your understanding, and reduce anxiety and feelings of helplessness.

3. Recognise that there are underlying issues that have caused the eating disorder; the person has attempted to deal with underlying psychological issues through practising an unhealthy relationship with food.

4. Be non-judgemental and supportive; let your loved one know that you are concerned for their health and have their best interest at heart.

5. Be aware that recovery from an eating disorder can be a lengthy process.

6. Eating disorders greatly affect family and friends; seek support and look after yourself.

7. Early intervention is a key aspect of recovering from an eating disorder. If you have suspicions, broach the issue being calm, honest and open about your concerns.

8. Secrecy is a key element of an eating disorder, so as part of the recovery process keep communication positive and open.

9. Accept your limitations as a family member or friend. You cannot deal with all the problems associated with the disorder.

10. Remember that eating disorders are a mental illness, not a choice, and the person does not want to be unwell, but they lack the ability to overcome the disorder without professional help.

Top ten tips for people with an eating disorder:

1. Admitting to yourself that you have an eating disorder is the first step towards recovery.

2. Seek professional help as soon as possible with someone who has expertise in treating people with eating disorders.

3. The first point of contact should be a GP who can provide an initial assessment of your physical state and diagnose the nature and severity of the disorder.

4. Confide in family and friends who can offer support.

5. When seeking help, be as widely informed as possible and be aware of all your options.

6. There are a variety of treatment options; seek information about the relevant approaches to find the most suitable option for you. A non-judgemental, supportive and encouraging environment is more likely to bring about change.

7. The main components of professional treatment for eating disorders are physical health management, nutritional advice and mental health management.

8. Support groups can be a great source of mutual support as they help to increase understanding and provide information.

9. Although recovery can be difficult, remember a healthier, happier, satisfying life is possible.

10. Recovery is a process. Anticipate there will inevitably be times throughout recovery when progress temporarily dips or even regresses. Remember that success is possible for you.

Yasmin Schaefer

EMOTIONAL OVEREATING

Using food to comfort emotions begins from the moment you are born. Your mother fed you to satisfy your hunger, dampen your discomfort, soothe and nourish you. As you received food, you also received other things from you mother such as feelings of love, nurturing, comfort, belonging, and acceptance. At the same time you may have felt satisfied, fulfilled, calm and relaxed. This occurs in most cases, unless you had a separation at birth, a mother who had postnatal depression other mental health issue, or who was not able to be fully available to you.

The connection between food and emotions can occur on multiple levels and can be reinforced via multiple sources:

From Infancy. Confusion begins from birth and the link between food and emotion cannot be separated.

Observation. You vicariously perceive the connection between food, emotion, reward, and/or celebration from family (e.g., mother, father, siblings, grandparents), peers/community and/or the media and you meld this into your own belief system.

Emotional/Traumatic Events. Something may occur later in life (i.e., adolescence or adulthood) that may trigger you to use food to cope with a situation due to the lack of emotional support (i.e., real and/or perceived) in your life. Each time you partake in emotional overeating, or a similar emotional event occurs in which you use food to cope with, you are reinforcing the link between food and emotional need/coping.

The main reasons why people emotionally overeat:

- Pleasure (food is your drug of choice).

- Reward and celebration (social events or alone; you will find any reason).

- Emotional relief (you need to have some timeout from negative feeling).

- Need fulfilment (something is missing and food is your surrogate).

The failure model of reducing/eliminating emotional overeating:

Many people who are emotional overeaters try to go cold turkey with the food and the behaviour. This is usually when you put yourself on a diet or realise that the behaviour is resulting in something you don't want in your life. Any change to your habits, environment, food, or diet results in an immediate stress response. This stress response then begins a domino effect of change in the rest of your mind, brain, body, thoughts, emotions, and behaviour. At some point, the change will become uncomfortable due to the build-up of cortisol and other biochemical changes. As cortisol continues to increase and flow throughout your system, it will make you crave foods high in fat, sugar, salt and refined carbohydrates. It is begging you to feed it and sabotage yourself. Eventually, you will get tired of feeling uncomfortable, having the cravings and constantly fighting them, so you turn back to the only thing you know that will take all of this away; food! Thereby, you reinforce the connection you have between the food and the emotional need.

The success model of reducing/eliminating emotional overeating

Understanding yourself, making gradual changes and implementing new ways of coping through a multi-layered strategy plan is the way to successfully overcoming emotional overeating.

Understanding

Step 1: What foods do you eat and what are you trying to achieve? You need to understand the foods that you eat, why you eat them and for what reason (e.g., pleasure, reward/celebration, need fulfilment and/or emotional relief).

Step 2: When, where and with what? Is there a pattern in the time of day (e.g., late at night, afternoon), where (e.g., at work, in the car, at home alone only) you eat and/or other behaviours you partake in at the same time (pairing behaviours e.g., watching TV)?

The change process

Step 1. Food changes — do only one of these at a time, not both together. You can still partake in your pairing behaviours during this phase.

- *Reduce.* If you normally eat a full packet of cookies you gradually want to reduce the amount by 20–30% at a time e.g., instead of 12 cookies reduce it to 9 cookies for 2–3 weeks; 7 cookies over the next 2 weeks.

- *Replace.* Find an alternative food that is healthier that you could switch to first and then eventually begin the reduction technique (e.g., ice-cream to gourmet yoghurt; oil-fried chips to oven-baked chips).

Step 2. Identify the emotions, needs and alternative coping strategies — the first thing that you need to know is that emotion is nothing to be afraid of. Awaking yourself to feeling and knowing how you feel is important to positively coping with and fulfilling your needs. Ask yourself these questions:

- Where do I feel joy and what are the signs (i.e., thoughts, feeling in your body)? Do this for all of the feelings throughout the week/month that are normal for example, fear, anger, stress, excitement, loneliness, boredom.

- What do I need when I feel (emotion)? This could be anything that you are using food to do for you (e.g., dampen, avoid, soothe, relax, security).

- What else could I do to fulfil this need outside of food? The answer will be dependent on the emotion and need. Let's take stress as the emotion and relaxation as the need. Alternative behaviours may include deep breathing, having a bath, exercising, socialising, having a massage, going for a walk, playing with the kids.

Step 3. Multilayered Plan — This is the key to everything! You need to have a minimum of 3 strategies, and up to 5 strategies, that you have sequenced together as your new coping plan. You will begin to implement this new coping plan as you are reducing and/or replacing your emotional overeating. Therefore, the more you practice the new coping strategies the sooner you will notice you will no longer need the food and you will break your connection between food and emotion. You may need to alter some of the coping strategies in the multilayered plan until you find something that really works for you.

Trial and error is the only way to true success!

Kellee Waters

TRAUMA RECOVERY

Trauma is the ancient Greek word for a wound or damage. In modern use, trauma refers to serious physical injury with life threatening consequences or psychological and emotional distress from a traumatic event that has lasting effects. Traumatic events include life threatening accidents, physical assault, natural disasters, sexual assault, child abuse or neglect, war, and torture. Living through and surviving events of this kind can overwhelm our psychological and emotional coping abilities, resulting in strong feelings of fear, helplessness, or hopelessness.

Many people experience and then recover from traumatic events. However, it is easier to recover from single traumatic events than the complex traumatic reactions associated with frequent or sustained neglect or abuse in childhood, for example.

Symptoms and Effects

The overwhelming experience of trauma can be difficult to integrate. Psychological difficulties can arise if a person begins to organise their life and activities around avoiding the feelings and memory associated a trauma. Trauma survivors may experience symptoms rather than normal memories of the traumatic event. These symptoms can be summarised as RAA:

- *Re-experiencing.* includes a sense that its happening again and can appear in the form of flashbacks, unwanted memories and feelings, nightmares, and physical symptoms without a medical cause.

- *Avoidance.* includes avoiding situations, places, people, feelings or thoughts that remind someone of the traumatic event or events.

- *Arousal.* includes significant changes in a person's level of general excitement. Too much excitement (hyper-arousal) can be experiences of being overly alert, watchful, unable to sleep, easily angered, and irritable. Too little excitement (hypo-arousal) can include experiences of depression, numbing, and loss of interest.

The process of recovery

Recovery from trauma is, for the most part, a natural process. A normal process of recovery from trauma might be:

- There is a traumatic event and experience.
- There is some kind of emotional outcry of grief, anger, fear or terror.
- The memory of the experience is avoided as a way to cope.
- There is a re-experiencing of feelings and memories associated with the event.

A cycle may begin that oscillates between avoiding and re-experiencing until the memory is processed and integrated.

This process can be assisted with appropriate support. The conditions for assisting recovery can be understood as moving through three stages. The first stage requires safety. This includes safety from further harm (including self-harm), a secure and stable living situation, and an ability to calm down or self-soothe. The second stage requires remembering and coming to terms with the fear of memories about painful past events. These memories need to be integrated, or put in their place in the past, not re-experienced as symptoms in the present. The third stage involves re-establishing social connections, a sense that I'm OK, and hopes for a personal and work related future.

There is good evidence to show that some of the symptoms of trauma, such as re-experiencing, are a natural and important part of the recovery process. Problems occur when the normal process of recovery is interfered with in some way. Interference may include: the lack of a caring, supportive and understating social network; expectations or injunctions to get over it; too many previous unresolved traumatic experiences; reliance on unhelpful coping strategies such as excessive drug and alcohol use and other addictive behaviours.

Tips for recovery

Safety first! People who have experienced trauma need a safe, stable and caring environment.

Learn. Education about the effects of trauma and the process of recovery can help reduce the fear, shame and stigma that may become associated with the symptoms of traumatic stress.

Time helps heal. Appreciate that healing from trauma is a process that takes time. This may include ups and downs on the way.

Avoid. Substances that can over stimulate the sympathetic nervous system, such as caffeine, alcohol, tobacco and sweeteners.

Be here now. Pay attention to the fact that what is happening here and now is different to what happened there and then. That is, what can be noticed through seeing, listening, touching things now is real, current and different to memories and feelings that may arise in flashbacks. Meditation and other mindfulness practices can assist with this.

When to seek professional support

See your general practitioner or mental health professional if:

- you are thinking of suicide, or harming yourself or someone else.

- it is too difficult to function in your usual routines at work, home or at school.

- you feel frightened, distressed, or angry most of the time.

- the RAA symptoms persist without change for more than a month after the traumatic event.

Forrest James and Chris Lobsinger

LIVING WITH A PERSON AFFECTED BY A MENTAL ILLNESS

Mental illness is term that is used to describe a group of disorders or illnesses that affects a person's brain and result in changes in behaviour, mood, perceptions, and at times cognitions. The more severe the mental illness, the more likely it will affect the way the person relates to other people (including partners and family members), which will in turn affect them all socially and vocationally. People who live with a family member or partner with a serious mental illness need to be aware of how the illness affects the person, and the effect on themselves and the family as a whole. Severe mental illnesses include, for example, a psychotic disorder such as Schizophrenia, Personality Disorders, Dissociative Disorders, Bipolar Disorder and Major Depressive Disorder. Even if the disorder is not necessarily classed as severe, severity may mean how much the illness itself impacts on the individual's functioning and how severely if affects others around them. There are various ways of managing both how you are affected and how you can help and live with the person.

These tips will be useful for you to consider and implement:

- *Become informed.* Information about the illness is key to understanding how it is likely to impact on the affected person as well as how it may impact on you. Mental illnesses affect individuals in different ways. For example, one person who is diagnosed with Schizophrenia is likely to present with a range of symptoms and difficulties that differ to another person diagnosed with the same disorder. There are ranges of ways to become informed. The Internet is a good source as well as talking to the affected person's psychiatrist or psychologist (if the family member permits this). If you are not permitted to talk to their therapist, you can seek a referral to a psychologist, through your GP, to help you understand the illness, how to manage the effects on you and how to better support the affected person. There are also many community organisations and support groups that offer a wide range of resources for you. There may also be education and training courses for carers that you can attend.

- *Become aware.* How do the changes in the person's behaviours affect them, you and the household as a whole? Becoming aware of how you are affected helps you understand your boundaries and limitations. This helps you take care of yourself as well as helping the affected family member.

- *Be supported.* You need to take care of yourself and part of this is forming a good support network. This could range from other family members to friends, support groups or by seeking out counselling through a mental health professional when required.

- *Find a balance.* You need to find a balance between what you need and what you are able to offer the affected person. How can you realistically support the affected person is important to establish so that you are not pushed to the edge yourself.

- *Communicate.* It is important that you sit down with the affected family member and discuss how they feel impacted by the disorder. You need to establish communication to set your boundaries as well as finding ways to support them that will be useful to them. Remember, everyone is different and is affected differently. What works for one person may not necessarily work for you or the affected person.

- *Understand the role of grief.* Often when people are diagnosed with a severe mental illness, their behaviours and personality change. You may think they are not the same person. This is normal. Although the person looks the same, you may think you have lost the old one. You may feel the loss as if a person has passed away. You may long for their old personality, stories, affection, thoughts, sense of humour and many other things that defined that person for you. Allow yourself to feel the loss, sadness and grief as you get used to the new person that has now taken their place.

- *You are not alone.* Did you know that mental illness directly affects 20% of the population at some point in their life? And these are just the ones reported. There are another two thirds of people experiencing mental health problems that go undiagnosed, untreated and not reported. Seeking help through support groups will help you feel less alone.

- *Take time out for yourself.* You often may require time to yourself when caring for or dealing with the affected person. This is especially important when the person's symptoms are severe and/or fluctuate frequently. You may need to seek other supports and respite. Communicate this with the person when you talk with them about the effects of their illness.

- *Do not tolerate abuse.* Even though the person may be severely affected by their mental health issues, this does not give them the right to verbally, emotionally, physically, financially or sexually abuse you. You have to protect yourself and draw the line. If the behaviours are this severe or unpredictable, other caring and living arrangements may need to be found.

- *Plan.* Develop plans and daily routines with the affected person in order to give them and yourself a sense of structure. Due to the disruptive nature of severe mental illnesses both interpersonally, socially and vocationally, a sense of routine may make it easier for you and the person to get into some kind of daily normalcy.

Anna Rybak

8

Grief and Loss Issues

- Recovering from Loss
- Supporting Someone who is Grieving
- Pregnancy Loss
- Death of a Child
- Children's Grief
- Parenting Bereaved Children after Sibling Death
- Suicide Bereavement
- Death and Dying
- Facing our Mortality
- Sudden Infant Death Syndrome
- Recovery After a Relationship Breakup
- Loss of Employment
- Saying the Final Goodbye to Your Pet

RECOVERING FROM LOSS

Loss is when we are deprived of something or a person of attachment, either thru a natural process, an accident, neglect or misfortune. The loss may be tangible (e.g., death, disability, unemployment, divorce, bankruptcy, menopause, baldness) or intangible (e.g., confidence, trust, purpose, opportunities, friendship). When we lose something or someone we grieve. Grieving is the normal response experienced after the loss and a natural recovery process which involves changes in emotions, thoughts, behaviours, and bodily reactions. (Bereavement is the term for being sad after a death.)

Dealing with a loss is a very individual and lonely experience. It can destabilise your sense of control and safety, and remind you of other (real or imagined) losses in your life. Following a loss, there is a possibility for either personal growth or decline. You need to explore how you will address the pain. Ignoring the loss can have a negative impact on the natural grieving process, while also enabling reinvestment of energy in the future. Focusing on the loss can re-traumatise you, yet also enable meaning to be derived from the loss. Grieving is necessary to re-establish the equilibrium and to adapt to the loss. It is not a linear process and you may feel like you are taking two steps forward and one step back. This is not unusual. There is no expected time to get over a loss. It is more like a process of working through negative experiences, tackling challenges as they arise, while simultaneously getting on with life goals and responsibilities. You will move forward and continue to carry some pain.

Common signs of grief

- *Emotional.* Sadness, yearning, guilt, anger, loneliness, fear, shock, self-doubt, frustration, helplessness, numbness, shame, mood swings, anxiety, panic, emptiness, ambivalence, relief, acceptance.

- *Cognitive.* Confusion, disbelief, forgetfulness, dazed, denial, phobias, poor concentration.

- *Behavioural and Physical.* Crying, trembling, fatigue, appetite changes, tension, palpitations, nausea, diarrhoea, constipation, unusual dreams, nightmares, social withdrawal, headache, stomach ache, various infections, dizziness, tightness in chest or throat, breathlessness, sleep problems, restlessness, loss of sex drive.

Pathway to recovery

To acknowledge, understand and accept the reality of the loss or losses. Find out all the details, attribute meaning to what has happened, and see the loss as irreversible.

- Feel the pain of the emotions connected to the loss. Experience the range of feelings in spite of how uncomfortable and painful they will be.

- Adjust to a new life without the person or thing that was lost. Learn new skills, take on different roles, and redefine who you are.

- Withdraw emotional energy from the lost person or thing, and re-invest it in new relationships and activities. Caring about new people and other things doesn't mean you didn't care about who or what was lost. Develop and implement plans for the future.

- Be hopeful and expect to come through the painful time. Accept your inability to control the loss and understand that your feelings, thoughts and behaviours are normal. Channel your energy and efforts into re-establishing your life. Be sure to stay connected to others and engaged in activities. Seek personal and professional help from others you trust when needed.

Dr John Barletta

SUPPORTING SOMEONE WHO IS GRIEVING

When someone you know is grieving there is often a sense of helplessness about how best to help and a fear of saying or doing the wrong thing. However, yet doing or saying nothing at all can exacerbate their pain and leave them feeling isolated, confused, and hurt around the perceived loss of support. If you are feeling lost and can't find the words, one of the most precious gifts you can give someone who is grieving is not to try to fix them or fill the gaps with words but to sit in silence and listen.

- Accept that you cannot take away the pain or gloss over the loss with wise words and stories about your own and others' losses.

- A personal visit, phone call or hand written note can be comforting. Potted plants, flowers, or small personal thoughtful gifts are also an acceptable way to express your feelings.

- When someone is grieving their energy levels are low and they will tire easily, so be aware of keeping your visits short, or ask them to let you know when they want some time alone.

- Offer to be available to help out with the practical day-to-day chores, such as, driving, cleaning, cooking, shopping, gardening. Be mindful about asking permission before jumping in to help, and check out their specific needs.

- Realise that your friend is a unique individual and will grieve in their own unique way, in their own time.

- Give them permission to express their pain without judging or dismissing their feelings. Let them know they are safe and that it's okay to cry, shout, scream or be angry about their loss in your company.

- When we see someone hurting, it is a normal human response to want to ease their pain. However, with the best of intentions, our words can be insensitive. Avoid statements such as: *I know how you feel, It's for the best, Be grateful he/she didn't suffer, There are plenty of fish in the sea, You are blessed to have had so many years together, Get on with it, You've got to be strong.* Instead, validate their pain by listening and reflecting.

- Remember you don't have to say anything, sometimes your presence in their life is all they need.

- Make a note of the date of your friend's loss and give them a call or send a note on those days. Family holiday times may also be tough.

- In the initial stages of grief, there is a degree of shock and denial, and for the first few weeks or so they have lots of support and personal details to take care of. However, there comes a time when they begin to realise the finality of their loss. When this occurs they sometimes feel they are going crazy. You can help by making regular contact throughout the months ahead.

- While it is a privilege to walk with someone through grief, it is also important to nurture and care for yourself. Don't get onboard the guilt train. If you feel tired and overwhelmed, it's okay to take time-out to reboot your own energy levels. Taking a break for you will enrich your body, mind and spirit.

- Most importantly be proud that you have had the courage to face your fears and be available to make a difference to someone who's grieving.

- It is not unusual for those who are grieving to make statements about being with their loved one or verbalising a belief like they can't go on without them. If you are concerned about the mental health of the person you are supporting, talk to them, acknowledge their pain and ask the hard questions.

Jan Bond

PREGNANCY LOSS

Before reading this contribution, it is important to note that, not everyone who losses a baby to miscarriage will be significantly affected by their loss. Also, those who have terminated a pregnancy for medical or social reasons will differ in their reactions, with some people experiencing intense grief or a delayed grief reaction at sometime during their lives. The severity of the loss depends on circumstances, (social, psychological and spiritual) of the individual at that particular moment in time.

Those who have been significantly affected will grieve the loss of their baby. All too often friends, family and the greater community minimise the grief of parents' whose baby has died. Comments such as: *you will have another, it wasn't meant to be, it was God's will, there must have been something wrong,* are not helpful and can exacerbate feelings of isolation. When your baby died, life as you experienced it during your pregnancy changed, and the hopes and dreams of becoming parents to this child have shattered. You will find yourself assaulted by conflicting emotions which will ebb and flow in no specific order. No two people grieve the same and you will be doing yourself an injustice by comparing yourself to your partner or others. Grieving is natural, normal and necessary. As you work through your grief, you will learn to live healthily with your loss and find a safe place in your life to keep precious memories of your pregnancy and baby. Take time to communicate your feelings and needs to significant others, and give yourself permission to seek professional help if required. Sometimes finding a safe place to talk to someone who is impartial can be helpful.

Working through your grief:

- Avoid making major life changes for the first few months.

- Take a list of questions about this pregnancy or subsequent pregnancies to your GP or specialist obstetrician for discussion.

- Send notes to family and friends informing them of the birth and death of your baby.

- Keep a journal, write poetry or write a letter to your baby.

- Plan ahead for significant dates, (e.g., birth date, due date, Mother's Day, Father's Day, Christmas, Easter). Sometimes just lighting a candle in memory of your baby on these days can bring comfort.

- Try to establish some routine in your day and go to bed around the same time each night.

- Drink lots of water, maintain healthy eating and exercise (with medical approval).

- Discuss your feelings and needs with friends and family. Don't be afraid to ask for help or accept offers. Be specific about what you need and how you want to be supported.

- Considering contacting a pregnancy loss organisation, a support group, or an online forum. If you have spiritual beliefs, you may wish to seek counsel with a religious minister.

- Find some time for self-care, beginning with small steps e.g., short walk on the beach or park, time out with your partner or a friend, massage, pedicure.

- Remember it's okay and healthy to have some fun, sing, dance and laugh. This doesn't mean you are dishonouring your baby (feeling guilty about doing these things is also normal).

Creating Memories:
- Purchase or make a memory box large enough to keep pregnancy indicator stick, photos, birth records, wrist bands, lock of hair, ultrasound pictures, or medical reports.

- Create a scrapbook. A number of scrapbooking stores run classes specifically for memory albums.

- Choose a name for your baby, or name a star in memory of your child.

- Plant a tree or shrub in memory of your son or daughter.

- Paint or draw a picture of your baby or have professional artist paint or sketch from a photo or description of your child.

- Buy a piece of jewellery or keepsake. Some parents choose a tattoo in memory of their baby.

However your pregnancy ended, it is your journey and yours alone. Do not judge yourself harshly. You did the best you could at the time. If you find yourself struggling to cope, contact a counselling telephone line, support group, a counselling health professional or spiritual leader for support.

Jan Bond

DEATH OF A CHILD

Experiencing the death of a child is an event that violates the natural order of life. Parents who have such excitement and hope for their child's life often feel like their life has been shattered when their child dies. It is estimated that up to 60 people (e.g., parents, grandparents, friends, siblings, work colleagues) can be affected by the death of a child. It is important not to assume then that each family or person grieves in the same way. Each person's bereavement is unique to who they were before the death and to the unique relationship they had with the child.

Children not only represent a parent's hopes, dreams and in a way their share in immortality, but they also define the adult's role of being a parent which includes nurturing, protecting and watching over their children as they grow. When a death occurs it can really confront personal beliefs and assumptions about the world, including, the natural order of life, ideas of what is fair and just, beliefs about safety in the world, and beliefs about one's strength and capability.

Other People's Reactions

People in general are fairly naïve about grief and often expect the bereaved to be back to their old selves within a couple of months. When this does not happen, people start to feel awkward and tend to withdraw both physically and often emotionally, leaving the bereaved alone in a time when extra support can be essential. A common reason for this withdrawal is that people feel helpless and out of control amongst some of the chaos that the parents are going through. Due to this, people revert to comments to try to distance themselves from their own feelings and to try and get back onto a more normal footing. This is done through sometimes minimizing the loss and using clichés such as: *Think of your other children; You're still young, you can always have another child; I know exactly how you feel; At least they are in a better place now.* These clichés are seldom helpful, and at worst, extremely hurtful. If there is a need to say something, then a simple: *I'm so sorry, my heart is breaking for you right now*, is more than enough.

Gender Factors and Impact on Relationships

As mentioned above there is no right or wrong way to grieve. Each person is an individual and therefore must express their grief in a way that is right for them. However, stereotypically, there are some differences between how males and females express their grief. Women tend to be more emotionally and verbally expressive and are more able to feel their way through their experience. Women often find it beneficial to speak to others about what happened. Their feelings can be quite intense and are often expressed through crying and physical exhaustion. Men, however, tend to be more analytical and therefore think through their grief. They have the story etched into their mind and find relief in distractions and task orientated projects. Men are more likely to be in control of their emotions, but do often exhibit anger more readily than their partners. Men can feel quite stressed if they are unable to console their partner or ease some of their pain.

Men commonly seek comfort through physical or sexual connection with their partners. This however can cause tension in some relationships as women often will be completely focused on the death of the child and the emptiness this brings. Women can also link sex to reproduction, to having a child, to having a child die which may minimize their need for physical closeness with their partner due to the connection of possible future pain. Being aware of what your partner needs during this time can be helpful. Remember there is no right or wrong way to grieve and your partner's grief is an extension of who they are. Keep the lines of communication open and ask your partner what the best way of supporting them is and tell them how they can best support you through this journey of grieving and recovery. Things will never go back to normal, however a new normal will be developed over time.

Kristy Jeffcoate

CHILDREN'S GRIEF

We all grieve and loss is part of everyday life. Children experience loss when they have to part with their first special soft toy or loss of a pet, and they inevitably experience the loss of grandparents. Grief is a natural response to loss and most children go through grief without the need of professional help. Grief means slowly accepting the reality of what has happened and learning to live with the changes. Grieving isn't about forgetting the person who has died. It is about finding a special place for that person in your memory, where it does not stop you enjoying life. It is about managing a great life change and the feelings that follow and there is no right or wrong way to grieve. Grief is unique and special to each of us. Respecting the way people, especially children, grieve without trying to analyse or pathologise children' responses is the key for effective support. All children grieve, however they can often be misunderstood or their pain can be overlooked. You might observe emotional reactions like anger, guilt and happiness. Depending on their age and maturity, they may not have the thinking abilities to make sense of what has happened. They may not have the words to describe their feelings, thoughts and memories. They use the language they know. Just as talking is adult communication, playing, acting and behaving is the way children communicate.

What to expect at different ages

Preschool children have a limited capacity to understand what is happening when faced with grief. They may have difficulty in separating from their loved one even for a short period of time. They may feel they caused the person to die. They may repeatedly ask when the deceased is coming back or when they can see him/her again. This is often the child's way of checking out the reality and trying to make sense of what has happened. They may report the deceased appear to them in dreams or when awake; this is normal, however, children might become fearful. Some children regress in behaviour (e.g., they may start to wet their bed or have difficulty going to sleep) and they mask their feelings with temper tantrums.

School-aged children begin to understand the irreversibility of death. They are often curious and concerned with the process, consequently will ask how and why questions. They often fantasize about what they can do to repair the damage and make everybody happy again. When children experience a loss they may feel they are losing control over other aspects of they life. Small strategies such as allowing the child to check if mum is okay during school hours, or to create his/her own strategies to deal with the pain of the loss allows the child to regain partially a sense of control and reduce his or her anxiety. In play they may take revenge on the one they hold responsible. This changing or undoing through play also counteracts helplessness. At this age children can show regression, acting out, anxiety and withdrawal. One thing to keep in mind is that they learn how to grieve by watching adults around them and by modeling other's reactions.

Adolescence is a time in which young adults start to experience their independence from their parents and a time in which they start to negotiate physical and psychological changes. The loss of a loved one will add intensity to an already stressful time. They might increase conflict with parents and adult figures, and show lack of interest in parental figures, or be excessively protective of other family members. They may start or increase risk taking behaviours like drinking, dangerous driving, and risky sexual behaviours. They may struggle in managing the intensity of emotions, retreat in themselves and cut communication. They may struggle in defining who they are and what is their role in the family. They rely on friendship supports to get them through, consequently it is important to acknowledge and encourage that aspect of their social life.

What you can do to help

- *Clear and honest communication.* (Do I tell my child that her father is dying? How do I tell them without hurting them?) Often adults choose not to talk about death due to the fear of hurting their children but children sense that something is wrong. Choosing silence increases fear and anxiety. They need information and honesty to help them in their grief, and need to trust adults around them. We need to speak to children openly in language appropriate to their age and understanding. It is our responsibility to ensure children have understood the information given to them. They need have the opportunity to ask questions and have them answered as honestly as possible, without over-burdening them with too much information (they will ask if they need more answers!).

- *Involvement in rituals.* Find ways in which children can be involved when a death happens by participating in simple rituals. The main ritual is the funeral, but you can design different rituals according to the need of your child like writing goodbye letters or sending birthday cards in the sky to celebrate the birthday of the person who died.

- *Being with the child's feelings.* Don't be afraid to show them how you feel as this helps them know it's okay to feel the way they do. Children tend not to stay with very sad feelings for long; they go in and out of grief. This is a very healthy way to deal with an emotion that is too intense to maintain for a prolonged period. Parents often try to fix the pain of children (kiss it better). You cannot protect your child from the pain associated with losing someone, however, you can learn to be with that pain and share it together.

- *Memory work.* Keeping memories alive by remembering and talking about the person who has died also helps children. Constructing memory boxes or writing memory books can be very effective with children.

Seek help for children with the following attitudes or behaviors that may stem from unresolved grief

- Acting younger than usual for example, thumb-sucking, bed-wetting, babyish behaviour, baby-talk, demanding of attention, wanting more cuddles, excessive clinginess or reluctance to let you out of their sight.

- Excessive and prolonged periods of crying.

- Extreme changes in behaviour, such as frequent and prolonged tantrums, anger, aggression.

- Changes in school performance and grades, or refusing to go to school.

- Lack of interest in friends and activities to the extreme of apathy, numbness, and prolonged isolation.

- Nightmares and sleep disturbances (difficulty going to sleep, waking very early or unable to go back to sleep).

- Headaches, stomach-aches, physical complaints, weight gain/loss.

- Negative thinking about the future, or lack of interest in it.

Dr Elisa Agostinelli and Dr Brian Sullivan

PARENTING BEREAVED CHILDREN AFTER SIBLING DEATH

Supporting bereaved siblings can often be one of the most difficult things for parents to do after a child has died. At a time when parents are exhausted and struggling to put one foot in front of another, to be able to focus on the other children and try to keep to a normal routine for them can seem overwhelming. It is common and normal for parents to feel guilty about their lack of energy, time or patience with their other children during this time. Sometimes seeking outside help during this time can be beneficial and ease some of the pressure.

Children, irrespective of age, look to adults to show them what to expect and how to deal with all the troubling thoughts and feelings that may surface in their own grief. It can be helpful for children to be able to talk about their sibling. To have their questions answered honestly, to also be asked what their concept or understanding of the situation is, to be involved in family decisions regarding their sibling and significant family events, and to have the freedom to be accepted for who they are. Just remember to keep reassuring your child that you love them and choose times when you feel slightly more energised to spend some one-on-one time with them.

Another child?

Considering having another baby after the death of a child is a really big decision and needs to be discussed in-depth with your partner. It is important to be aware of the timing of this decision and to be able to allow your family time to be self-focused through their grief before needing to become more life-focused through the birth of another child. If possible, it is usually good to wait until after the first anniversary of the death of your child before starting down this path. Having another child can be a wonderful thing — not to replace the child —but to create an avenue of increasing wonder in discovery about new meaning in life, along with a unique bond to a new and precious family member.

What do bereaved parents need?

- Permission to express their thoughts and feelings without judgment.
- To be able to grieve in the way that is best for them.

- Time to be alone, to grieve or to be with others if needed.

- To retain their individuality and the uniqueness of their grief to their relationship.

- Empathy and understanding for what they are going through.

- An advocate/support person who can act on family's behalf as needed.

- Practical support with the small things.

- That their child will not be forgotten and having people share memories of their child.

In some cases, if your grief is interfering significantly with your ability to deal with life's challenges, or you are unsure how to best support your own child through this difficult time, be sure seek help from whatever/whoever you know will be most supportive.

Kristy Jeffcoate

SUICIDE BEREAVEMENT

The term "survivors of suicide" is often used to describe those who have been impacted by the death of someone to suicide. Survivors may include relatives, friends, co-workers and other individuals who knew the person who died.

Bereavement is a process of grief and mourning that includes all of the physiological, psychological, behavioural, and social response patterns displayed by an individual following the loss of a significant person or thing. Grief and mourning make up the two parts of bereavement: Grief is the expression of feelings (e.g., pain) through an emotional response; and, mourning involves the social customs and rituals that help a person grieve through expression of feelings, thoughts, and memories that include the deceased.

Impacts of suicide bereavement

For the majority of the population, the grief experience following bereavement (of any type) appears to represent a normal or non-pathological process, whereby typical grief reactions are experienced, particularly in the first few months, up to a year following the death of a loved one. These typical grief reactions are experienced by suicide survivors as well as additional unique reactions.

Grief reactions that are more extreme or severe than normal, perhaps reflecting depression, anxiety or even post-traumatic stress disorder, usually only occur in a small minority of the population, including some suicide survivors. Several factors determine these grief outcomes, including previous experiences of grief, current or previous mental illness (especially depression), previous and current life stress or crises, the quality of the relationship with the deceased, age and gender, personality type, religious and cultural factors, availability and access to social support, and changes that may occur following the death of the deceased such as financial hardship, relationships, and change in employment.

Suicide survivor grief

In addition to typical grief reactions, suicide survivors have specific and unique grief reactions, which are not dissimilar to the experiences of those bereaved by sudden traumatic death. This is most likely because of the shared similarities associated with (a) the unexpected nature of the death; and, (b) the, often, violent or traumatic nature of the death.

However, there are also other unique differences between suicide and sudden death bereavement which are related to the bereavement process itself. For suicide survivors, the bereavement process may be longer and perhaps even slower and more difficult to process (particularly in the first two years after the death).

The following experiences are more prominent in survivors of suicide, versus sudden death and natural death. It is normal for suicide survivors to have one or more of these experiences, and for up to 2 years, or more, following the death of a loved one.

- Guilt and self-blame (*Why didn't I prevent it? I should have seen it coming? What if?*)

- Shame (*I am so different now. I can't be around others. No-one will want anything to do with me or my family.*)

- Anger at oneself and/or others (*How could this happen to me? Why didn't anyone* (health workers) *prevent this happening? Someone has to be responsible and accountable.*)

- Psychological pain associated with the inability to explain the death (*My heart is too heavy. I can't rest my brain. I can't stop ruminating about what and why?*)

- Fear associated with another family or peer suicide (*I'm worried about myself and my family. What if someone else in our family suicides?*)

- Feeling stigmatized and socially isolated (*No-one can possibly understand, so there is no point talking about it. The way people look at me, and the way they avoid any discussion of the topic just makes it worse. I may as well just keep away.*)

- Feelings of rejection and abandonment (*How could they do this to me? Didn't they love me enough to just talk to me?*)

- A stronger need to find meaning in the death (*Why did they do it? I thought I knew him/her so well?*)

- Struggle to make sense of the motives and frame of mind of the deceased (*How could they possibly get the motivation/courage to take his own life? What was going through their mind?*)

- Increased impacts on family interactions, dynamics and communication patterns (*No-one wants to talk about them or it; and so now there is an absence of talk. Our family roles have changed and our relationships will never be the same.*)

- Increased risk of suicide and psychiatric problems (particularly increased suicidal thoughts, depression and anxiety.)

It is often helpful to talk about these experiences, feelings, and the pain associated with loss to suicide. This is because many of these normal feelings, such as guilt, self-blame, and anger, if left untouched, can lead to future negative psychological and emotional problems as they are not fully understood or processed.

A commonly asked question by suicide survivors: Why?

Often there is no completely accurate answer to this question since the causes of suicide are multi-faceted and complex. No single factor contributes to, or causes, suicide although a particular situation or event may trigger the suicide, or may act as the last straw that broke the camel's back. There is substantial research, however, which supports the high probability of several important contributing risk factors for suicide, and also points to differences in risk factors for different age groups across the lifespan. However, it is important to note that nobody will ever know with 100 per cent accuracy, why someone took their own life.

Coping in the aftermath of suicide

Coping with loss to suicide is a very individual process, and different strategies and support mechanisms will be more or less appropriate at different periods throughout the grief journey. However, several ways to assist you to cope in the aftermath of suicide have been suggested by both survivors themselves, as well as professionals who work specifically in this field of suicide.

- *Talking about your loss.* It is most important to talk with someone who will listen, even if you need to keep reaching out until you find that special person who can truly hear you and your pain. A good listener will not necessarily understand your pain, rather you will know and feel that they care enough for you to be there and listen. Often family members stop talking about their loved one to each other, but this in fact can increase the negative impacts of loss. By opening up to your family, it is often revealed that others are actually sharing the same or similar thoughts and feelings. Talking with other suicide survivors has also been reportedly a helpful and positive experience.

- *Seek professional help and allow yourself to be helped.* It can be difficult to ask for help/support when you feel guilt, shame, pain and especially when you feel isolated, but this is a very important step to take along your grief journey if you feel you are not coping. This is especially critical for those suffering suicidal thoughts, or who lack the desire to keep living without their loved one. Your emotional and physical load will be lessened if you can speak with a professional or someone who is knowledgeable about the facts associated with suicide and suicide loss. Importantly, factual knowledge acquired about suicide (and its causes) can significantly reduce cognitive and emotional distress, as well as dispel myths which often lead to negative and unhelpful stigmatising attitudes and beliefs.

- *Access factual information and resources.* There are numerous books, websites and research articles available on the topic of suicide and suicide bereavement. Together with providing factual information about suicide and suicide bereavement, often this information can increase insight into both your own grief reactions and other's responses to you in respect of suicide loss.

- *Writing down your thoughts (journaling).* Often this process allows you to reflect on your own thoughts, your decisions and feelings about the loss and about your own experience and your future. It is important, however, not to dwell on the why, rather to try to seek answers where information is available to you. Coronial counselling services as well as professionals in the area of suicide prevention and suicide bereavement can be of help in discussing your reflections.

Some simple coping strategies include:

- Cherish memories of your loved one by looking at photos and memorabilia.

- Celebrate the life of your loved one at the anniversary of their death or their birthday; your loved one will always be a part of your life.

- Take time to be on your own when it feels right to do so.

- Cry when you want to; it is normal and an important release of your energies and pain.

- Accept that you will get irritable, forgetful, unhappy, and that you will have both good and bad days.

- When you feel really down or low, make sure you contact a friend or someone who you can trust to talk with.

- Pray, exercise, or listen to music.

Remember

Healing and grieving takes time. While the intense pain and emptiness may feel endless, it will not go on forever. The pain does lessen, and over time, the number of good days will outweigh the bad days. But feeling better about yourself and your loss over time, does not ever mean that you have stopped loving nor that you've forgotten your loved one.

Jacinta Hawgood

DEATH AND DYING

Life is a precious gift; its loss is our most difficult, yet inescapable, experience.

Here are some words that may help us understand, accept, prepare for, and face the life transitions of death and dying.

All living beings are impermanent by nature, which means having been born we will eventually die. The length of our life is not certain and the time of our death is also uncertain. In our culture, we typically associate death with illness and old age, but the truth is that young and healthy people die every day. Some people die suddenly and unexpectedly, and for some the end of life is gradual and expected.

Thinking about death is anxiety provoking for many of us but if we have the courage to think about it perhaps we may be able to reframe our perspective, and as a result replace fear with confidence. Exploring ideas and our own thoughts about death and dying may also enable us to give purpose to life and meaning to death.

Most of us believe some element of our being continues on after death — our mind, our soul or even the ongoing effect of our actions. This continuity means we can use our present life to attain more far-reaching and personally satisfying goals than momentary happiness based on material possessions, which ultimately we have to let go of anyway.

Some things to consider as you come closer to the end of life

It is common for priorities to shift when you see your own death as imminent. Spending time with family and friends, as well as (re)connecting with your own form of spirituality often becomes more important.

Make sure you acknowledge and attend to your physical, mental, interpersonal and spiritual needs:

Physical

- Thinking about medical treatment as a battle or fight against illness is not always helpful. It creates failures and losers in a process that is as natural as birth and breathing itself.

- Don't put up with physical pain. There are many sources of pain relief available through health services.

- Our breath is our connection with all of life. Breathing in, feel yourself inhaling that loving connection and breathing out, offer it back to all.

Mental

It is normal to experience some fear about death and the process of dying. To achieve a state of mind where you are at peace and content with the life you have lived, acknowledge your mistakes. Experience regrets, feel love for yourself and rejoice in your achievements. Feel love for others and remember their kindness and feel comforted by universal love/God.

At the end of life, our self-identity continues to change, as it has through life. How we see ourselves changes when we are dying, as we must let go of previous activity-based roles and goals. You are much more than what you do, so this is an opportunity to connect with your deeper self.

Interpersonal

- Make efforts to resolve any unfinished emotional business you have with others. Create peace for yourself and others by seeking and giving forgiveness.

- Be generous with your possessions; create a special memory/keepsake for those you care about.

- Let others be generous with their caring for, and kindness towards, you.

Spiritual

Spirituality can be described as the need to be connected to, and in harmony with, yourself, with others and with something or someone greater — a divine being, the universe, or nature. The meaning and purpose we find through this connection is our source of strength and tranquillity as this life draws to an end. Developing an understanding of and familiarity with our spiritual framework throughout our life becomes a refuge at the time of death.

Some suggestions on how you can help someone who is dying:

- You may feel helpless and uncomfortable, but you can be a source of comfort by being present and willing to listen should they want to talk. Gentle touch, such as holding their hand, can communicate care and reassurance.

- Provide comfort by creating a quiet tranquil environment and being calm.

- Talk to them as if they can hear you, even if they appear unconscious. Talk about and celebrate the person's positive qualities and actions throughout their life.

- Encourage the person in their own source of refuge, be it spiritual or religious. Don't force your beliefs on them.

Practical preparations

Leading up to your death, and after you have gone, your family will be in the process of grieving. You can help them by ensuring your wishes are clear so they do not have to make these difficult decisions on your behalf.

- *Legal documents* — plan what will happen with your financial and material possessions. Have documents such as a Will, Enduring Power of Attorney and an Advance Health Directive prepared.

- *Organ and/or tissue donation* — if you would like to donate, register and make sure you let your family know about your wishes as they will be asked for consent.

- *At home or residential care* — discuss with your family and your health service provider about the options for at home or residential care during your illness and whether you would prefer to die in your own home.

- *Spiritual or religious rituals* — explore spiritual or religious rituals you would like performed before and after death and discuss these with your family and the person you would like to perform them.

- *Funeral arrangements* — talk to your family about how to best celebrate your life and how to say goodbye in a meaningful and joyful way. Make arrangements with a funeral service, perhaps with the help of a loved one, including whether you would like to be cremated or buried.

Venerable Yeshe Khadro

FACING OUR MORTALITY

Most, if not all of us, do not want to die and yet at the same time we know deep down that death is inevitable. Death is not an option; it is an unnegotiable certainty. Life is always lived in the shadow of death. As one philosopher has put it: There is no cure for birth or for death, except to enjoy the interval. Extreme fear of death and a frantic avoidance of facing our own mortality do detract from the enjoyment of life.

A rite of passage

Throughout history, all cultures and societies have marked death with beliefs and ceremonies that vary but are universal in function. Rites of passage, the celebration and significance of the rituals attached to transitional stages in human life, are part of our daily lives and mark our transitional phases. In terms of death and dying, in our society, we have funerals, eulogies, memorials, wakes and obituaries to mark our final rite of passage and to help those still living to share the pain and loss of their loved one's death.

Denial of death

Before our modern times, death and dying had been a more open and accepted aspect of daily living. Now it seems talk of death and dying and is taboo to many and with that an opportunity for wisdom and integration is lost. We live in a culture where there is great fear, anxiety and avoidance around death. With Botox and cosmetic surgery, and a culture that idolizes youthfulness and idealises external beauty, the reality of ageing and eventual death can be denied or at least evaded. As well, many advances have been made in prolonging life and in improving the quality-of-life for patients with life-threatening illnesses. Overall, the average age of dying is increasing. Even when we do die, we want to go out looking presentable, so there is a beautifying industry in the embalming process. If we do not face our own mortality, we can live lives of pretence, living in a dream world where we fantasize that death may be for others but not for us.

Facing our own death

However as we grow older, face illness or tragedy, or if someone we love dies, we will at some time be confronted point blank with our own mortality, questions about our own inevitable death and our final moment in this life. And this may lead us to ask ultimate questions that philosophers have grappled with over the centuries: Who am I? What am I doing in this world? What is my living for? What does it all mean? Is there life after death? Do heaven and hell exist? Is there a supreme being? And so on. Whether you are religious or not, whether you consider yourself spiritual or not, all human beings at times in their lives ponder questions of such weighty significance. How can we face our own death without denial, without terror, without undue anxiety? How can we face death with courage, acceptance, respect, and grace? In facing our mortality, it is possible to treat death as our great teacher rather than as a monster such as the grim reaper to be either escaped or conquered. The wise men and women of all the world religions and wisdom traditions believed that life is lived more fully and more deliberately when death becomes one's wise mentor for our living rather than the grim reaper of our final harvest. Escape from death is not an option. Our death is inevitable and is our final act in this life. Healthy functioning means we learn to face our reality, not with resignation but with hope and acceptance.

A good death

While some will have peaceful and uncomplicated departures, many will not. Some of us will have some time to prepare, others will not. Death can be hard and messy work. Is there a way we can die well? Is there a good death? Is there a right way to do this and an unhealthy way to die? Some have thought that there are certain criteria for dying a good death. These include:

- A natural death, (accidental death, suicide and homicide do not fall under the criteria of a good death), through which one can prepare.

- Dying after one has experienced a full life and living one's life to the end, with strong relational ties with family and friends.

- Finalising one's necessary financial and legal requirements.

- A death which is accepted, where the dying process is attended by open family communication.

- A good death must be generative, in other words, it must confer wisdom to younger generations.

- A good death must be sombre and sorrowful. The person will be missed. No life is completely complete. There will be a mixture of emotions that need to be experienced and expressed.

- A good death is peaceful. A peaceful death is one where the dying person is surrounded by love and support. Pain is minimised and appropriate medical and palliative care is provided.

- Causing as little pain to those who are left behind as possible. A good death is a gracious death, where complaint and resentment are minimal.

Since we all die in unique and personal ways, it doesn't make sense to stereotype our lives and our deaths into categories that must be checked off before a death is evaluated as good. Because we are all individuals, then each of us will experience death in our own unique way. While there may be no universal checklist for how humans should die a good death, most would agree that if at all possible, retaining some control over what happens to you, decisions over pain management and palliative care, choice over where death occurs (home or hospital), having a say in who is present, having time to say goodbye, having access to any religious, spiritual, or emotional support requested, being allowed to die with dignity and respect, being able to leave when it is time to say goodbye, may be positive contributors to a good death. Even so, the time will come to relinquish control and let go of this life.

So in response to the earlier question: How can we face death with courage, acceptance, respect, and grace? The answer seems to be embedded in another question. Because death is one part of our life and significantly the end part, then the better question maybe: How can we face life and live life with courage, acceptance, respect, and grace? If we can live our life in that way, with meaning and purpose, then we will die our death in that way, or at least that is the hope. Having lived our life with honesty, integrity, purposefulness, kindness, and compassion will be great preparation and foundation for our final moment in this life.

Dr Brian Sullivan and Dr Elisa Agostinelli

SUDDEN INFANT DEATH SYNDROME

Sudden Infant Death Syndrome (SIDS) has been called a parent's worst nightmare. In an instant, the hopes and dreams that parents hold for their baby are snatched away, along with their baby. There are many causes of infant death. The most common causes are Neonatal Death and Sudden Infant Death Syndrome.

Neonatal Death (death during the first 28 days of life) occurs in approximately 4 in 1000 births in Australia, and 6.3 per 1000 in the USA. The causes of neonatal death include congenital defects, extreme prematurity, low birth weight, maternal complications, cord and placenta problems and birth complications.

Sudden Infant Death Syndrome refers to the sudden death of an infant that is unexpected and remains unexplained after a thorough forensic autopsy. With around 150 deaths annually in Australia, SIDS is the most common cause of death in babies between 4 weeks and 1 year of age. Although studies have identified many risk factors for SIDS there has been little consensus about the syndrome's biological cause. In Australia, the leading organisation for SIDS research, information and support is *SIDS and Kids* (in USA and Canada it is *SIDS*).

Prenatal (before birth) Risk Factors for SIDS

- Maternal smoking.

- Use of other drugs or alcohol.

- Poor prenatal care or nutrition.

- Subsequent births less than a year apart.

- Teenage pregnancy.

- Infant or mother being overweight.

- Infant's sex — 60% of SIDS cases occur in males.

Postnatal (after birth) Risk Factors for SIDS

- Exposure to tobacco smoke.
- Low birth weight.
- Premature birth.
- Baby sleeping prone (on tummy).
- Not breastfeeding.
- Hot or cold room temperature.
- Exposure to mould.
- Infant's age — highest incidence between 2–4 months.
- Co-sleeping with parents or siblings.

Research

According to an American study, babies who die of SIDS are more likely to have abnormalities in the brain stem which helps control functions like breathing, blood pressure and arousal, and abnormalities in serotonin signaling. A British study discovered that the common bacterial infections Staphylococcus aureus and E. coli appear to be a risk factor in some cases of SIDS. SIDS cases peak between eight and ten weeks after birth, which is also when maternal antibodies are starting to disappear and babies are less protected.

The loss of a baby

Because the current infant mortality rates are dramatically less than fifty or a hundred years ago, many parents have never considered the possibility that their baby might die and probably haven't met anyone who has experienced the death of a baby. The shock of losing their child can be overwhelming. As well as the physical loss of their baby, parents may suffer other losses, including a sense of safety and fairness, loss of status as a parent, loss of future dreams and loss of income. It is common for most important relationships to be altered, including spousal, family and other relationships.

Common feelings

It is common to feel great shock and grief for an extended period of time, and for feelings of loss to come in waves, long after the event. Parents are likely to experience guilt (that they didn't keep their child alive), shame (that others judge them differently) and fear (that they won't be able to keep future babies or existing children safe). They may feel very isolated but incapable of reaching out. It is common to avoid anything that reminds them of babies or pregnancy. If they choose to have another baby, for some it can be an anxiety provoking time.

What helps

Friends and family can best help by allowing parents to talk about the baby (if they wish), and encouraging them to grieve their loss. Most bereaved parents fear that their baby will be forgotten, so mentioning the child's name will usually be welcome, even if it brings tears at the time. Remembering the baby's birthday or anniversary of death will be appreciated by most parents. Practical help with driving, shopping and child minding may also be required. Above all, avoid platitudes — better to just say that you're sorry and that you will be there for them in whatever way they need. Friends can remind parents that support services exist, and access those services themselves if needed.

Linda Male

RECOVERY AFTER A RELATIONSHIP BREAKUP

In spite of the fact that over 40% of marriages and committed relationships end in separation or divorce, the decision to terminate a relationship can be an agonising, frightening, depressing and guilt laden experience. For some it may well be the most difficult decision they have had to make in their life, with no certainty that it was the right one. Nevertheless, it may well be the most courageous and constructive course of action. Divorce as a life crisis has within it the seeds of both danger and opportunity. There is a future after divorce, but the outcome depends on whether one can grasp the opportunities. There are four pathways along which you have a choice to travel following divorce. Three spell danger, the other offers opportunities.

Revenge

The goal here is to get your own back. It reflects a continuing one-sided view of the relationship and why it ended. Much energy is invested in attributing blame, punishing or playing the victim. The anger and bitterness maintains the battle and the crisis remains unresolved. Not only is all hope for a new beginning stalled, but research shows that post divorce conflict is the most salient factor affecting the adjustment of children.

Rebound

A divorce can bring changes in your social network. You cease to be part of a couple and this may affect the way family, friends and society view you. Your normal day to day routine will be disrupted and you may lose valued sources of affection, reassurance and companionship. The insecurity, isolation and dislocation can lead to a frantic search for a replacement partner. This may fill the vacuum bringing immediate comfort and relief. However, relationships formed to fill voids and provide release from emotional pain have a high risk factor. The consequences may well be another unhealthy relationship with more conflict and pain.

Retreat

Suddenly there is no one to come home to, no adult to talk to, and no feedback regarding dress, behaviour or attitudes. Shocked, immobilised, depressed, there is the temptation to withdraw from social commitments, contact with people, from life itself. The result is months, even years of drifting along, with no sense of direction, feeling abandoned and bereft. You do not think well of yourself and it is unlikely that others will warm towards you. It marks the beginning of a vicious cycle of plummeting self-esteem.

Rebuild

An essential prerequisite for rebuilding is review. Behaviour patterns left over from the previous relationship can affect any new relationship. Reviewing the past also helps you clarify what you would do differently, and what you want to give and receive in a new relationship. Rebuilding means establishing your own identity to enable you to be more self-reliant and self-contained. Becoming an individual in your own right is a rewarding and enriching experience. This new-found autonomy helps you come alive, and find significance and meaning in what is ahead. This requires commitment of time and energy.

Real or psychic divorce is more difficult to achieve than a legal divorce. If there is such a thing as a good divorce then, like a good relationship, it is a mutual enterprise, not easily achieved, but well worth the effort. Do not miss the opportunities for a new beginning. A qualified counsellor can certainly assist you discover this.

Karol Misso

LOSS OF EMPLOYMENT

As job loss or redundancy frequently occur, the average person is highly unlikely to remain in just the one job for their entire career. However, rather than occurring as a result of an individual's behaviour or poor work performance, it is often the result of a business' economic difficulties. Although this situation may be very painful to work through at first, you can eventually see it as an opportunity to discover your dream career, to learn new skills, to make new plans, and to act on them. Right now though, if you have lost your job, you are probably dealing with a lot of different feelings (e.g., confusion, rejection, fear or even anger). If you are worried about how you are going to make ends meet, the first thing you need to do is to test your eligibility for government benefits.

If redundancies are widespread within your current industry, you may want to consider a career change to an area of work where there is growth, stability or an identified skills shortage. The most difficult part, however, may be recognising what you really want to do. Finding yourself, knowing your values, interests, transferable skills and personality traits will assist you in listing what it is you want in a career.

Whether you decide on a career change or not, you will ultimately need to sharpen your job searching skills:

- Take time to evaluate your situation and make sure that passion is your motivation — not money.

- Write a list of your employment preferences.

- Research the career requirements, job description, educational qualifications, knowledge and skills and whether your preferred occupations are facing skills shortages.

- Consult a career counsellor for career testing or your local job service to assist you in generating an initial list of careers.

- Network with people who have first-hand knowledge of the occupations you prefer, or consider volunteering in that particular field before you make the final decision.

- Create a plan to achieve your new skills, and then act on it.

- Find ways to remain involved in the lives of your former colleagues, clients and networks (e.g., e-mail articles of mutual interest, invite people for coffee and attend professional events).

- Ensure that everyone knows the type of work you are looking for.

- Use online and offline networking resources (e.g., employment and corporate websites, private and government funded recruitment organisations, as well as temping agencies).

- Sign up for e-mail updates from job search websites.

- Research companies where you would like to work and market yourself directly to them. Find out if someone in your network is connected to someone who knows someone in the company you are interested in — then ask for an introduction.

- Consider taking an "in the meantime" job to protect your finances and mental health.

Resumes:

- Your resume needs to highlight your strengths and help you to stand out from the crowd.

- Carefully read each job description, research the company, and identify key words the employer may be using.

- Customise your resume to the job and the company.

- Start your resume with a short, factual executive summary which is tailored to the job advertised and which outlines your key selling points and objectives.

- Make sure your resume is accomplishment-focused, highlighting accomplishments along with tasks which you have performed for example, explain how you exceeded quotas by implementing a more efficient production strategy. It's what you did that matters, not what you were supposed to do.

- Proof read your resume and then come back to it later. It's amazing the changes you'll want to make once you've had time to clear your head.

Job search tips for older workers:

- Age-proof your resume.

- There's no need to mention every job you've ever had. Omit training and graduation dates as well as job dates. List the number of years in each job and include only your most recent positions (perhaps the last 10 years). You may even like to downplay job titles so that prospective employers don't assume you are over-qualified.

- Focus your resume only on the requirements of the job for which you are applying.

- If some of your previous employment duties and experience don't address the job requirements — don't highlight them.

- Amplify relevant accomplishments, and, where possible, identify financial benefits to be gained by the new employer for example, highlight how a particular strategy you utilised positively impacted the bottom line for your previous employer.

- Everyone, regardless of age, needs to be computer literate. There are free or low-cost classes available within your community (e.g., your local library).

- The more current your skills, the better your prospects of finding employment.

One of most difficult things about being out of work for an extended period of time is keeping a positive attitude. It is, however, imperative you do so for both your own emotional wellbeing as well as the impression you make with potential employers.

Whilst time spent job searching is important, it is also imperative that you spend a few hours each week doing something you enjoy — taking long walks, reading, meeting friends for coffee or learning a new skill.

Volunteering in an area of interest is a good way of learning new skills, having a new referee to add to your resume, and keeping your confidence and self-esteem intact. It may also lead to an offer of paid employment!

Sue McLaughlin

SAYING THE FINAL GOODBYE TO YOUR PET

Regardless of the reasons behind it, the decision to euthanase a pet is never an easy one. Even in the face of sound medical evidence that euthanasia is the kindest option, making that decision is often overwhelmingly difficult for pet owners. Often the pet has been part of the family for a long time, and even if they haven't, they are almost always valued members of the family. Unfortunately the majority of pets don't just die quietly in their sleep without suffering, which means a lot of pet owners face the decision to euthanase their pet at some point — often towards the end of their pet's life.

How will I know when its time?

When trying to make a decision whether or not to euthanase a pet or how to time that decision, owners often ask veterinarians whether their animal is in any pain. The clinical signs of pain in an animal can be variable depending on the source and the severity of pain, and may include: reduced appetite or not wanting to eat at all, reluctance to move if movement causes pain which can lead to toileting in inappropriate places such as bedding, and personality changes such as depression in a usually boisterous pet. Of course the presence of debilitating pain is an important factor to consider when deciding if euthanasia is an appropriate course of action. However, it is not the only thing veterinarians take into account when monitoring a pet's quality of life. Veterinarians usually consider several parameters to assess an animal's quality of life including, but not limited to: their interest in food, which can be reduced by symptoms such as nausea even if there is no overt pain, their ability to toilet independently, their ability to show interest in activities they have always enjoyed such as going for a walk or being stroked, and perhaps most importantly the owner's perception of their pet's quality of life. Even though veterinarians can advise and support you, because you know your pet and their personality best and have often lived closely with them for a long time, you are also often the best judge of their quality of life.

Talking to your Veterinarian

Pet owners are sometimes reluctant to broach the subject of euthanasia with their veterinarian, but it is important to discuss any questions or concerns you have about euthanasia with them. Veterinarians are there to offer advice without judging, and help you make an informed decision about whether or not it is time to make this most difficult decision. Talking through it with a veterinarian if it is on your mind and addressing any concerns you have beforehand unfortunately will not make the decision to euthanase your pet any less painful, but it can mean the decision making process is easier than if you were tackling it on your own. The death of a pet or having to have a pet euthanased is a loss that can't be measured. Everyone has a different relationship with their pets, but there is no doubt that for the majority of, if not all, pet owners, a pet's death affects them deeply. The importance of acknowledging the role our pets play in our lives and allowing ourselves to grieve in whichever way suits us as an individual best, can't be overstated.

Grieving

It can be easy to be surprised by the depth of grief caused by the death of a pet. I had to make the decision to euthanase my old cat several months ago. He was at least fifteen years old, a stray — so I didn't know his exact age. I was nineteen and in my first year at University when he allegedly followed my younger sister home from the shops. He was a scruffy, chocolate brown, Persian-cross with yellow eyes. He won my parents over on the first night with the loudness of his purr, and stayed on until now, fifteen years later, when as a veterinarian I had to face the decision to euthanase him. I tried to talk to myself professionally. I told myself that not only was he very old, but that he had been unwell for some time and was ready to die. My mother had told me over the phone that he had lost all interest in food in the last two days, and he was barely moving. I knew I didn't want to put him through a barrage of diagnostic tests and procedures and have him spend his last few days or maybe weeks in and out of hospital. I knew on a logical level that that would not have been kind to him. I tried to will myself away from grief because I knew from a humane point of view, and very likely from a medical point of view this was the right decision. And yet ... there was doubt, because I did not want to let this cat go, let alone be the one to make the decision to let him go. I was getting ready to drive to my parents' house to euthanase him when my mother phoned to say he'd died. He had saved me from having to make and carry out the decision to euthanase him. I was relieved and devastated.

We all grieve differently and process grief differently. The most important thing is not to follow what many of us perceive as social norms and suppress grief over the loss of a pet. Acknowledging your grief and finding a way to honour the memory of your pet that you are comfortable with will help you through this experience. It could be burying your pet in the garden with their favourite toy. It might be printing, framing, and hanging a favourite photograph of them with the rest of your family photos. It might be planting a tree in their honour. It might be having them cremated and scattering their ashes. It might be sharing memories of the funniest or naughtiest things your pet did in its life, with other family members. It might be keeping their collar or a little bit of their fur tied with ribbon. It might be making a donation to an animal welfare organisation in their name. There are many different ways to grieve.

The afternoon that my old cat died, I did what I needed to do to help me look my grief in the face and cry. I did what I needed to do to let go of my professional voice that wanted me to view such an emotional issue with logic. I wrote:

In Loving Memory of Kaspar

The little brown cat followed my sister home from the shops.

Supposedly.

Knowing my sister, she probably led him with a scent trail of something tasty. Golden pools of late afternoon sun for eyes and the chocolate swagger of his tail begged my parents for asylum from stray-catdom. His real cat's purr — loud enough to hear across a room — was loud enough to make his case for joining the family.

He stayed comfortably draped across our lives, perfectly meeting an unspoken need for his soothing presence in the house, until this Sunday when he slipped unobtrusively out, leaving many memories and a little brown cat shaped hole in each of us.

Dr Anita Link

9

Sexuality Issues

MISMATCHED LIBIDOS

Libido is another term for sex drive, which is the passionate desire for sex. Libido can be classified as high or low but it is actually more complex than how often a person desires sex. It has elements including what triggers arousal and what dampens it, the importance of sex compared to other parts of a relationship, the meaning of sex for each individual and what is pleasurable during sexual activity. Mismatched libidos used to refer to partners who differed in how often they wanted sex; mismatched partners were either high or low libido. Certainly some people are aware of a regular need for sex whereas others feel they wouldn't care if they didn't have sex again. However, two people can want sex at the same frequency but can differ in the meaning of sex (e.g., is it about emotional intimacy or "hot" activities) or what is pleasurable. This mismatch in wants and needs can lead to one partner gradually withdrawing from sex.

Concept of libido types

Although we acknowledge that there is a wide range of individual differences in human sexuality, we don't seem to talk about them very much. We tend to expect our partner to be like us and to enjoy sex in the same way we do, yet logic says that just as there are, for example, personality differences, there must be great diversity in sexuality as well. Think about, how often you are interested in sex — once every month? once a day? more often than that, or less often? Then add in what activities you enjoy: are you comfortable with a usual routine or do you crave variety and long sessions of passionate sex? Is your sexual desire strong and persistent or subdued and easily lost? Is the main satisfaction you get from sex the emotional intimacy or the physical release? You don't have to continue any further with this exercise to conclude that all the possible combinations of the range of sexual characteristics give us an incredible variety in normal sexual individuality. These different combinations create libido types e.g., the sensual libido type — values emotional connection above sexual performance, while the erotic libido type wants sex to be intense, varied and passionate, if not every time then at least some of the time.

When mismatched libidos is a problem

When a couple differs in ways that have significance to one or both partners, confusion and distress can begin to undermine their relationship. A good example of that is the importance of who initiates sex, how often, and in what way. While some couples are quite comfortable if one partner mostly initiates, some people feel unattractive or unloved if their partner does not initiate sex at least half of the time in a hot, can't keep my hands off you way. The hurt and frustration that is caused by such misinterpretations gets in the way of the couple finding other ways of getting their needs met that are acceptable to both.

Working together on the mismatch

While there is no therapy program that can guarantee that every couple with mismatched libidos will resolve their differences so that they get the sex life they really want, there is much you and your partner can do together to develop a good enough, mutually satisfying sex life.

- Recognise that you are different but equal: the differences in wants and needs do not make one person right and the other wrong.

- Be respectful, courteous, and encourage each other with generosity and gentleness to say what is true for each of you. Don't be surprised or defensive when your partner says something that you disagree with: listening to another point of view doesn't mean that you have to agree with it.

- Describe, don't judge. Using words such as cold or selfish, or insisting your partner has a problem leads to defensiveness which blocks communication. State the problem in objective terms: *I would like to have sex more/less often; I would like more/less variety in our sex life.*

- Be willing to really listen to your partner. Ask about your partner's opinion: *What do you think about this? What do you think would help here? What would you like to do? I would like to solve our problem in this way. What's your view on this?* If you are asking because you genuinely want to know the answers and are not merely using these questions as a form of attack, you will encourage an open and frank atmosphere that might reveal previously hidden solutions.

- Challenge your interpretations. Misinterpretations are common in cases of mismatched libidos.

Taking action:

- Identify what you would like your partner to do to achieve a more satisfying sex life for you. Keep your requests in line with your hopes for a good enough sex life rather than your ideal sex life, and start with what your partner is likely to be able to do. There is no point in expecting your partner to suddenly increase sexual frequency or initiate sex in a passionate way if you know he or she has a lower sexual desire than you. What first step would you like your partner to take that demonstrates he or she is willing to work on your problems?

- Now comes the point where you have to take responsibility for your part in developing a mutually satisfying sex life: What are you prepared to do now and over the coming weeks that goes toward meeting your partner's needs, as described? Can you make that first change your partner has requested? Don't wait to see what your partner does; you can only change your own behaviour. If you both take responsibility for change, and your focus is on meeting your partner's needs rather than concentrating on yourself, ultimately your sex life should move toward your mutual wants and needs.

What typically happens as you follow this process is that instead of working against each other and feeling hurt and let down, as you each put yourself out to please the other person, you feel more loved, secure and empowered. As you accept your partner is a different libido type, and you develop your ability to give your partner more of what makes them feel good, your confidence as a lover and partner grows. A good lover is first and foremost a sensitive person who can be flexible and reasonably adapt to the wants and needs of the partner, and the realities of life circumstances. This is not always a simple process to achieve the changes you have both agreed upon, but couples discover by working together to solve challenging sexual problems, they experience new depths and strengths in the relationship that make the struggle worthwhile.

Dr Sandra Pertot

WOMEN'S HEALTH AND INTIMACY

Many women find themselves caring for their families, friends and special people in their lives and often juggling either full-time or part-time work. If this is you, imagine life as a game where you juggle five balls — work, health, family, friends and spirit, and you keep them all in the air. Understand that work is a rubber ball and if you drop it, it will bounce back, but your health, family, friends and spirit are made of fine glass, and if you drop one of these your life will could be shattered.

Following are some tips that will assist you to maintain the balance in your life and keep all the balls in the air:

Work:

- Work efficiently during your hours at work and leave on time.

- Where you can with your household budget, income requirements, and the age of your children, work only part-time.

- Part-time work helps you maintain your energy levels and family-life balance, and enables you to socialize and maintain a level of independence that is essential to your spiritual and personal wellbeing.

- If you don't like your job, change it; remember it is a rubber ball and will keep bouncing back; don't allow the stress associated with a job to impact on your health, family, friends and spirit.

- Take your allocated holiday breaks.

- If your job allows, some days, work from home.

- Don't be a martyr — ask your partner, children, family and friends to help wherever possible. Even small chores done by someone else can lighten the load.

Health:

- Only a very small percentage of the female population can eat whatever they want and not gain weight, the vast majority have to work to maintain a healthy weight.

- Cardio-vascular exercise at least 30 minutes a day (e.g., walking, jogging, swimming, skipping, boxing, gym classes and even sex) assists in cardiac function and helps with weight maintenance.

- A well-balanced diet with emphasis on fresh veggies and fruit is critical.

- Drink plenty of fresh water and reduce cordials and soft drinks.

- Research suggests that drinking a daily coffee latte or long black may minimize risk of Parkinson's disease, cancer and Type 2 Diabetes, due to the anti-inflammatory compounds in coffee. Too much coffee is however harmful.

- Don't smoke! Lung cancer is now the leading cancer killer of women having surpassed breast cancer.

- Breast screening and breast checking is vital for all women, but particularly for women with a family history, or genetic tendency, of breast cancer. Talk to you GP about self-examination and the most effective time during your menstrual cycle to examine your breasts.

- Cervical and ovarian checking is essential for all women, and your GP or gynecologist can advise you, as well as women's health clinics in your local area. If you are sexually active, have the checks yearly; it takes very little time. After menopause consult with your GP about the frequency of checks.

- Vaccinations are essential and they include:

> Tetanus-diphtheria booster
>
> Measles, mumps, rubella and chicken pox
>
> Human Papillomavirus (HPV)
>
> Meningococcal
>
> Hepatitis A and Hepatitis B
>
> Influenza and Pneumococcal

Most of these vaccinations are received as a newborn, and then as a child, however it is essential to have a vaccination record, especially when considering pregnancy. For older women, influenza and pneumococcal vaccines will assist in fighting off those winter colds and chest infections.

- Perimenopause is the transition stage before menopause, which may start as early as 35 years, however, most women notice changes in their mid to late 40s. This perimenopause phase may last for five to ten years. It is different for every woman, with some experiencing uncomfortable and obvious changes while others appear to sail through the change. Perimenopause, and menopause, can also have an impact on libido. It is important to consult your GP, a specialist physician, or natural therapist about healthy management of the physical and emotional changes you may experience.

Family, Friends and Spirit

Family and friends are important contributors to a woman's health and well-being. Enjoying a balance is paramount for health and the spirit. Family and friends need to be supportive and respectful of your commitments and also make time for them.

- Take time to spend with yourself — read a book, go to the movies, have retail therapy (as your budget allows).

- Smell the roses, walk in the garden, do some gardening.

- Do simple pleasurable activities like picnics with family, have a day at the beach.

- Have a weekend away with your partner, re-affirm your relationship, enjoy this time.

- Give yourself permission to be selfish so you can de-brief and relax.

Intimacy

A "passion prescription" contributes to good health and harmony for the spirit. Sometimes when we get into comfortable relationships we forget that intimacy and sexual attraction can benefit from a little mystery and excitement.

- Make the time to communicate about sexual intimacy.

- Get dressed up and go on a date with your partner, making the effort to look your best.

- Talk about sex in a positive way, make sure there is a no blame game being played.

- Take a weekend away — vacation sex can sometimes be explosive and fun.

- Be spontaneous and enjoy every moment.

- Menopause can change a woman's libido; be aware of this and speak to your GP to discuss treatments to assist with symptoms that may affect sexual function/enjoyment.

- Always kiss your partner hello and good-bye; and warm, caring hugs are great too.

Actions usually speak louder than words, so be deliberate with plans to get what you want for your health, relationships and in life generally.

Jan Lloyd

MEN'S SEXUAL HEALTH

Sexuality is a key aspect of human life and has long since gone beyond its biological function of reproduction. Problems with sexuality may destroy personal relationships, and are best overcome when both partners openly communicate and have a strong desire to treat the problem.

Erectile Dysfunction is a common problem that affects at least one in three men over the age of 40 years, increasing to about two in three men over the age of 70 years. Persistent Erectile Dysfunction is uncommon in young men. All men experience failure in achieving erection at some time in their lives, particularly when tired, under stress or the influence of alcohol, or during a major illness.

Erectile Dysfunction is the inability to maintain an erection that is rigid enough and lasts long enough to permit sexual intercourse. It is not the same as infertility nor is it the same as premature ejaculation. Erectile Dysfunction can occur at any age, although it is more common after the age of 40. There are well-recognised changes that occur as men age. It takes longer to be aroused, the penis needs more direct stimulation and does not become so rigid. Any distraction may lead to the loss of the erection, and the climax (orgasm) can be less intense.

What causes Erectile Dysfunction?

The ageing process — this is by far the commonest cause. It happens to some men in their 30s to 40s but other men not till their 70s and 80s. One thing is for sure, if you live long enough on this planet, sooner or later you will have some sort of erection difficulty. Contributing to this ageing process are things like high blood pressure and high cholesterol.

- Smoking — smoking affects blood vessels and your penis is one big blood vessel.

- Diabetes affects nerves and blood vessels, and erectile dysfunction is a common complication of diabetes.

- The psyche affects erections in a positive way or a negative way.

- Alcohol will affect erections if you have had too much of it (brewer's droop).

- Medications such as commonly prescribed anti-depressants can affect erections.

- Diseases of the nerves such as Multiple Sclerosis will impact erections.

- Prostate cancer treatments such as a prostatectomy, brachytherapy and external beam radiotherapy can in some cases cause total impotence.

Here are some tips to bear in mind with respect to hopefully minimising your chances of developing Erectile Dysfunction:

- Beware of the ageing process. Try to keep negative ageing health problems at bay, keep blood pressure down, keep cholesterol under control; exercise regularly, get regular sleep, have a good diet and don't allow yourself to get overweight.

- If you are Diabetic, good control is essential — once again, watch your weight.

- Keep calm — penises can be very stubborn — the angrier you get with it, the more likely it is to do nothing.

- Use alcohol in moderation.

Men's Sexual and Reproductive Health Issues — some general rules:

- Sexually transmitted infections — unless you are totally confident about the partner you are with, always wear a condom.

- Testicles — any unusual lumps or bumps particularly if you are under 40 years of age, go straight to the doctor.

- Prostate — any suggestion of obstruction to flow of urine such as difficulty starting, poor stream or end-dribbling; again, go directly to your doctor as it could be serious.

Although men's health issues can be embarrassing for you to talk about, be aware that your doctor discusses these issues on a daily basis, and will be able to put you at ease. Men's sexual health issues are just another part of your physical health, and are so very important to examine. There are some specialist clinics that guys can access which focus particularly on men's issues, and are worth the effort finding in your local community.

Dr Richard Clarke

COMING OUT — TELLING FAMILY AND FRIENDS

Regardless of age, coming out to family and friends can be the hardest thing you will ever have to do. Many experience stress and anxiety because they are fearful of their family's reaction. However, once you are able to deal with such reactions, things can improve with the right kind of support. Additionally, the response from parents to coming out often isn't half as bad as you had imagined it was going to be. Here are some issues for you to consider to help make the process less confronting.

Before coming out:

- Understand you are not the only person going through these confusing emotions about your sexual orientation.

- Seek support even if it is an anonymous telephone help-line service. Check your local telephone book or the Internet for assistance.

- Take your time coming out. Wait until you feel comfortable in yourself and be prepared for a range of questions.

- If you are concerned about other's reactions, have emotional support, financial independence and a place to stay organised if things do go very badly.

- Find information to give to your family so they know you are serious and can seek help immediately if they wish.

- Never ask one parent to keep it a secret from the other, especially if they are living in the same house, or have a close relationship.

- Remember, being gay or lesbian doesn't mean you will lose your morals, or become a deviant as some myths and outdated beliefs might suggest.

- Homosexuality is a natural sexual orientation just like heterosexuality. It just isn't as common.

- Even though there may be tough times when you first come out understand things will get better. You will get more confidence and your family will begin to understand with support and your help.

- Be patient and don't expect parents to understand in a day. Remember you took time coming to terms with being gay or lesbian and so will they. This doesn't mean they think being gay or lesbian is bad, it just means it isn't what they expected.

- Understand that people fear what they don't understand and many don't understand diverse sexual orientation, which can make it difficult for people when they initially come out.

- If you lose friends because you disclose to them, they were never your friends, and let them go.

- It isn't uncommon for young people to experience their own self-loathing or internalised homophobia. Just know you are a good and worthy person and these feelings will pass.

- No person chooses to be gay, but you can choose to be happy.

- Be yourself, you don't have to prove anything.

- Being gay or lesbian doesn't mean you have to be an extrovert or party person if that isn't you. Take your time, you will find your niche.

- You can still have a successful career and relationship. It will be just a little different to what family and perhaps you once expected.

- Never apologise for being gay or lesbian. You have done nothing wrong.

- If you believe in a God, then you know that you are loved by them.

- Be true to yourself and live your life as honestly as you can.

When you disclose to someone that you are gay or lesbian it isn't telling them what you do in bed. You are telling people about who you are and what you are. It's all about being honest to others whilst remaining true to yourself.

Shelley Argent

WHEN YOUR CHILD TELLS YOU THEY ARE GAY

When a son or daughter comes out it isn't unusual for parents to go through shock, anger, denial, blame, guilt, shame, grief, fear for their child, and feelings of paranoia and isolation. Homophobic beliefs emerge with people believing the outdated misinformation that still persists in some circles. Additionally, it isn't unusual for these feelings to continue for months. Seek quality information and emotional support and you will soon come to the realisation that the only person that really cares that you have a gay son or lesbian daughter is you. Often when a loved one comes out it is totally unexpected and we can behave in a manner we could never imagine. While you are struggling to understand what has gone wrong, think about how your son or daughter is also struggling. The hardest thing they will ever have to do is tell parents they are gay or lesbian. They know at worst they will be rejected by family and at minimum cause disappointment. Here are some issues to consider when dealing with the news.

- Don't be hard on yourself if you cry a lot, find it hard to sleep and feel your child is now a stranger to you. Many feel their child has died and a stranger is now standing in front of them. But don't worry, this is common and these feelings will pass.

- Understand it isn't a choice. You as a parent have done nothing wrong and neither have they. People may decide to come out or keep their feelings hidden but this doesn't change their sexual orientation.

- Most parents look for a reason, but there is currently no clear scientific evidence as to why people are heterosexual or homosexual.

- Ask questions, don't interrogate, and listen to what they have to say. Tell them you don't understand but you want to.

- Encourage them to bring their friends home, the same as you would a heterosexual son or daughter. Make a genuine effort to get to know their friends.

- Don't have double standards. What you would permit for your heterosexual sons and daughters you should allow for your gay son or lesbian daughter.

- Therapy to bring young people to their senses, to straighten them out, will not help them. However, therapy may help your relationship and give you some insight.

- Homosexuality is not a mental illness. It is a natural sexual orientation and was removed from the list of mental illnesses in 1973!

- Young people don't automatically lose the family values or morals that their parents have taught them just because they are gay or lesbian.

- Some people think their child is gay because of bad parenting. If this is you, now is the time to step up and be a parent who can accept and support them, and generally be there for them, because when a person first comes out, it can be a very stressful and challenging time for them.

- Don't use the thinking that this is their choice and you (as their parent) have no control. Remember they also have no control, as they didn't choose to be gay. However, they can choose to do things to make them happy. They chose to be honest with you, the person they care about the most, and that is very important.

We all want to live our lives honestly and so do our gay sons and lesbian daughters. Accepting parents soon learn that sexual orientation is really only a very small part of a person and doesn't make someone better or worse than anyone else. We eventually wonder what the fuss was all about. Hindsight is a wonderful thing.

Love, understanding and acceptance is the prescription for keeping your family united through this difficult time.

Shelley Argent

Stress Management and Time Management Issues

- Controlled Breathing for Stress Relief
- Progressive Muscle Relaxation for Stress Relief
- Reducing Stress: Mind-Body Strategies
- Stress Management
- Adult Anger Management
- Meditation to Relax the Mind
- Avoiding Road Rage
- Time Management
- Overcoming Procrastination

CONTROLLED BREATHING FOR STRESS RELIEF

Controlled breathing is a great stress relief technique, which you will find very useful exploring. It is learned easily and is extremely effective for relaxation and anxiety. Practice daily for 15 minutes when you are relaxed so it will have some ongoing impact, and also do it whenever you want to reduce the impact of stress.

Sit comfortably upright

Sitting upright is better than lying down or slouching as it increases the capacity of your lungs to fill with air.

Control the rate of your breathing

Breathe in through your nose and out through your mouth in a steady rhythm. You may find it helpful to count one, two, three as you breath in, and one, two, three as you breathe out.

Use your diaphragm (lower chest muscle) to breathe

Your diaphragm is the big muscle under the lungs. It pulls the lungs downwards which expands the airways to allow air to flow in. When you become breathless you forget to use this muscle and instead you use the muscles at the top of the chest and shoulders. Each breath is more shallow if you use these upper chest muscles. So, you tend to breathe faster and feel more breathless if you use your upper chest muscles rather than your diaphragm.

You can check if you are using your diaphragm by feeling just below your breastbone (sternum) at the top of your abdomen. If you give a little cough, you can feel the diaphragm push out there. If you hold your hand there you will feel it move in and out as you breathe.

Relax your shoulders and upper chest muscles when you breathe

It is best to take the weight off your shoulders by supporting your arms on the arms of a chair or your lap. Gentle massage of your shoulders by a trusted person will help you relax. They can stand behind the chair and gently rub your shoulders and encourage you to relax.

Relax your mind too

Anxiety will make breathing problems worse. So, refocus your mind when you are short of breath. For example, shut your eyes and to concentrate on pleasant, peaceful thoughts or events. Some people find it easier to relax by listening to quiet soothing music.

If persistent anxiety is a problem you believe is making your breathing worse, see your GP, psychologist or relaxation specialist. They will be able to advise you on relaxation exercises, courses or other useful approaches to manage your breathing, stress and anxiety.

Dr John Barletta

PROGRESSIVE MUSCLE RELAXATION FOR STRESS RELIEF

Progressive muscle relaxation (PMR) is a technique for reducing anxiety by tensing and relaxing your muscles. Since muscle tension often coexists with anxiety, you can reduce your level of anxiety by learning how to relax your muscular tension. Progressive muscle relaxation incorporates both physical and mental components. The physical part involves tensing and relaxing muscle groups in the entire body. With eyes closed, and in a sequential pattern, tension in specific muscle groups is purposefully done for about ten seconds and then released for twenty seconds. Then you move to the next muscle group; and so on and so forth to other groups of muscle.

The mental part focuses on the difference between sensations of the tension and relaxation. Given the eyes are kept closed, you concentrate on the tension and relaxation. For some people who are anxious, the mind has thoughts such as: *Relaxation exercises are not something I can do!* To test this belief, focus your attention on the warmth and heaviness feelings of the tensed muscle group, and mental relaxation will be felt as a consequence. With regular practice you will become more expert in how to relax and therefore keep anxiety and panic at a distance.

Each of the following alternating tension and relaxation exercises is done while focusing on the breath. Tense each body part to its maximum as you inhale. Hold the tension as long as it is comfortable; then let go of the tension slowly as you exhale.

1. Make fists with your toes. Relax.

2. Pull the feet back, bringing the toes towards the knees. Relax.

3. Tense the thigh muscles as if you were trying to lift your legs against a weight. Relax.

4. Pinch the buttocks in and up, making them hard; as if you are seated upon a rock. Relax.

5. Take a big chest breath and pull the abdomen in, hardening it. Relax.

6. Take a big chest breath and tense the whole upper body. Relax.

7. Make fists with your hands. Relax.

8. Pull your hands back at the wrists, as if to bend the hand up towards the elbow. Relax.

9. Raise your shoulders up to your ears. Relax.

10. Raise your eyebrows and furrow the forehead. Relax.

11. Squeeze your eyes shut. Relax.

12. Smile, pulling back the corners of the mouth and baring the teeth. Relax.

PMR is a quick, simple and effective and you will find it useful to help you relax and control anxiety and panic symptoms. Remember, practice makes perfect.

Dr John Barletta

REDUCING STRESS: MIND-BODY STRATEGIES

How great would it be if you could be one of those people who never seem to be over-stressed and takes everyday hassles in their stride? If you are wondering how they do it, and what can you do to be part of that elite group, keep reading. Some say stress and the resultant anxiety and fatigue are an inevitable part of modern living, but more tranquillity amid the busyness of life is absolutely achievable. Implement one, or more, of the following sure-fire strategies to help you take control of your life. By engaging in these practices you will not only significantly improve your stress management but also improve your physical health and immune system.

Exercise

Reasonably vigorous exercise such as jogging, swimming, gym, or bike-riding are excellent ways of breaking the stress cycle. Exercise increases growth factors in your brain increasing its health, improving serotonin levels and lowering the stress hormones. Exercise is a fine aid to good brain and mental health. In addition to stress reduction, regular exercise enhances cardio-vascular fitness, physiological health and mood, while social connections can also be developed.

Meditation

This is a great mind-body exercise because as stress rises, the mind goes into over-drive. With over-thinking and negative thoughts becoming present, these activate physical changes in your body and your nervous system ramps up as do cortisol and adrenaline levels. When you focus during meditation, concentrating on the present enables you to let go of concerns about the past and the future. As your mind reduces worrying thoughts, your nervous system comes back into balance and stress hormones dramatically reduce. This process allows you to deal with the racing, unhelpful thoughts that seem to come at stressful moments. (Pilates, yoga, and Tai Chi also reduce stress in this way).

Breathing

Another excellent mind-body technique is controlled breathing which lowers heart rate and reduces anxiety. Sit comfortably upright as it increases the capacity of your lungs. Control the rate of your breathing, by inhaling slowly and deeply in through your nose and out through your mouth, and use the lower chest muscle (diaphragm). You breathe faster and feel more breathless if you use your upper chest muscles rather than the diaphragm. Check if you are using your diaphragm by feeling just below your breastbone (sternum) at the top of your abdomen. Also, relax your shoulders and upper chest muscles when you breathe, and relax your mind too. Anxiety makes breathing problems worse so quieten your mind by closing your eyes and concentrating on pleasant, peaceful thoughts (or listen to soothing music). You know this works when you feel noticeably calmer in your mind and body. Like any technique, it takes practice as you learn how to replace patterns of stress with patterns of calmness. Once this skill is learned it is possible to switch off stress just by deciding to do so.

Massage

The experience of stress can lead to physical tension in the body, which is the tightness people feel in their back, neck and shoulders. Massage therapists and physiotherapists can easily lessen such discomfort by releasing tightness from tendons, soft tissue, and muscles. A trusted partner can also be extremely helpful by providing gentle massage to aid relaxation; this in turn can enhance a couple's interpersonal connection. Touch is powerful psychologically and physically as it increases the sense of bonding and support, increases natural feel-good brain chemicals, and reduces stress hormones.

Trialling just one of these strategies will get you feeling less stressed and able to deal with life's trials and tribulations — try one and you are sure to benefit from the results!

Dr John Barletta

STRESS MANAGEMENT

Stress is the body's natural response to challenging situations and can occur when we are threatened or the balance in our life is somehow upset. An imbalance occurs between the demands placed on us, and our ability or resources, to deal with them. These demands may come from your thoughts and emotions, your schedule, your environment or relationships.

Tolerance for stress differs widely between individuals. When the nervous system perceives a threat, either real or imagined, it responds by releasing a flood of stress hormones, particularly, adrenaline and cortisol. These hormones automatically prepare the body for action in a process known as the fight or flight response.

To live a rich, full life it is inevitable that we will all, at sometime, experience pain, loss, fear, anger, frustration and great joy. Not all stress is bad. Whilst it can energise us to finish a worthwhile project and achieve goals, prolonged stress may have negative effects.

If you are constantly feeling frazzled and overwhelmed with life, the following strategies may assist you to make positive changes to increase your wellbeing. A balanced life allows time for work, relationships (family, friends and colleagues), socialising and staying healthy. The time ratios for these activities will differ over your lifespan.

- Take care of yourself; if you are not healthy you are not able to care for anyone else. If you think that you may be stressed, there is a good chance that you are. Take some time-out to assess the situation. The world will function without you for a while. Research suggests a link between long working hours and life-style illnesses such as obesity, alcoholism and cardiovascular disease.

- Mental health or personal days are recognised within progressive organisations. People work faster and more effectively when they are physically and mentally in good shape. It is a waste of your time, and your employer's money, and has a negative impact on your health if your stress levels are not managed.

- Learn about your stressors by listing, in order of importance (from 1–10), the main causes of stress in your life. Then consider making small changes to reduce their impact on you. For example, if the traffic stresses you going to work, leave ten minutes earlier, take a less busy route, or listen to soothing music in the car.

- Wellness weekends can be achieved by booking into a retreat to relax, unwind and eat well. Have a couple of days by the beach or in the country, or stay home, schedule a massage and take time out and do some of these nurturing self-care suggestions.

- Self-soothing activities can be tried in a group or class environment, or alone, depending on your preference: Yoga, Meditation, Progressive Muscle Relaxation, Visualisation and Guided Imagery; there are numerous books/CDs and DVDs available at bookshops or your local library to help guide you through these techniques.

- Learning and practising Mindfulness is a gentle way to calm your racing thoughts and focus your concentration on the present moment. This assists by reducing worrying thoughts about the past or the future. Daily practice may decrease the influence of difficult and painful experiences by lowering your reactivity to them.

- Take 10 breaths and discover a simple yet effective way to slow things down, wherever you are. Breathe normally through your nose and concentrate all your attention on your breath going in and coming out. Random thoughts will intrude but gently refocus your attention back to your breathing.

- Reduce the negative influences in your life. These can be friends, family or colleagues at work. It may also be unhelpful habits that have developed over time such as too much TV or computer time, or eating junk food. If spending time with certain people leaves you feeling drained, limit time spent with them. You only have so much physical and mental energy to spend in one day, don't waste it on negativity.

- De-clutter your life by organising or cleaning out your office/home/schedules. Home can be a sanctuary and by de-cluttering you can create a peaceful, organised space.

- Create a garden or grow plants in pots to have a tranquil place where you can meditate, read quietly, have a cup of tea or just enjoy the feeling of watching nature at work. Quiet times away from constant stimuli (including TV) gives our nervous system a well-needed rest.

- Exercise is a great stress buster. Join a gym and have an age/fitness appropriate program designed. If you don't like gyms, walk, swim or cycle. Set reasonable, achievable goals and consult with your GP first about any medical issues. An exercise physiologist or qualified personal trainer may be helpful to get you started.

- Exercise and socialise by playing golf, tennis, netball or touch football. Join a hiking group. Attend dancing lessons or put on your favourite music and dance at home; excellent for increasing fitness and releasing the feel-good endorphins!

- Keep a journal and write down your feelings and thoughts on a regular basis, and make it detailed. "Bad day" is not enough. Getting things out may be a release valve and allow you to reflect. It may also highlight patterns of behaviour or events that increase your stress levels; include positive and negative experiences.

- Eat more natural foods such as vegetables, fruit and lean meat or fish. Cutting down on caffeine and sweet drinks is helpful. Strict dieting is not healthy and may cause cravings, so allow yourself a treat sometimes. A dietician can provide further information on eating well.

- Family meal times can be difficult to achieve in this busy world and can be noisy and chaotic. They can also be special events that allow you to reconnect, discuss events, make plans and achieve that human interaction that is so vital for our wellbeing.

- Alcohol free days (AFDs) are recommended for two consecutive days per week. Reliance on any drugs, alcohol or prescription medication may leave you drained, tired, dehydrated and feeling down. Discuss any concerns with a health professional and assess the benefits of your relationship with these substances.

- Time management, prioritising and delegating may help people who are time poor and struggling to fit everything in. Effective results may be achieved by designing a realistic schedule, identifying urgent issues, and tackling one task at a time in order of priority. If possible, delegating work to people with fewer responsibilities may reduce seemingly insurmountable workloads.

- Saying "no" and the 24 hour rule are ways to reduce spur of the moment decisions that lead to increased commitments and workloads. Taking 24 hours gives you time to consider your present commitments and whether you can comfortably take on any more. Practise saying "no" in a firm but pleasant manner.

- Seek out professional help to improve communication skills, anger management, problem solving and coping skills and to learn more about the impact of your thoughts and emotions on your behaviour.

- Be kind to yourself and strive for excellence, not perfection!

Margaret Davoren

ADULT ANGER MANAGEMENT

Anger is a normal healthy emotion and it's how you deal with it that matters. Anger is experienced in response to perceived powerlessness, threat or mistreatment, which evokes a defensive or offensive response in the individual. Anger is a powerful energy source which, when used constructively, can be beneficial but if not thoughtfully directed can be very destructive. Anger provokes both physical and emotional responses. The physical responses are related to autonomic arousal that prepares the body for fight or flight. The autonomic nervous system increases adrenaline which can result in physical muscle tension, increased heart rate, increased blood pressure, dilated pupils, jaw clenched, rapid shallow breathing and increased acid to stomach. Emotion responses to anger are evident in behavioural and thinking changes like impulsiveness, poor judgement, physical violence and reduced objectivity. The experience of the adrenaline rush can feel very seductive and provides the angry individual with some perceived short-term benefits that reinforce the behaviour. Long-term perpetuating behaviours develop as perceptions initiated in times of anger reinforce a view that the world is not living up to expectations and refocusing the blame on the outside world, some person or events, rather than on unrealistic expectations or ones own vulnerabilities. Forgiveness of our fallibility can be difficult to acknowledge, yet is a huge step towards empathic forgiveness of others.

Chronic anger leads to problems whether anger is outwardly expressed or held within. Outwardly expressed anger causes defensive or aggressive responses in others. Inwardly directed anger, passive aggression, results in behaviour that sabotages relationships — sulking, stonewalling, bitterness, avoidance. Both expressions of anger can lead to health issues such as depression, anxiety, increased blood pressure, poor immunity, ulcers, Irritable Bowel Syndrome, heart disease and stroke.

On the spot management of anger:

- Stop, breathe, count to ten and assess.

- Don't let it build up, recognise the early physical signs and defuse.

- Reduce signs by doing the opposite for example, breath deeply, relax muscles, be as objective as possible (empathise), remove self from triggers (physically or thoughts), time out.

- Do something constructive with the energy — exercise, write it down, or talk about it.

- Give yourself time for the adrenaline rush to pass.

- Observe your thoughts and challenge their subjectivity, be flexible with your thinking.

- Choose to let go of anger.

Maintenance in anger management:

- Understanding and ownership of ones emotions is the first step.

- Identify personal triggers — who, what, when and how.

- Learn meditation/relaxation/mindfulness methods to reduce stress.

- Address irrational thinking and learn assertive communication.

- Maintain a healthy/active lifestyle to improve tolerance and patience.

- Sleep well.

- Practice on the small stuff at every opportunity.

- Seek professional or group support when necessary.

> *Everybody can get angry, that's easy. But to be angry with the right person, with the right intensity, at the right time, for the right reason and in the right way, that's hard.*
>
> *Aristotle*

Siobhan Burgess and Tracey Saxton

MEDITATION TO RELAX THE MIND

The stress of high-paced life in modern society contributes to both physical and psychological ill health. While work tasks generally are less physically demanding than in the past, technological advances have caused the mental demands of work to increase exponentially. And not only at work. Riding the bus, driving your car, walking down the street, sitting down to eat — all day you are bombarded with information from computers, telephones, televisions, radios, newspapers, magazines, billboards, posters, and junk-mail in a never-ending stream.

The mind has an amazing capacity for dealing with all this information. Even so, there comes a time when you just have to give it some rest; to go for a walk in the forest, or go fishing, or simply go and sit on a rock by the ocean. The reality is, though, that you usually can't just take off to the forest or the ocean whenever you need to relax the mind. This is when the practice of meditation may be of help.

Meditation has been practised in various forms since the beginning of time. It is recognised as an essential component of all traditions of spiritual practice. During the last few decades meditation has also become integrated into contemporary psychological treatments for a range of conditions, and neuroscience researchers have been able to identify the beneficial effects of meditation on brain functioning.

The most extensively researched meditation form, mindfulness meditation, has its roots in 2,500 years old Buddhist psychology. Currently, applications of mindfulness meditation are increasingly used as part of the treatment plan for people dealing with chronic pain, depression, anxiety, obsessive-compulsive disorder, drug addiction, eating disorders, sleep disorders and stress.

Mindfulness meditation aims at disengaging from the frantic activity of the thinking mind. While the thinking mind is busy producing mental commentary about your experience, or is fantasising about somewhere and/or sometime else, your actual experience takes place where you are, in the present moment. In mindfulness meditation you practise bringing your awareness back to, and remaining in contact with your actual, lived experience. Thus, your involvement in the activities of the thinking mind decreases, and the mind gradually begins to settle down and relax.

Breathing-mindfulness is the most fundamental of all mindfulness meditations. It can be practised at any time in any place and — as long as you are still breathing. However, you may find it easier to practise in a peaceful environment, particularly when you are new to the practice.

- Sit comfortably, yet preferably with a straight back, on a chair or on the floor. If you slump or lie down you may fall asleep, which may not be what you want.

- Let your eyes be half-closed, and your gaze point down somewhere in front of you, without looking at anything in particular. Or simply close your eyes.

- Notice any tensions in your body (e.g., around the eyes, forehead, cheeks, jaw, neck, shoulders, arms, chest, abdomen, back, buttocks, legs), and gently release them — let them go loose and limp.

- Then let your awareness be drawn to the breathing. Simply become aware of it, without changing it at all. Just let the breathing happen as it happens naturally by itself, and notice the gentle movement as the breath comes in … and goes out …

- Rather than observing the breathing from your head, as if from the outside of yourself, place your awareness at the very centre of the breathing, and feel the breathing happen throughout the whole body surrounding you. Feel yourself filling with air … and emptying … filling … and emptying … feel yourself expanding … and contracting …

- Stay with the gentle rhythm of expanding and contracting, and anytime that you discover that you have become engaged in thinking activity, just calmly return your awareness to the breathing. Don't get upset, don't waste time analysing the thoughts or how they came about, and don't waste energy fighting with the thinking mind. Simply disengage from it, by gently returning your awareness to breathing-mindfulness.

The benefits of meditation increase over time as you continue to practise. Just as with getting fit or losing weight, there are no quick fixes or shortcuts. Whether your first meditation leaves you feeling calm and peaceful, or not, you may need to meditate for several weeks before you can truly appreciate the benefits of meditation. Therefore, it is strongly recommended that you commit to regular meditation practice over an extended time period, to reap its full benefits.

Fit meditation into your daily routine at a regular time every day. Some people find meditating in the morning useful to start the day in the right frame of mind. Others prefer meditating after they come home from work, or at the end of the day to release the accumulated stresses of the day.

Formal mindfulness meditation can also be complemented with informal mindfulness practices, where you, even momentarily, disengage from the thinking activity, by drawing your awareness to your actual experience of the present moment — perhaps just noticing the patterns formed by the gaps between the leaves when looking at a tree, or listening to one particular instrument in (the background of) a piece of music, or paying specific attention to the feeling of your feet touching the ground as you walk.

Eating-mindfulness is an interesting example of informal mindfulness practice which may increase your appreciation of the flavours of your food immensely. The example below is formulated around eating a grape, but can be modified and used for anything that you eat.

- Hold a grape between your fingers, and notice how it feels to touch. Look carefully at its skin, and notice the patterns of veins under the skin. Also notice the point where the flower once was attached, and on the opposite end where the grape was once attached to the vine.

- Lift the grape to your nose, and find out if you can detect its fragrance, and whether the fragrance is different at one end compared to the other.

- Touch the grape to your lips and tongue, and notice how it feels and tastes, without biting into it.

- Listen to the sound, as you bite off a chunk of the grape. Notice the intensity of the flavour of the juice that is released into the front of your mouth. Also, look at the flesh of the piece of grape still in your hand. Notice its inner structure, including perhaps the seeds at the centre.

- Slowly move the piece of grape around in your mouth, and notice how different flavours appear on different parts of your tongue.

- As you begin to slowly chew, listen to the sound the chewing makes. Notice the flow of juices, and the intensity of the flavours on different parts of your tongue. Also, notice how your tongue automatically manoeuvres the pieces around your mouth, positioning them for chewing.

- Notice the urge to swallow, when the piece of grape has been chewed sufficiently, and when the swallowing happens, follow the movement all the way down toward your stomach, until it disappears out of awareness.

- Notice how your tongue continues to chase up any little pieces around your mouth and in between your teeth, and as all the pieces have been swallowed, remain aware of the lingering flavours.

- If you wish, you can extend this exercise to a full meditation, by continuing to be aware of any lingering flavours in your mouth, for as long as any remain. Anytime you discover that you have become engaged in thinking, disengage and again return to awareness of flavours.

If you are interested in further explorations into the practice of mindfulness meditation, and/or how it can be applied to various psychological conditions, contact a therapist who specialises in mindfulness-based therapy, and who has experience of their own mindfulness practice.

Lars Andersson

AVOIDING ROAD RAGE

Road rage describes a range of aggressive and dangerous driving behaviours directed at other road users. The phrase involves images of uncontrolled temper and the open display of anger and frustration. A common alternative term is aggressive driving with road rage seen to be a manifestation of extreme aggressive driving.

The psychology of road rage

Road rage perpetration, in its more serious forms, appears to share similar determining factors, frequency and symptom patterns with the condition known as Intermittent Explosive Disorder. A number of nonspecific psychological factors may contribute to road rage as well. These include the tendency to displace anger, and attribute blame to others, as well as unrewarding and stressful employment situations. Contributory factors may include high levels of general stress, displaced anger, illogical attributions, psychiatric disorders, as well as the strains of modern urban living. Alcohol and other drugs play their part in heightened aggression.

The sociology of road rage

The emotional experience of road rage is seen at least partly as a consequence of socialisation and acculturation. Emotions are integral to our self-concept and are used to give meaning and provide explanation for our lives. Emotions locate the individual within the world of social interaction because they are generated by interactions with others.

Common Signs of Road Rage:

In Self:

- Heightened perception of other road users' thoughtlessness.
- A feeling of urgency to complete the journey.
- Persistent anger at the perceived inadequacies of other drivers.
- A belief that you have priority and right of way on the road.
- Escalating verbally-abusive outbursts at other road users.

- Reducing the following distance and tailgating the vehicle in front.
- Flashing your headlights.
- Using the car horn to gain attention.
- Weaving and randomly surging and braking.
- Dangerous lane changing with or without signalling.
- Threatening and/or obscene gestures to other road users.
- Ongoing enraged eye contact.

In Others:

- Other vehicle consistently invades your safe driving space.
- Tailgating occurs whether you speed up or slow down.
- Horn blasts or light flashing directed at you by the other driver.
- Verbal abuse, curses, and threatening and/or obscene gestures are directed at you or your passengers.
- Physical injury or damage is threatened either verbally or by a weapon being displayed.
- Physical assault and/or vehicle damage is experienced with vehicles either moving or stopped.

Avoidance tips:

- Keep alert to signs of heightened tension within yourself as early warning indicators.
- Be aware that congested traffic conditions and stressful driving environments (e.g., lane breakdowns, heavy rain, peak hour congestion) can contribute to road rage. If possible and practical, pull out of the traffic to park and wait for conditions to ease or drive a less direct and more leisurely route to your destination
- Avoid arguments and highly charged conversations with your passenger/s as this can increase driver tension and stress. Play relaxing and calming music on the in-car audio system. Breathe deeply and calmly to relax. Use a relaxation intervention
- Pay attention to giving other road users courtesy gestures such as acknowledging a safe merge, indicating well in advance, and keeping a safe following distance.
- Avoid any non-essential use of lights and horn to express displeasure at others' behaviours.

- Avoid threatening or disapproving direct eye contact. Any eye contact made should be helpful, courteous, and aimed at making the other drivers behave similarly.

- Keep alert to recognise common signs of aggression and potential road rage in other drivers.

- If threatened, avoid eye contact and drive as normally as possible without excessive speed or braking to put other road users at risk.

- If persistently threatened in a stopped situation (e.g., red lights), raise windows and lock all doors. If possible, driver or passenger/s should dial for Police assistance. Note other driver details, car make and model, and registration number.

- If threatened in a driving situation, seek off-road staffed premises e.g., garage or restaurant and immediately ring Police. Ask staff to note details of the aggressor and his/her vehicle.

Remember that avoidance is better than confrontation. Recognise the early warning signs of aggression either within yourself, or in other road users, take a calm measured approach to de-escalate the situation, and leave potential conflict behind.

Dr Herbert Biggs

TIME MANAGEMENT

Listen to someone's conversation long enough and you will come across statements such as *I don't have enough time*, or *I need my time in my life*. I am sure you have heard it as well. Have you maybe said it yourself? The simple reality is that we all have the same time there is in the world! Each and every one of us has 24 hours in a day. No more. No less. It is what we do with our time that determines our effectiveness.

The issue of time management is really life management. Life is simply broken down to allocations of time. Time and life are both precious and limited commodities. So if you want more time in your life, or what appears to be more life, you have to get the most out of each day. That means getting the most output, simply by using 24 hours in the best possible way.

Here are seven of the simplest yet most powerful tips to get more done and get more time. — seven ways to get more life out of your day.

A Warning Though! If you are quick to dismiss these seven proven strategies as just another nice time management tip-sheet, here is a challenge for you. Starting today, do each one of these things daily and check them off as you do. A daily ritual, if you like. Do that for twenty-one consecutive days and watch how much more you get done.

Here we go

- Ask yourself this question, first up in the day. What is the most important thing to do today? It is the task that, if not done, has the most serious consequences. It could be the biggest loss you will make, or the greatest cause of emotional pain. If you are honest with yourself you will find that there will always be something that is the most important thing to do. Get serious with yourself. You may not like it, but you know what it is. Identify it.

- Do that most important thing, immediately. Or do it at the soonest time that's most practical. Best if you can to do it before anything else and then discipline yourself to complete it until it is finished. Rearrange your daily patterns if need be, so you can accomplish this — it's vital. Imagine how you would feel if, everyday, you started your day doing your most important task. How would you then feel for the rest of the day? How much more energy, patience, and peace or mind would you have for the rest of the day? It is better to be in front of the game rather than be behind, playing catch-up all day.

- Separate the urgent from the important. If we don't guard ourselves, the urgent things for the day sap us of all our productivity. Some urgent demands are important but if we stop and evaluate, we may find that they are not so important, and that they can wait. Try it. You don't have to answer every phone call, every email, or respond to every person who comes into your office. You must schedule a time in your day to do your most important tasks and block off, say "later", or schedule a time for all the urgent issues to be dealt with.

- Learn to say "no" to some things. Most people have an inability to say no. They get involved in more projects, committees, activities, and unimportant issues. Their mind loses focus, and it simply reacts to the next thing that comes along. Learning to say "no" — in a polite way — puts you back in control. You don't have to be rude. Simply decide to put the emphasis back on your most important task and schedule a later time for the other things, or eliminate them altogether if they really don't add value to your life. People will respect you more and will be less likely to waste your time in the future

- Work with a list. This one may sound obvious, however it is surprising the number of people who think in their head and never on paper. Use a to-do list, a diary, a whiteboard, anything you need, as long as you write things down and get organized. You can use a range of sophisticated devices, software and equipment to remind you, prioritise, and alert you of any tasks. If it is written down, it won't get lost, because even those with the best of memory can lose track of some things. Just feel the peace of mind from not constantly having it in your head for a change.

- Separate your list into ABCDE priority. Allocate a letter to each task you need to do, from A to E; 'A' represents the most important tasks. There can be serious negative consequences if you don't do an 'A' task. 'B' stands for something important; something you should do, but not something as important as an 'A' task. 'C' is for something that would be nice to do, 'D' is for task you can delegate to some else, and 'E' is for an unimportant task that can instead be eliminated from the list. The rule is doing your 'A's first, never letting a 'B' or 'C' tasks get in the way.

- Continually ask yourself this same question with every activity you engage in. Is this task that I am doing helping me move towards what's important: my goals, my values, my income, or is it taking me backward? It is either generating a benefit to you, or a waste of time. Be honest with your answer, and remember, don't kid yourself — you are only robbing your own time and life. If the answer is yes then it is adding value to you, if not, replace the activity with one that does.

Remember, we only have one true moment of power in our life, and it's in this moment called now. Treasure it. Don't waste it. Once it's gone, it is gone forever, and you never get that moment back. Besides, who knows how many moments of now we really have? Apply these simple principles to your life for the next 21 days, and prove to yourself once and for all how much potential and power you really do have.

Do it now!

Sam Tornatore

OVERCOMING PROCRASTINATION

Procrastination is essentially the act of putting off urgent and important tasks and replacing them with low-priority tasks.

Everybody falls victim to procrastination to some degree at some stage, however when it impedes normal day-to-day functioning, it can become a problem.

Not only does the delaying of high-priority tasks create problems in the delivery of outcomes, the associated guilt, stress and decrease in personal productivity compound to create a stressful cyclical dilemma.

People procrastinate for a number of reasons:

- Lack of personal interest in task.

- Lack of understanding of the reason for the task.

- Perceived lack of capability to perform the task.

- Real lack of capability/skills to perform task and therefore an avoidance altogether.

- Inability to distinguish between urgent and important; urgent and not important, non-urgent but important, and non-urgent and not important tasks.

- Lack of information required in order to prioritise tasks which leads to a lack of confidence to make a decision.

- Overload of tasks such that the person is overwhelmed, and consequently choose the easiest, menial tasks to perform.

- Personal fear of failure, or perhaps a fear of success.

- The desire and need for perfection — If I can't get this done perfectly, then I can't possibly do it!

- Rebellion against the standards or expectations imposed on you by others.

In order to reduce the procrastination in your life, consider the following:

- Establish a clear focus. This may refer to a specific task in question, or to your overall direction.

- Be clear with exactly what and how much you need to achieve in a certain timeframe.

- Prioritise tasks into *high, medium* and *low* depending firstly, on their level of Importance and then on their level of Urgency. If you do not have enough information to make this judgement, seek it out.

- In the event that procrastination is a result of a fear of failure or fear of success, face the reality of what life would be like if you were not afraid. What would it look like? What strategies would you need in place to handle the failure or success? In the best selling book *Who Moved My Cheese*, Spencer Johnson asks the pertinent question, What would you do if you weren't afraid?

- Refer back to your personal values when dealing with personal issues you are procrastinating about. Ask yourself if the task at hand is aligned with your values. If it isn't, why are you doing it? Follow your internal compass!

- Establish and communicate with involved others regarding their, and your, expectations and standards to ensure you are on the same page.

Bronwen Edwards

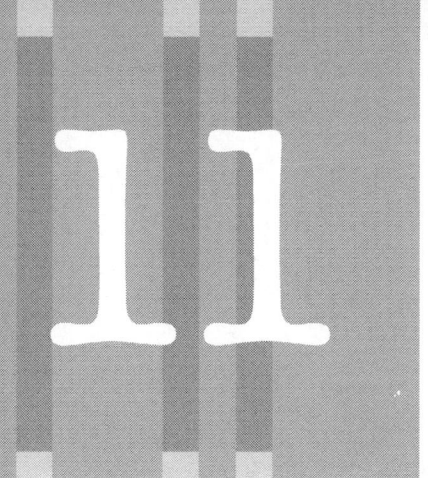

Addiction Issues

REDUCING THE HEALTH RISKS OF ALCOHOL

Alcohol has a complex role in Western societies. It serves a mixed role in the economy — generating employment, export income and tax revenue; while at the same time causing significant cost to industry through absenteeism, lost productivity and early retirement. It also plays a role in society — predominantly used for enjoyment, celebration, socialisation or relaxation; however alternatively used due to peer pressure, boredom, to escape, or to drown sorrows, amongst other things. Many people have tried alcohol, and many drink at levels causing few problems. Nonetheless, harmful alcohol use is responsible for a considerable burden of death, illness and injury. Alcohol-related harm is not limited to the drinker but has relevance for families and the broader community, as alcohol often plays a part in road accidents, violence, relationship break-ups, child abuse and neglect. As a result, the National Health and Medical Research Council reviewed a wide source of research literature and published guidelines so that individuals could make informed decisions about their alcohol consumption.

What do the guidelines recommend?

- For healthy men and women, drinking no more than two standard drinks on any day reduces your risk of harm from alcohol-related disease or injury over a lifetime.

- Drinking no more than four standard drinks on a single occasion reduces the risk of alcohol-related injury arising from that occasion.

- Children under 15 years of age are at the greatest risk of harm from drinking. Not drinking in this age group is especially important. For young people aged 15 to 17 years, the safest option is to delay drinking for as long as possible.

- For women who are pregnant, planning a pregnancy, or are breastfeeding, not drinking is the safest option.

What are the health risks?

The health risks from alcohol use increase progressively — the more you drink, the greater the risk. Drinking alcohol can affect your liver, or cause brain damage, heart disease, high blood pressure and increases your risk of many cancers. Alcohol impacts on mental illness as it can exacerbate symptoms of depression or anxiety, impair the effectiveness of antidepressant medications, and contribute to impulsive suicide attempts. If consumed during pregnancy, alcohol can cause a significant risk to unborn babies such as growth defects and brain development problems (e.g., Foetal Alcohol Spectrum Disorder). It may also increase your risk of injury through road trauma, falls, violence, and accidental death.

What is a standard drink?

A standard drink contains 10 grams of pure alcohol. It is important to understand that drink serving sizes are often more than one standard drink and that glass sizes can often vary. The label on an alcoholic drink container usually tells you the number of standard drinks in the container.

Tips to reduce the risk to your health when drinking

There are a number of things you can do to make sure you stay within low risk levels, not get out of control, but still have fun:

- Set yourself limits and ensure you stick to them.

- Drink slowly.

- Try drinks with a lower alcohol content.

- Start with non-alcoholic drinks and alternate with alcoholic drinks.

- Eat before or while you are drinking.

- Try including some non-alcoholic drinks in drinking rounds.

- Never leave your drink unattended.

- Plan safe transport home.

Tips for parents

Even if a teenager has already started drinking, parents can always positively influence drinking habits in the following ways:

- Set a good example in your own alcohol drinking.

- Provide education about alcohol laws and the possible consequences for breaking them.

- Inform teenagers that drinkers under 18 are at greatest risk of road accidents, injuries, violence and self-harm.

- Reward good behaviour if a responsible attitude towards alcohol is displayed.

- Discuss issues such as dealing with peer pressure to use alcohol and the problems with binge drinking.

Tips for breastfeeding women who choose to drink

- Avoid alcohol in the first month after your baby is born and until breast-feeding is well-established.

- After that, limit alcohol consumption to no more than two standard drinks a day.

- Don't drink alcohol immediately before breastfeeding.

- Consider expressing milk in advance if you want to drink alcohol.

What support is available?

There are many private and community services that can provide help if needed. If you or someone you know needs support and treatment to reduce or cease alcohol intake, you should contact:

- Your doctor.

- The local community health service.

- An alcohol or other drug helpline.

- A therapist with specialised training in alcohol.

Dr Matthew Hocking

SMOKING CESSATION

Approximately 20% of the population smokes tobacco, and we know that tobacco smoking is both physically and psychologically addictive. This means that your body experiences withdrawal symptoms (e.g., headaches) when you stop smoking. Nicotine is the dependence-forming substance in tobacco products. When you intake nicotine into your body, the positive experience you get from nicotine only lasts around one hour, so you inevitably need to smoke many cigarettes throughout the day to achieve the positive affects.

Researchers have found that the level of nicotine content of cigarettes you smoke is associated with the number of cigarettes you smoke. However, if you choose to smoke cigarettes with less nicotine, you will probably just smoke more of them. In one sense tobacco use is far more habit-forming than other drugs of dependence because you have to give yourself this drug many times per day.

Giving up cigarettes can be a challenging, and it often takes several attempts to stop.

Here are some key points to help you:

- Ask yourself if you are ready to give up smoking. If you're confused or ambivalent it means that you're thinking about giving up, but the pros of smoking outweigh the cons. Try making a list of these pros and cons and compare how many you have in each list. Sometimes you may have many reasons to keep smoking, but for you there can be just one very important reason to stop. Some people conclude that life is short, that smoking makes it shorter, and that they would rather stop smoking and have as much time on Earth to spend with their loved ones as possible.

- If you are ready to stop smoking, your GP can prescribe you a medication called Varenicline (sold as Champix or Chantix). This medication is specifically designed to stop the craving and desire to smoke. Your GP will ask you to choose a cessation date. You keep smoking while taking Varenicline for about one week, and then stop.

- Nicotine replacement such as nicotine gum, patches or inhalers is also a good option to consider. These approaches work by slowly reducing the amount of nicotine you take until you don't feel the need for nicotine anymore.

- All of the above approaches are effective ways to cease smoking. However if you add counselling to one of these interventions, your chances of being successful at giving up will increase.

Receiving professional counselling as well as using the above interventions is helpful if you lapse into smoking while you're trying to give up. People who lapse often experience the abstinence violation effect where you feel like a failure or guilty. Lapses are really only temporary setbacks and a professional counsellor can help you get back on track. You can do it.

Dr Jason Dixon

HARM MINIMISATION IN USING ALCOHOL AND OTHER DRUGS

Are you one of the 90% of the population who have consumed alcohol or another drug that can be abused? While most illegal substances, including alcohol, present little risk to health with only occasional use, for some people their use gets out of control. Prolonged use of alcohol and other drugs builds tolerance. This means that you have to take more of the drug to achieve the same affect. You may also find that although you used to use alcohol and other drugs for recreation, more of your daily activity is becoming more drug-focused. You may turn to alcohol and other drugs when times get tough because there are short-term rewards to using such as feeling good or feeling better, or both. The information below will assist you in minimising the harm associated with alcohol and other drug use.

Plan your use. Less use means less harm to your health, work, and social relationships. Plan to use only on the weekends. It's better to use on a Friday or Saturday, which will give your body and mind some chance to recover on Sunday. Put aside how much you are going to use and only use that much. It's better to tell yourself that, This is as good as it gets, rather than taking too much and dealing with the consequences later.

Choose carefully with whom you will use. This is by far the most important aspect of using safely. It is important that you trust the people you are using with and where you will consume alcohol or other drugs. Ask yourself if you can trust the people you're using with to help you if you get into trouble.

Eat before you use. No matter what substance you're taking, extra demands are put on your body when you use. This is especially the case with stimulants such as Speed or Ice. Your body needs more energy reserves from food when you use.

Important tips for reducing harm from alcohol and other drugs:

- While you may well be aware that alcohol affects your ability to drive or operate machinery safely, however consuming Cocaine and alcohol together your produces a chemical called Cocaethylene in your body. This chemical is toxic to your heart. It is better to restrict your alcohol consumption if you plan to use Cocaine.

- If you're going to use MDMA, sometimes called Ecstasy, being with people you trust, avoiding alcohol, drinking plenty of water, and taking breaks from dancing or other rigorous activity is important. This keeps your core body temperature down. Also it's often difficult to know what's contained in a pill so it's safer to take a ¼ or ½ a pill first to see how you will react before taking more.

- Prolonged Methamphetamine use, (Speed or Ice) is associated with malnutrition. It's important to consume healthy food beforehand, and also afterwards when you regain your appetite. It's also better to eat while you're taking. While you are using, consider making a milkshake with fruit, milk, yoghurt and other healthy ingredients that are easy to palate.

- There is debate as to how much alcohol consumption harms or promotes good health. It depends on gender, age, body weight, metabolism, and physical activity. For men and women it's best to consume no more than 2 standard drinks a day (and alcohol-free days are recommended).

- Opiates such as Codeine (an over-the-counter medication), and Heroin are substances that cause physical as well as psychological dependence. When you stop using substances such as these after a long period of use, your body can experience flu-like symptoms, stomach cramping, sweats, nausea, anxiety, agitation, vomiting, and diarrhoea.

- Such symptoms above are called physical withdrawal and can be life threatening if the main substance you've being using is alcohol or Benzodiazepines (e.g., Valium).

It is very important you seek professional help if concerned about withdrawal or any aspect of drug use that is chronic or out of control.

Dr Jason Dixon

GAMBLING ADDICTION

Gambling is most often perceived by society as a form of entertainment. Even in countries such as China where the Government prohibits casinos and public gambling, it is still widely perceived by the culture for thousands of years as a form of recreation and leisure. When gambling becomes problem gambling or it becomes an addiction, then this behaviour often creates a devastating impact for the gambler and for those who are close to them. Problem gambling can drive people to lie, rob, and steal in order to get money to maintain their gambling behaviour. In doing so, problem gamblers destroy relationships and trust with their family and friends, break laws, and put themselves and their family into financial crises.

Problem gambling often starts with the reward of winning in the beginning. Problem gamblers become lured by the money and the excitement of winning and they continue to gamble with the hope of winning more money and obtain more excitement. When they start to lose, they become obsessed in trying all sorts of gambling strategies and approaches to chase their losses which then leads to greater and quicker losses. Some gamblers will even start to creatively come up with reasons and theories about why they lost or won and how they should conduct their gambling strategies next time. These beliefs often enter the realm of irrationality and superstition, yet they keep problem gamblers in the vicious addiction cycle.

The feeling of guilt is prevalent amongst problem gamblers, and the common reasons are; guilt about the money they have lost; guilt of maintaining secrecy of their addiction from their family and friends; guilt of maintaining the lies they have made to those that have emotionally and financially supported them; and judging of their gambling addiction and knowing how destructive it is in continuing the addiction. Stress, anxiety, depression, and poor physical health can be typical symptoms from ongoing obsession and compulsion to gamble. In some cases, problem gamblers also engage in substances such as cigarettes, alcohol, and illicit substances to help them feel better and less stressed.

There are many theories on why people become addicted to gambling and they contribute in some degree toward a very complex picture that is problem gambling. These theories include:

- Learned behaviour from a significant other such as a family member or friend.

- Genetic predisposition that makes people more prone to becoming problem gamblers.

- The thrill of winning.

- Psychological addictiveness of the gambling game itself.

- The need to chase losses when they lose more than they intended to.

Most problem gamblers have at some stage tried to stop gambling out of guilt and desperation, and they would be successful for periods of time. However, when the urge to gamble builds up and their will and determination subsides, they inevitably get drawn back. Some problem gamblers who seek intervention from a therapist to help them stop also do not have much success in stopping permanently; they tend to want a quick fix solution. After one or two sessions with the professional, they might start to realise there is no quick, magical solution that the professional can prescribe to miraculously stop them from gambling. Then they start to lose interest in continuing their treatment and stop going to the sessions.

Giving up the gambling addiction is difficult and requires more than determination. The willingness to accept help from family, friends, and professionals is vital in breaking the cycle. If you or someone you care about is trapped by gambling addiction and you or your loved one want to give up gambling, the following points are worthwhile:

- *Be clear that trying to give up the gambling addiction on your own is very difficult.* Even if you are able to give up gambling for some time, the chance of relapse is almost certain to happen. Be open-minded to accept help from people you trust and know that they will be committed in helping you.

- *Self-barring or self-exclusion from the gambling venues is an option you can take.* You may be able to access the self-exclusion application form for your State on the Internet. You can contact one of the venue managers and speak with them about your intention to self-exclude and they will assist. If abstinence is your choice, you may join your local Gamblers Anonymous group for ongoing support. These groups are empowering when you are giving and receiving support from people you share a clear common goal with. Your emotional struggles with gambling are acknowledged and validated in the group and the sense of connection with members means you would not be isolated in your quest to quit gambling.

- *Consider involving someone you trust to assist you with financial management.* If this needs to be more extreme, it may mean you give them control of your money for the period that you are susceptible to relapsing. Thus you are only allocated an amount of money for living expenses but not for gambling.

- *If you are in debt and have difficulty meeting payments, it could be useful to consult a financial counsellor from a community organisation.* They help you with money managing strategies and make suggestions with regard to your dealing with people and institutions that you are indebted to.

- *Seek counselling for your gambling addiction.* Many community organisations provide free gambling counselling service — so use them! Remember it takes many attempts to stop gambling, and when the gambler has finally stopped gambling, their relationships and financial matters are in tatters. There are gambling helplines that have 24 hour service and consultants will be able to refer you to your nearest gambling help service and other services such as financial and relationship counselling.

- *Understand that gambling is often a way of emotional coping that you may not be fully aware of.* You need to create other ways to support your emotional self as removing this coping mechanism (i.e., gambling) may make you feel vulnerable as you quit your habit. For example, many problem gamblers who are addicted to poker machines report a sense of being in a trance or a numbed state where nothing else matters. They feel so relaxed, soothed, and at ease such that they do not know or care how much they are gambling, until all the money is all gone and guilt and self-blame sets in.

- *If you are addicted to poker machines, some questions you could ask yourself:*

    What is it in life that I am trying to soothe and relax from?

    What are some stressful feelings that I often feel but I do not feel them when I am playing poker machines?

    How long have I had these feelings?

    What do I feel when I am right in the midst of playing?

    Is there any anger, frustration, grief, and/or sense of purposelessness that I have been sitting with that I do not know how to resolve, but that gambling helps to alleviate those feelings?

Explore these questions deeply and you will gain valuable insights into how you use and maintain your gambling behaviour. Games like horse racing and casino card games evoke stimulation and excitement when you win. Problem gamblers addicted to these games report a great sense of mastery and control when they win. They feel they have been masterful in generating their game plan that has beat the system. If you are addicted to such games ask yourself:

In general, how excited and stimulated do I feel in life?

How much control do I feel I have in creating the life I desire?

How strong is my sense of purpose and meaning in being alive?

How would I experience life in general if I did not have the excitement and stimulation I get from gambling?

What feelings am I not allowing myself to experience when I put so much focus on gambling?

It is recommended you explore the self-reflective questions above with a therapist who has the professional expertise to facilitate you to explore deeper into your emotions and thinking. Whilst practical strategies are important in helping you break the addiction, abstinence from gambling is usually only long-lasting if there is awareness and insight into how you use gambling for emotional coping to the point where it has become a destructive problem.

Webb Lin

INTERNET ADDICTION

The Internet is an amazing device designed to establish instant contact throughout the world. Like all modern conveniences, it is not without a dark side, and that is the side of addiction. This is a new problem, in some ways similar to other addictions, and in other ways a new frontier. The types of addictions are numerous but the common ones involve social media, games, and pornography.

Social media addiction is more common among women but can effect anyone. It includes Facebook and similar sites, chat-rooms, and virtual life experiences. Game addiction can be fantasy play, gambling, or video games which are played either alone or against others. Pornography addition, which is a predominantly male problem, involves visual stimulation via images, movies, or other material which can be free or on paid sites.

While the reasons for becoming addicted are many and varied, there are two main pathways; one is as a way of dealing with (or avoiding dealing with) emotions, and the other is for arousal seeking.

Signs of addiction

It has been said that admitting a problem is 90% of the solution. The point where normal use becomes addiction is subtle as it happens across time with a gradual blurring of the boundaries so most people do not readily accept they are addicts. The key indicator is when the behaviour is interfering with day-to-day real life. Whether that is wasted hours and failing to fulfil normal tasks; chronic tiredness from late nights or early starts; fights with spouse or parent as they feel disconnected from you; fights of jealousy about your online friends; the behaviour intruding into work-time; or day-dreaming about the next fix, are some of the signs that you have crossed the line.

Irrational beliefs

To maintain a behaviour, you develop thought patterns which enable justification of what you are doing. I am not hurting others, it's just for fun, I'll catch up the sleep on the weekend and I'll miss out if I am not online. Make list of all your beliefs about the behaviour on sheet of paper that has line down the middle. On the other side, write all the reasons why the belief is faulty. This is beginning of challenging your false reasoning.

The ABC of the problem: All patterns of behaviour have an antecedent or trigger (A), the behaviour (B), and a consequence or payoff (C). Think about the last time you were online. What was the trigger (A)? What did you do (B)? What happened afterwards (C)?

A — Sometimes it is an emotional trigger like a fight with a partner or feeling depressed; other times the trigger may be the sight of a computer. Knowing what triggers it, means you can address the cause. If emotionally triggered you need alternate ways of dealing with the emotions — call a friend, do counselling, have a walk, write feelings in a journal, or something else.

B — The patterns of the behaviour help you manage the situation. Was it night or day? Could you stop? How did you get started? Use this information to rearrange your life. Set a time limit on the computer; make a rule not to use the computer at night; check your emails only in the morning; put the computer in the lounge; go to bed at the same time as your spouse; or some other means of managing the action.

C — How did you feel afterwards? If feeling guilty or negative, seek help when feeling bad. If you feel lonely, make some real friends. Also consider how you addressed the guilty feelings. Did you engage in another self-destructive behaviour? Similarly, you may be using the Internet to escape depression, or the problems from the use may be the cause of depression.

Giving up is difficult. You may relapse. However, if you try these ideas and are still relapsing, seek professional help as early as possible.

Dr Phil Watts

INTERNET PORNOGRAPHY ADDICTION

The use of pornography is an emotive issue which society views across a range of values including it is a sin or evil, through to whatever someone wants to do in the privacy of their own home is okay. Irrespective of your belief, there are four important benchmarks to know you have a problem:

- The pornography controls you so you cannot stop even if you try.
- It is interfering in your life or the life of those you love.
- You are engaging in behaviour that is against you normal moral beliefs.
- You are engaging in behaviour which is illegal.

If any one of these four indicators is present, you have a serious problem.

For many people addicted to pornography, there is an important cycle. When online they go into an altered state of awareness. I call this the tunnel. Using the images creates a level of arousal which feels good and numbs reality. A user can stay in the tunnel for hours. However, when out of the tunnel the reality feels negative, lonely and isolating. There may be guilt. There will be mounting problems. Therefore, the cycle is a downward spiral because depressive feelings increase, self-esteem is shot, and problems increase. Often this either creates, or makes worse, symptoms of depression. And the solution you are using when in this state? To look at more pornography!

Another important consideration is that each time you think a thought you brain lays down a neural pathway. Each look at pornography activates a pathway. Over time your brain is altered so as to create not a pathway but a six-lane super-motorway! These changes are permanent even if you do not activate the path again. These pathways may deteriorate if never activated, but they will never disappear. The more you have used, the harder it is to give up.

These two aspects lead to the critical realisation that any activation of the pathway will make it worse. Once in the tunnel, the altered awareness makes it difficult to stop, therefore never go near the tunnel. There can be no controlled viewing, only abstinence or avoidance. To get your life back you must completely cease using pornography.

Ultimately there are two parts to addressing the problem. The first is management. The second aspect is addressing the underlying need for pornography. It is likely that professional help is needed for the second.

Management begins with cleaning the computers; installing protective programs (giving passwords to someone else); and moving computers to a public area in the house. Triggers can be external (e.g., seeing a magazine cover in a shop), external (e.g., a fight with your partner), or habit (e.g., checking emails then looking at pornography). Until you can understand the triggers, you will be out of control. Each relapse needs to be an experience to learn from. Even if you do not go online, analysing the times when you get an urge to go online can be helpful in understanding the emotional patterns.

The ABC of the problem: All patterns of behaviour have an antecedent or trigger (A), the behaviour (B), and a consequence or payoff (C). Think about the last time you were online. What was the trigger (A)? What did you do (B)? What happened afterwards (C)?

A — Sometimes it is an emotional trigger like a fight with a partner or feeling depressed; other times the trigger may be the sight of a computer. Knowing what triggers it, means you can address the cause. If emotionally triggered you need alternate ways of dealing with the emotions — call a friend, do counselling, have a walk, write feelings in a journal, or something else.

B — The patterns of the behaviour help you manage the situation. Was it night or day? Could you stop? How did you get started? Use this information to rearrange your life. Set a time limit on the computer; make a rule not to use the computer at night; check your emails only in the morning; put the computer in the lounge; go to bed at the same time as your spouse; or some other means of managing the action.

C — How did you feel afterwards? If feeling guilty or negative, seek help when feeling bad. If you feel lonely, make some real friends. Also consider how you addressed the guilty feelings. Did you engage in another self-destructive behaviour? Similarly, you may be using the Internet to escape depression, or the problems from the use may be the cause of depression.

If your partner is using pornography?

Partners are often tremendously damaged when they find their spouse is using pornography. As many women have difficulty separating sex from love, they often see the partner's use as a betrayal. It is often seen as an affair. For most men it has nothing to do with their partner, it is an emotional coping strategy due to a lack within themselves. For women, they need to know that it is not about them. However, the deception can be a problem for partners. They feel that they have been lied to as the partner lead a double life. Complete honesty is necessary. As a couple, relationship counselling will be necessary.

What do you do if you find your teen using pornography? As exposure to Internet pornography is now happening in the early teens due the ubiquitous nature of internet, you should teach children in a preventative manner. Of course teens are curious however, take the situation seriously if you catch them viewing pornography. It is easier to prevent than cure because once the brain is changed, it is tough going back.

Dr Phil Watts

CODEPENDENCY IN RELATIONSHIPS

Most people are self-reliant and have relationships that are mutually support-ive. However some people get trapped in unique ways of relating to others that end up in conflict and suffering. You may have heard the word codepen-dent if you know someone who has had a drug or alcohol problem. People who are codependent become absorbed in the problems of the person with an addiction and ignore a lot of their own needs, living instead mainly in reaction to the behaviours of the other person. However codependency-like behaviour is not restricted to people in relationships with someone with substance dependency. In fact, contrary to what some people say, codependency is not a disease and not a clinical term. Nevertheless it is helpful to think in terms of codependency to help people work through dysfunctional relationships and improve quality of life.

Ask yourself these questions to explore if you are in a codependent relationship:

- Is there someone in your immediate family who has had an ongoing problem in life such as, relationship problems with friends and coworkers, alcohol and other drugs?

- Is your quality of life dependent on how well the other person is doing?

- When the other person in your life is not doing well, does your own self-esteem suffer or you feel depressed?

- Do you self-sacrifice to try and make the other person feel better and then you feel good about yourself?

- Do you feel that you're always ready to help others (enable) but find that when you have a problem there is no one to go to for support?

- If you answered "yes" to some of these questions, there are several things you can do that will bring to you a sense of freedom, confidence, and improved quality of life.

- Clearly define what problems the other person has. Repeatedly remind yourself that it is their problem not yours!

- Altruism, the desire to help others, is a good way to improve your general sense of wellbeing, but self-sacrificing altruism (sometimes called the Martyr Syndrome), ultimately leads to inequity of wellbeing in your relationships.

- Contemplate the idea that selfishness is a virtue. In other words, sometimes you need to be a bit selfish or self-nurturing so that you have emotional reserves to help others. Helping people is a wonderful experience with many benefits, but only when you are responsible in meeting your own needs.

- When the important person with the problem in your life makes unreasonable requests, establish a relational boundary by calmly and sensitively saying that you can't help them. Be strong and don't give in to the emotional tactics the person you love will use. They will eventually give up on draining you emotionally.

- When you've successfully repeated step four above on many occasions, and after some time, the loved one will give up seeking or demanding unreasonable support from you.

- Be sensitive to the chance when you can caringly suggest that your loved one should seek professional help. This needs to be done in a calm, sensitive, and respectful way. Make sure you are emotionally ready and confident before you try this. You might have to be patient and make several attempts before they seek help.

- Don't spend time researching and arranging appointments for the other person! Empower them by asking inquisitive questions about helping professionals in general. If you sense any resistance, calmly drop the topic.

Seek support yourself from a counsellor who will give you strategies to help maintain your own mental wellbeing despite the problems your loved one is working through.

Dr Jason Dixon

12

Abuse, Neglect, Violence, Bullying and Crime Issues

- Child and Adolescent Abuse and Neglect
- The Problem of Domestic Violence
- Men Helping End Family Violence
- Becoming Free from Domestic Violence
- Childhood Bullying
- Cyberbullying
- Sexual Assault
- Dealing with Traumatic Incidents
- Victims of Crime

CHILD AND ADOLESCENT ABUSE AND NEGLECT

Child abuse is defined as any act, or acts, by a parent or caregiver that inflicts harm on, or threatens harm against, a child or adolescent. This harm can involve physical, sexual, psychological and or emotional maltreatment or neglect. It may consist of single or multiple incidents. The failure by an adult to act to prevent the known harming of a child by another person is also deemed abusive. Child abuse describes acts perpetrated against a child or young person by someone older, usually an adult, or where there is a significant age gap (e.g., an older sibling, relative, neighbour or babysitter). It constitutes an abuse of the power held by the adult or older person over someone who is younger, weaker, dependent and or vulnerable. The perpetrator may be a stranger but more often than not, it is someone known to the child (e.g., a parent, relative or family friend). Both offenders and victims can be either male or female. Children and adolescents from every background can be the victims of abuse, regardless of class, culture, race, gender and sexual orientation. In Australia, statistics suggest that 1 in 5 children will be sexually assaulted by the time they turn 18.

Physical abuse involves aggression directed towards a child or adolescent by a parent or caregiver. It may involve punching, kicking, shoving, slapping, burning, hair pulling, stabbing, choking or shaking. The signs of physical abuse vary between individuals and in some children there may not be obvious clues that they have been intentionally harmed. However, more obvious signs include physical injuries such as bruises, cuts, broken bones, brain damage or even death. Shaking a baby or child can result in shaken baby syndrome and may result in a variety of physical injuries, brain damage or death.

Psychological and or emotional abuse may include name-calling, ridicule, harming or threatening to harm a pet, criticism, humiliation, withholding communication, love and or affection. Children may blame themselves, develop extremely low self-esteem, display a learned helplessness functioning style and struggle to trust any adult caregivers (such as a teacher). This can also lead to difficulty in developing and maintaining healthy relationships as an adult.

Neglect is indicated when a parent or caregiver fails to adequately provide for a child's physical, emotional, educational and/or medical needs. For example, failure to provide adequate food, clothing, hygiene, medical care when required, nurturing and affection all constitute neglect. Neglect may be indicated by malnutrition, failure to thrive, sleep deprivation and fatigue, dental decay and or poor hygiene.

Child sexual assault is a form of child abuse whereby an adult or older person engages a child in acts of a sexual nature for their own gratification. Such acts may include indecent exposure to a child, exposing a child to pornographic material or forcing or allowing them to witness sexual activity, sexual contact with a child including attempting to engage in sexual intercourse with a child or using a child to produce pornography. Sexual assault may be indicated by physical symptoms such as sexually transmitted infections, genital and or anal soreness, bleeding or injury. Post-pubescent adolescent girls may be put at risk of unwanted pregnancy. Some children may display sexualised, age-inappropriate behaviours such as excessive masturbation or sexually acting out with peers, and may utilise force or coercion.

Other indicators include behavioural issues such as aggression, social withdrawal, sleeping problems (such as nightmares, insomnia related to fear around night-time or the bedroom), flashbacks, disruptions to appetite, self-harming, and suicidal thoughts amongst others. Emotional symptoms may include anger, anxiety, shame, guilt, confusion, depression, dissociation and fear.

Some children and young people may have experienced multiple forms of abuse, physical, psychological, emotional and or sexual. The impact of such trauma can include both short and long term psychological problems which can impair the child's academic, occupational and or social functioning. Children may develop symptoms of post-traumatic stress disorder or other psychiatric disorders, such as eating disorders. They may fail to report the abuse as they may be pre-verbal, feel threatened by their abuser, feel confused or guilty or fear that they won't be believed amongst other reasons.

How to respond

Most parents and caregivers have an innately strong desire to protect their children from harm. The idea that someone may intentionally harm your child is devastating; especially if it is someone you trust and perhaps love. Some parents and caregivers may also be aware that some of their own behaviours are inappropriate and in these cases it may feel impossible to talk to anyone about these concerns for fear of the potential legal repercussions. If this is the case, it is highly recommended that you seek help from a psychologist or therapist to work on healthy parenting techniques or issues such as substance abuse, to develop healthier boundaries between yourself and your children. If you are still unsure, try a confidential telephone counselling service where you can get support and advice whilst remaining anonymous. Remember, the safety and wellbeing of your child is your priority.

The most important thing to do if you have concerns that a child or young person may be at risk of harm is to put their needs first. Children are extremely vulnerable and depend on their parents and caregivers for safety and affection. Children need to know that when they confide in us they will be believed. If a child or young person tells you that someone has hurt them in the past or is currently hurting them you need to let them know you believe them and you will try to help make them safe. Do not interrogate your child and try to force them to answer questions. This can be emotionally overwhelming for the child and may also contaminate any future legal proceedings. If there is an allegation that someone is abusing a child or young person, this must be reported to the police or appropriate child protection authorities in your state or territory for investigation. Your role as a parent is to support your child emotionally.

Prevention

It is strongly recommended that all children and young people receive personal safety education primarily as an attempt to prevent abuse by teaching children about their bodies, their rights, and appropriate versus inappropriate behaviour. Remember, knowledge is power, and giving children an age-appropriate understanding of what is and is not okay, and more importantly what to do if someone is harming them, empowers our children. It is also important to educate children who have unfortunately already experienced abuse, to help lessen their vulnerability to re-victimisation.

Treatment and recovery

Many parents or caregivers feel that they are simply not equipped to respond appropriately if they discover that their child has been abused or harmed. However, it is important to remember that your child needs you right now. You are the adult and you can help them. The best way to help them is to let them know that you believe them and will try to keep them safe by reporting the abuse or assault to the authorities. It may be beneficial to speak to a counsellor or psychologist, as these professionals can assist you to adequately and appropriately support to your child. They can also give you practical strategies to assist with specific issues such as depression, anger outbursts, sleeping or eating issues that have arisen as a result of the abuse. There is no doubt that being abused or neglected is a traumatic experience for a child. However, when a child feels heard and believed, when steps are taken to protect them from further harm and when the child receives the appropriate care and support, it is possible that they can recover. The abuse does not need to define the child —it is not who they are, but rather something terrible that they have experienced.

Remember, that they still have their whole life ahead of them and with the right support they can still enjoy a happy and healthy future. Access the help that is available for both you and your child and never lose hope.

Sam Vidler

THE PROBLEM OF DOMESTIC VIOLENCE

In the 1970s, social activists and advocates became increasingly concerned about the level of men's violence towards women, and the lack of social and legal responses that would keep women and children safe and protected, and would hold offenders answerable for their actions. Victims were isolated, living in fear and shame, under threat and trapped in their own homes. More often than not, society at-large either turned a blind eye, kept its head in the sand, or did not act with authority to keep victims safe and offenders contained. In the last 40 years, our understanding of the phenomenon we call domestic violence has expanded. In that time, our social and criminal justice interventions have developed to the point where we have legislation against domestic violence, training in appropriate criminal justice responses, shelters and services for victims, rehabilitation programs for offenders, and a more cohesive community awareness of and intervention for this extensive problem in our society. However, we still have much work to do. Still much domestic violence is unreported and underestimated in our community, or else responded to ineffectively and therefore unsafely. Our systems still let victims down, not prioritising their safety.

Results from police statistics and outcomes of international research show that this is a deeply entrenched socio-legal and public health problem and is widely spread across cultural, religious, and economic levels. Some have not unrealistically called this problem an epidemic. It is an epidemic which is gender-based. Predominantly, domestic violence is a pattern of men's violence towards and abuse of women and children. This is not to say that all men are violent. Of course that is not the case. It is to conclude though from the evidence that men are the perpetrators of most of the violence in our communities, against other men as well as women. One in four women (maybe higher) will be a victim of domestic violence and/or sexual assault over the course of her life. This statistic is unacceptable and cannot be tolerated. This is an issue of highest priority because of its human rights and social justice implications.

Effects on women and children

Domestic violence includes physical, sexual, social, economic, spiritual, and emotional abuse. As well as the physical assault on women's and children's bodies, there is the serious effect on mental health. Women who are victims can develop low self-worth, depression, anxiety, suicidal behaviour, drug and alcohol abuse, and post-traumatic stress disorder. Abused women are at higher risk of miscarriages, stillbirths, and infant deaths. Infants of abused women can manifest poor health, weight problems, difficulty eating and sleeping, and excessive irritability and screaming. Early school-age children can exhibit high levels of distress and adjustment difficulties. They can show signs of fear and terror and become withdrawn, feeling constantly on alert and unsafe. School age children can develop learning difficulties and social problems. They may blame themselves for the violence. Boys may become aggressive and girls withdrawn or dependent. Teenagers who witness or experience violence at home can express rage, shame, and betrayal. They may manifest these emotions by oppositional behaviour and delinquency, running away from home, sexual promiscuity, truancy or dropping out of school completely, or by using drugs and alcohol. Alarmingly, girls are at increased risk of becoming victims of abuse in dating relationships, and boys are at increased risk of becoming abusive men in adulthood.

Keeping victims safe

As a society, the safety of our members is a priority. We cannot overlook, or ignore the safety of any sector of society, women included. Every year in our community, people die from domestic violence; people are severely physically injured and damaged emotionally. Children's healthy development is jeopardised. Lives are torn apart. Women and children are traumatized and trapped. Unless we put a stop to this wave of violence, the effects will be felt well into the future through the intergenerational transmission of violence. The next generation of abusers will learn their trade.

Victims, when they seek help, need reassurance that his violence is not her fault and that she does not deserve this treatment. Victims need to know that help is available and that a caring professional will stand by her and support her in the difficult and dangerous process of separating (if that is what she wants to do). Strong and safe police responses, nurturing and compassionate women's services, rigorous court support and safety planning, as well as appropriate sanctions and strict conditions for offenders, will go a long way towards ensuring victims are validated and respected. Victims need a sanctuary of safety and support in which to rebuild their lives free from violence and abuse, where safe housing, medical services, childcare, education and employment opportunities are available.

Holding offenders accountable

Men who are violent towards the women and children in their lives use physical and sexual violence, and other abusive strategies, to coercively control their partners. Men will use violence to stop arguments, to stop their partners from doing something, and to punish them for disobedience. Men will use violence and abuse to get what they want, when they want it, how they want it, or to punish their partners for not getting it. Men's violence to their intimate partners is not about loss of control, or about seeing red, or about his being stressed out, or even about the booze. These are all excuses and fail to address the core of this behaviour. Men's violence is always chosen behaviour, it is intentional, instrumental, strategic, deliberate, and purposeful. It wins for him male dominance, privilege, and entitlement over women and children. He believes that this is his right. Men's violence towards women is not just about individual acts or incidents of abuse or physical violence. It is a whole pattern, context, environment and atmosphere of intimidation, threat, coercion and control over women and children. It is about what is around and between the individual acts of violence as well, not just the isolated acts.

Sanctions for violence

Denying the offender's violence, trivializing the damage it does to the victim, and blaming her for provoking him, does nothing to help a man change his abusive beliefs and behaviours. If we deny it, minimize it, and blame her, as a society we have confirmed him in his violence, and further made our society an unsafe place for her, and for others. Swift and certain court referral to an accredited behaviour change program, which adheres to strong standards, and is embedded in a collaborative community response where there is effective criminal justice involvement, consequences for non-compliance and recidivism, and close monitoring of offenders, has a better than even chance of leading to behaviour change for participants, and safety for victims. Men who complete programs that are comprehensive and which are components of collaborative community responses to domestic violence have lower recidivism rates. For a community to speak out and side with the victim, to be active and aware is to create safe systems and safe society for all. That sends a clear and loud message to offenders that we do take his violence seriously and will act to end it. To the victim, the message received is that her safety matters and that she will be protected. Victims then become survivors.

Dr Brian Sullivan

MEN HELPING END FAMILY VIOLENCE

Violence against women has been called the most shameful violation of human rights in our world today. Men cannot claim to be making real progress towards equality, development and peace, if violence against women and children continues at the present alarming rates in our society. While it is true that men are the predominant perpetrators of violent and abusive behaviour, the good news is that most men are not violent and abusive. Most men are respectful and considerate of women and children. And most men are not comfortable or in agreement with other men who are violent, sexually, physically and psychologically to women and children. But most men do not know what to do or how to go about expressing their unwillingness to support a violent status quo toward women and children. Most men do not know how they can intervene in an effective and safe way for all. Most men want to be allies and advocates for women and children, but many men are static bystanders and witnesses to the violence around them, paralysed by fear and silenced by confusion and uncertainty. The following points offer some direction to men who are not violent and abusive as to how they can respond to other men's abusiveness and how they can be allies and advocates for the human rights of women and children.

Learn the facts

We should be aware that this is a social problem for many women and children in our society, not the isolated misery of an unfortunate few. Domestic violence and sexual assault have been called epidemics in our society, and this is men's violence directed towards women and children. Statistics has shown this is a serious problem for 1 in 4 women over the course of their lifetime. These are not nameless faces and anonymous statistics. These women are someone's mother, sister, aunt, grandmother, daughter, colleague, and friend. They are in your neighbourhood. For women, the end result of such behaviour can be: fear and intimidation; social entrapment and isolation; mental health problems, from depression, anxiety, drug and alcohol abuse, post-traumatic stress disorder, to suicidal ideation. For children, the effects of violence and abuse can lead to learning difficulties, social, emotional and behavioural problems, post-traumatic stress disorder, future relational problems, and sadly in too many cases, for both women and children, serious injury and even death.

Listen to women and girls

Allow yourself to be guided by them, to understand them, and to interact with them as equals and get to know them as human persons. This especially holds for the women in your life: your mother, your sister, your daughter, your partner, your wife, and others. Spend time with the women in your life. Give them priority. Husbands can arrange to be with their wives to listen to her needs. Dads can make time for their daughters to listen to their hopes and aspirations, and encourage them in those.

Believe that this is a men's issue

Believe that domestic violence and sexual assault are men's issues. The harsh reality is the men are the predominant offenders of these crimes. Associate with like-minded men who are not violent and abusive and discuss how you can contribute to ending gender-based violence. The harsh reality will only be transformed if the majority of men allow their resistance to other men's violence be heard and seen.

Examine your own attitudes and watch your language

What are your beliefs, behaviours and attitudes when it comes to men's roles and women's roles in our society? Should you have entitlements and privileges over women and children because you are a man? How do you talk about women when you are in the company of other men? Using terms such as *bitch, skank, slut*, is not respectful and does not build equality. Does your language need to change? Language change can lead to changes in thinking and behaviour.

Be an ally to women who are working against violence

You can do this by funding and supporting a domestic violence shelter or a sexual assault service. Be a part of a rally for non-violence or against sexual assault. Men's presence is a sign of solidarity with women and a stand against the problem. It is a powerful symbol to men who are violent and abusive towards women and children that the majority of men do not support such behaviour and beliefs.

Refuse to fund sexism

Do not buy into music, magazines, DVDs, websites that objectify, depersonalise, brutalise, and disrespect women. Sexism is a violation of human rights. Sexism of any kind in any way does not help men and boys to relate respectfully to women, and it can form in men rigid negative attitudes and unreal expectations about women in their lives. This can in turn lead to unhealthy and even dangerous behaviour in ways of interacting with women.

Distance yourself

When you find you are part of conversations, jokes, and comments that demean, humiliate or disrespect women, distance yourself. Would you like someone talking about your mother, sister, or daughter in that way? If you stay and say nothing, you could be colluding with those other's attitudes. Take a stand and speak out.

Mentor boys and adolescents

Take opportunities to teach and mentor boys and young men how they can grow to be men without demeaning, disregarding, or disrespecting women and girls. Collaborating and cooperating with women and girls as equals is an important aspect of being a respectful man.

Encourage men to seek help

If you know men who are abusive, aggressive and hostile to women and children, encourage and urge them as a friend to seek professional help to change their behaviour. Gently ask him: *What kind of man he wants to be? How is what he is doing showing he loves his partner? How does he want his children to remember him?* This may not only improve the lives of those women and children, but the men who are behaving that way as well.

Support human rights and social justice

Violence against women is the most shameful violation of human rights in our world today. Domestic violence, sexual assault, and child abuse are urgent human rights and social justice issues. They constitute illegal and criminal behaviour. They are not just personal problems but societal problems that we as men can do something about. Ending domestic violence and sexual assault will mean a safer and healthier world for all. Refuse to be a silent bystander and don't believe for one moment that you can't do anything to alleviate this problem.

Dr Brian Sullivan

BECOMING FREE FROM DOMESTIC VIOLENCE

Violence can occur in any relationship and in any setting. However it is predominately men's violence towards women and children in intimate spousal-like relationships that is commonly referred to as domestic violence. A man's violence and abuse towards his partner may be perceived by some to be normal or even trivial. It is in fact and in law, illegal, unethical, serious, and always harmful to those who experience such abuse. It can have serious health consequences for women and children including homicide and suicide. Women do not usually overestimate their risk in being in a relationship with a man who is violent towards them. Frequently, though, they may underestimate the risk. If you are afraid of your partner; feel powerless in standing up to him, feel coerced to do things that you do not want to do, feel controlled, manipulated, and oppressed by him, if you are called names, insulted and humiliated by him, if you as a mother, wife, lover, woman are devalued and belittled and this is a pattern over time – then you may be a victim of domestic violence and abuse. Abuse can take many forms: physical; sexual; psychological; financial; social; and spiritual. You do not deserve this abuse; you are not responsible for causing the abuse and it isn't your responsibility to stop it. You are not alone. Research shows that 1 in 4 women over the course of their lifetime will be victims of domestic violence and sexual assault.

Healthy relationships are safe relationships

Mothering through domestic violence is a risky business. For you and your children to live a preferred future, his violence has to stop or you have to extricate yourself from his abuse. His abuse is about controlling and oppressing you. It is not loving, respectful, or intimate behaviour. You are not being treated as his equal. You are not being treated justly, or fairly. Your rights as a human being are not being respected. This is not the way a healthy relationship should be. Domestic violence affects your own physical and mental health. As well as physical injury, anxiety, depression, suicidal thoughts, trauma, drug and alcohol use can be the symptoms. Regardless of whether you decide to stay or leave an abusive partner, your safety and the safety of your children takes priority.

Leaving or staying?

Many women do not want to end the relationship but they do want the violence and abuse to end. Women who leave violent husbands, boyfriends, or male partners do so for a variety of significant reasons. Given the widespread and traumatic consequences of violence and abuse, we need to understand these reasons, from the victim's perspective. These include being: badly injured and fearing for her life or the lives of her children, unwilling to endure the abuse anymore; encouraged and supported by family and friends to do so; receiving appropriate interventions by police, courts, doctors and others, afraid of the effects of abuse on her children; fearful for her own mental health; wanting an abuse free future; desiring respect and love in a relationship, among others.

Many women will choose to stay, again for a multitude of significant reasons that we need to understand from her perspective. Many of these are based on her perceived level of risk and threat to her and her children, to other family members, and even to pets, or her financial dependence, or the difficulty in marshalling and mobilising the resources needed to establish a new and safe living arrangement for herself and her children. Some women live in the hope that he will change. Some women may feel embarrassed or ashamed of the situation, or even afraid of the future — better the devil you know. We, as a society, do not usually expedite a woman's choice to leave a violent partner, so from past experiences, she may doubt that anything can be done to stop his violence and protect her.

Seeking help and making choices

Whether you are staying or seeking separation, your safety and the safety of your children must become your priority. Some things to consider that enhance your safety are: police intervention and support, and a domestic violence protection order against the perpetrator. The law is there to protect you. The support of family and friends will be invaluable. You may need the safety and shelter of a women's refuge for a time. Domestic Violence Women's Services, Women's Health Services, or Women's Legal Services may be able to support you with information, resources, and counselling to help your decision-making and to achieve your goals. Becoming financially independent and able to support your children and having suitable and safe accommodation will be critical to your future. Separation does not immediately equal safety! Abuse may escalate when he fears losing control of you. Leaving can be a high risk and dangerous time so make provisions for your safety. Express your safety concerns strongly to police and service providers you ring or visit.

Safety planning

A safety plan can assist you if you are staying, needing to leave in a hurry, and then staying safe once you have left. Consider:

- Developing a list of safe people to contact, and having a code word or sign that can alert family, friends, teachers, work-mates that you need help and to call police.

- Have a safe room to go to, if his violence escalates. Avoid rooms where weapons may be accessible (e.g., kitchen). Avoid rooms with no exits (e.g., bathroom).

- Have change with you, so you can use pay-phones or pay for taxis.

- Have a list of important phone numbers that you might need.

- Pack an emergency bag and leave it with a friend or family member.

- If you decide to leave, the following suggestions are for you to consider taking with you:

    Your credit cards, driver's licence, health cards.

    Important documents — Birth certificates (self and children), your marriage certificate (if applicable), passports, insurance policies, bank statements, income statements, and mortgage statement (these could be photocopied in advance).

    Domestic Violence protection order (if applicable).

    Medicine and prescriptions.

If you have left the relationship, then it may be safe to consider:

- Alerting police as to your location (and his).

- Contacting school and workplace and advising them of safety concerns.

- Obtaining an unlisted phone number and screening all calls.

- Changing locks and ensuring your new place has adequate safety.

- Varying your routines if travelling to work, shopping or picking up children.

- If you have to meet him, do so in a public place in the presence of safe people.

- Saving and documenting all emails, phone texts, letters, messages from your partner.

- Photograph your injuries, damaged property or goods inflicted by your partner as this could be useful evidence if needed for court.

Sadly, becoming violence-free in your life can be difficult, complicated, and challenging work. This is an indictment on our society, not you. You will come into contact with multiple services and organisations, some who understand your situation and others who won't. Whatever the case, believe that you and your children deserve freedom from abuse, that you are of infinite value, keep hope alive, and never resign yourself to abuse in your life. You and your children have a human right to be free from violence and abuse.

Betty Taylor and Dr Brian Sullivan

CHILDHOOD BULLYING

Many of us have experienced being a victim of a bully at some time in our lives. We know how humiliated and hurt we were. If you find out your child is being bullied you might want to jump in and sort it out immediately. However, it is better to remain calm and have a conversation with your child, not an interrogation, and make a plan. About a quarter of children say they have been bullied at some time and yet many will not tell us for fear of retaliation from the bully or because of what we might do.

Signs to look for in a child who is being bullied:

- Any change in behaviour.
- Difficulty sleeping — not sleeping or sleeping too much.
- Difficulty eating — loss of appetite or overeating.
- Any torn clothing, scratches or bruises.
- Loss of interest in school or friends.
- Not wanting to go to school.
- Excessive nervousness.

How to talk to your child

First make sure your child is indeed a victim of bullying and is not actually fighting with another child. While bullying is aggression it is a special kind of aggression where there is a power imbalance, that is, your child cannot easily defend himself or herself and it is repeated. Because of this it is important to encourage your child to tell you what is happening but for you to remain calm, to model how to listen and solve problems.

- Tell your child that you are pleased that you are having this conversation and that they are very brave for telling you as you realise how scared they must be.
- Tell them it is not their fault — they don't have to change anything, whether it is the colour of their hair or their demeanour. Especially don't encourage

them to stand up to the bully because if they could easily have done that they would have. Remember the bully has power over your child.

- Ask your child how they would like to be helped. Don't take over however much you want to. A victim by definition feels powerless to stop the bullying. We don't want to add to that by disempowering them further. Let them be part of the problem solving process.

- Make a plan: What does your child want to do? Do they want to learn how to remain calm? How to use humour? How to enlist their friends?

- What do they want you to do? — Do they want you to go the school? Or the bully's parents? Or the sporting club?

- In your plan discuss with your child expected reactions and realistically what you would like others to do.

Each family's plan will be different but the one thing we know is that there are three things that families can do which help. First is to show you care by being warm and supportive. The second is that brothers, sisters and friends show they also care. The third is to keep your regular routines and calmly solve the problem.

Dr Marilyn Campbell

CYBERBULLYING

Cyberbullying is any bullying through technology, usually using mobile phones and the Internet or combinations of these. Methods used to bully include texting derogatory messages on mobile phones with young people showing them to their friends before sending to the victim; bad-mouthing or excluding someone from a chat room; inviting comments on nasty blogs or placing embarrassing or bullying videos on YouTube. It is important to distinguish if it is bullying or fighting using technology because that determines how it is best handled. Just because young people send a nasty text or use instant messaging to berate someone, it could be fighting between equals and not the intentional, aggressive, repeated acts of someone with more power, which defines bullying.

Cyberbullying is still a social relationship problem and not a technological one. Most adults still view electronic technology as a practical tool, while adolescents increasingly see it as an essential part of their social life and interaction with peers. Because of this seamless offline and online relationship that characterises young people today, it is very important to understand that cyberbullying is about social relationships, the destructive, hurtful side of relationships. This is illustrated by the fact that most cyberbullying victims are also victims of traditional bullying and most cyberbullies also bully in the playground.

Contrary to what many adults believe, cyberbullying is not as widespread as traditional bullying. Studies show about a quarter of all young people experience traditional bullying with about 14% being a victim of cyberbullying. However, it seems because of the potentially large audience and the 24/7 nature of this bullying, coupled with the fact that cybervictims are also being bullied in the playground, the mental health consequences are more serious.

What to do to prevent cyberbullying?

- Talk to your child about not bullying anyone, how hurtful it is and that it is not just fun. Just because you can't see the victim's reaction doesn't mean it should be fun for you.

- Talk about how to resist peer pressure to join in bullying. Even to sit by and watch emboldens the bully, so better to log off.

- Encourage your child to be an involved bystander who defends a victim. This is easier to do in cyberspace where there is no physical danger. Your child can send a private text or instant message to a victim with a message of support without the bullies knowing.

- Tell you child not to give out their password to anyone because others can use it to bully by pretending to be them.

- Surveillance or supervision? There is much advice to keep the computer in the family room. However, it is difficult to constantly watch what is being written or received and with mobile phones it is impossible, especially now the Internet can be used on mobile devices. Reasonable supervision not surveillance is more practical.

- So should we ban the technology? As adults can we solve this problem by online filters? Or by even more extreme measures of not allowing our children access to the Internet or a mobile phone? No, because it is not technology but the social relationship which is the cause of cyberbullying.

- Carefully consider the family rules before buying the technology. It is like buying your child their first bicycle. You don't give it to them and say it is good to exercise, now off you go to play! You explain the dangers and give the rules about wearing a helmet, busy roads and being home before dark. In the same way mobile phones and computers have wonderful benefits but also have dangers. One doesn't need to exaggerate them, just explain them and what the rules are.

- We also need young people to learn to tell the difference between tattling and reporting. Tattling is when the child wants to get someone else in trouble but reporting is when there is harm to themselves or others. We are actually unable to see cyberbullying even less so than traditional bullying so we rely on young people to tell us. Make sure your child feels comfortable in talking to you about bad things that happen online right from when they start to use the Internet or mobile phone.

- You can't bully-proof your child but it is possible for them to learn not to bully.

What if your child is cyberbullied?

- Talk to your child. Tell them you feel they are very sensible for reporting this harm to you and you will do everything you can to help.

- Tell them it is not their fault they were cyberbullied, it is a problem that the bully has.

- Ask them how they would like to be helped.

- Make a plan. Each family's plan will be different according to the circumstance. What does your child want to do? What does your child want you to do? In your plan discuss with your child expected reactions and realistically what you would like others to do.

- Don't ever think about taking away the technology if your child is a victim as you will be punishing them and this a major reason children don't tell parents about cyberbullying.

- Report serious incidents to the police. However, remember that the police can only uphold the law and unfortunately there may be no laws about being nasty or hurtful. The cyberbullying must usually be a crime, such as a death threat, for the police to be able to take action.

- Report to your Internet Service Provider if there is offensive material about your child on a website. However, remember this might be only one way in which your child is being bullied.

Finally children learn from what they see you doing in your relationships with others. So model pro-social behaviour and solving conflict appropriately yourself so your children will too.

Dr Marilyn Campbell

SEXUAL ASSAULT

Sexual assault is an assault of a sexual nature against a person, or sexual acts perpetrated against a person without their clear consent. Child sexual assault is when the victim is a child or young person and the perpetrator is someone older, such as, an adult or an older youth. Sexual assault is often thought to refer to rape, that is, sexual intercourse without consent, such as forced vaginal, anal or oral penetration (penile or digital penetration or penetration with an object). However, sexual assault also includes acts such as showing someone pornographic material without their consent or understanding, making sexual comments or unwanted sexual advances, inappropriate touching or unwanted sexual contact, forced kissing or torture of a sexual nature. It is often assumed that sexual assault is an act committed by an adult male against an adult female, however perpetrators can be either male or female, and victims can be of either gender, and can be adults (including the elderly), adolescents or children. Often the offender is known to the victim, such as a parent, caregiver, relative or friend, in a much smaller number of cases the offender is a stranger. Perpetrators may use force, coercion, violence, threats, intimidation, or drugs (e.g., in the context of drink-spiking and date rape). Another closely related issue is that of sexual harassment in the workplace, which again consists of unwanted and inappropriate sexual attention, comments or contact.

Symptoms, signs and indicators

Sexual assault can be a terrifying and traumatic experience, which can have profound short-term and long-term psychological effects. Symptoms vary between individuals and some may not be as obvious as others. The victims of sexual assault may sustain physical injuries such as bruises, cuts, broken bones, genital and or anal injuries, sexually transmitted illnesses and or unwanted pregnancy. However, even after any physical injuries heal, the emotional and psychological scars may remain. These can include anger, anxiety, shame, guilt, confusion, depression, dissociation and fear. The trauma of being assaulted can lead to nightmares, flashbacks, insomnia, sleeping issues, disrupted appetite and even suicidal thoughts or behaviours. Other possible effects include denial, helplessness, self-blame, numbness, promiscuity (to regain a sense of control over one's body and sexuality), loneliness, social anxiety and difficulty concentrating. The impact of such a traumatic experience can impair an individual's academic or work performance and or their social functioning. It can have a detrimental impact on the victim's relationships, as they may struggle with issues around trust, power, control, sexual and emotional intimacy and their sense of safety. Family members may struggle to deal with what has occurred and may unknowingly react in an unhelpful manner, for example by focussing on revenge or by denial and minimisation of the event or its effects.

If you become aware that a child or young person has been harmed (or is at risk of harm) you must put their needs first. If a child or young person confides in you that someone has sexually assaulted them, touched them inappropriately or made them feel uncomfortable you need to let that child know you believe them and will try to help make them safe.

Do not interrogate the child and try to force them to answer questions. This can be emotionally overwhelming for them and may impede any legal proceedings. Rather than asking questions about exactly what has occurred, focus on exploring how they are feeling. Open and gentle questions (e.g., how did you feel when that happened?) can be a relief for the child and are more appropriate than closed or leading questions (e.g., did it only happen that one time?) which may cause a child to feel guilty or ashamed and thus shut down. If there is an allegation that someone is abusing a child or young person, this must be reported to the police and or the relevant child protection authorities in your state. Children need to know that they can confide in us and will be believed. If a child or young person tells you that someone is harming them you have a duty of care to intervene appropriately.

Parents or caregivers often feel that they are not equipped to respond appropriately if their child has been abused or harmed. However, it is important to remember that your child needs you to believe them and try to keep them safe by reporting the abuse or assault to the police or child protection authorities in your state. It may be beneficial for parents or caregivers to speak to a counsellor or psychologist themselves, as these professionals can give you the emotional support you needs in order to fully support your child. They can also give you practical strategies to assist with issues such as anger outbursts, sleeping or eating issues.

Response — emotional, psychological, physical

If you or someone you know has been sexually assaulted you may need to seek medical assistance immediately. This can be a scary and confronting experience as a physical examination may be required, so having a support person with you may help. You may also decide to report the incident to the police. Again this is not an easy thing to do, but remember, you have done nothing wrong. The person that harmed you has broken the law and by stepping forward, you may prevent this person from harming another innocent person. Contacting a sexual assault counselling service can provide you with the advice and support you require to make decisions at this difficult time.

Treatment and recovery

Sexual assault can be a terrifying and traumatic experience, and depending on the circumstances it can also be very confusing. If the person who assaults you was someone you loved and or trusted it can generate complex and conflicting emotions within you. Sometimes the victim of a sexual assault can wonder if they are somehow responsible for what happened. It must be clearly stated that any kind of assault or abuse against you is not your fault. The person who hurt you is the one at fault. They are the one who should be held accountable and they are the ones who should feel guilty and ashamed.

Many people find that attending counselling with a specialised sexual assault counsellor can be helpful in letting go of self-blame and reclaiming a positive sense of self. Counselling may help to reduce the feelings that can follow being hurt, such as depression, suicidal thoughts, nightmares, and anxiety. Remember, if you don't feel comfortable with a new counsellor, keep looking until you find someone who you can trust. Also, it is up to you whether or not you wish to discuss the assault itself, you should not feel pressured into talking about anything you do not wish to discuss. You can benefit from counselling by focussing on the impact of the assault (such as nightmares or feeling depressed) without discussing the assault itself if you do not wish to. Counsellors who work with child or adolescent victims will focus on feelings, rather than the assault itself to avoid re-traumatising the child and impeding possible legal proceedings. However, some people may choose to discuss the details of the assault as they find that it is therapeutic to tell someone what they experienced. This is okay too. If you do not feel that your therapist is able to listen and support you, find someone else — do not give up.

Sexual assault is a traumatic experience for anyone. However, with emotional and psychological support, recovery and healing is possible.

Sam Vidler

DEALING WITH TRAUMATIC INCIDENTS

Despite what is in the media or what we think is ideal, a stress-free life is undesirable and unrealistic; stress is associated with almost every aspect of life and with things we enjoy — planning an overseas holiday, or organising a family occasion can be stressful and yet we would say these events are the most positive in our lives. The stress associated with these and other significant events are the things that help us develop coping and the adaptive skills necessary to deal with things which are less enjoyable or are more challenging. So, some stress is good. This is when stress to which we are exposed overwhelms our capacity to cope or involves a distressing or traumatic event, that we struggle. A one-off distressing event may, for example, be when one loses a wallet, one is frantic about the loss of important valuables and after searching one has to accept the item may not be found and steps have to be taken to cancel credit cards and replace other items. Such an event is stressful but one soon acknowledges the loss, and over a period time the stress associated with the event passes and we return to normal.

About traumatic incidents

In a different context, the sudden and unexpected shocking story that one sees on the TV news or reads about in the newspaper, may be distressing and unpleasant. We distance ourselves from the event by changing channel or putting the newspaper down. This may not be the case if one is involved in a motor vehicle accident, or if one's house is burgled, or if one is the victim of a natural disaster. These events generate stress, and depending on the degree of direct impact on us, we probably have or display signs of distress that are physical, cognitive, emotional and interpersonal (i.e., behavioural). These reactions are normal and let us know we are not a statue. Remember that stress is not just in the mind. No matter how calm or resilient we may think a person is, the reality is that no two people cope in the same way, no two people have had the same experience in life, and therefore no two people will cope with or respond in exactly the same way. Traumatic incidents are problematic when one's coping capacity is overwhelmed by an event which is beyond our control and beyond our normal coping. It is very important we understand that these events are exceptional, and "An abnormal reaction to an abnormal situation is normal" psychiatrist Viktor Frankl wrote.

Normal reactions to abnormal events

Having experienced a traumatic event, the mind and body responds in a normal way to deal with the experience in what has become known as the fight or flight response. This response is natural and takes place when a threat, or a perceived threat, to danger occurs and prepares our body to either fight or to escape, or sometimes freeze. Whilst we may not think that the event warrants either response, the body nevertheless reacts in this way. This fight or flight response can be traced back to our primitive past when our bodies required a rapid burst of energy and mental focus to flee from, or deal with, danger (e.g., predators or enemies); this response is important and normal. The brain responds whether the danger is real or imagined. Science has helped us understand and categorise behaviours which people experience in three general categories; arousal is the word we use to describe feeling anxious, fearful and worried after a significant event; the arousal sometimes leads to changed behaviours; this is when people show or engage in behaviours that are different from usual and which they may not recognise or understand themselves. The behaviour may be more isolating, avoiding the usual circle of friends or contacts; and finally our cognitions — the way we think about things. This is often due to the necessity to make sense of (or normalise) what has been an overwhelming experience; we may feel as though we can't get it out of our mind.

These are some of the reactions you may recognise:

- *Arousal/Emotions* — fear, denial, avoidant, feeling numb, irritability, feeling lost, sad, anger, shock, feeling isolated.

- *Behavioural/Physical* — substance abuse, conflict, distancing from relationships, avoidant of reminders of the event, not wanting to talk, busyness, rapid heartbeat, headache.

- *Cognition/Thinking* — slow thinking, difficulty making decisions, sense of confusion, difficulty concentrating, memory problems, poor attention span, distressing dreams, intrusive unwanted thoughts and memories (of the event).

Helpful hints for those who have experienced a traumatic event:

- Rest a bit more often, and maintain a good healthy diet and exercise regime,

- Keep the use of drugs and alcohol to a minimum,

- Stay in touch with friends and relatives who are supportive,

- Remember that flashbacks, recurring dreams and irritability can be normal in the circumstances.

For family and friends:

- Family and friends should keep in mind that once the practical necessities have been dealt with, and the person's circumstances are no longer in threat or danger, to offer care and support to the individual.

- Allow the person to talk but don't push them to talk it they don't want to.

- People will deal with their experience and share their experience in their own way and in their own time; pressure to talk just adds further pressure to their already difficult set of circumstances.

- Listening is more important than giving advice; so listen in a non-judgemental way to the person's experience.

- Using expressions such as, *I know exactly how you feel or You're lucky it wasn't worse* are not helpful and serve to alienate the individual rather that support the individual.

- Acknowledgement and validation are important to the person's sense of security.

- Normalising reactions in a non-judgemental and supportive way are essential.

- Encourage the person not to use alcohol or drugs to cope, but guide them to seek assistance in other forms e.g., relaxation, exercise, health eating habits, and counselling.

Seeking assistance

If the individual has behaviours or symptoms which last for more than a month, they should be encouraged to see their doctor and/or a mental health professional to seek advice and assistance. Sometimes, professional intervention is necessary to ensure complete recovery.

Children and traumatic events

Children of all ages who have been involved in or connected with a traumatic event should be the subject of special care and attention. The child may be directly involved or impacted simply because the event has been shared within the family. Children respond to tragedies and traumatic events in different ways from adults. Additionally children are often thought not to be able to appreciate the event as adults might, (sometimes children are thought not to be affected at all). This is not the case as children are affected but reveal it in different ways. It is essential that parents, carers, teachers and others who are involved with children make every effort to be informed about and are able to develop an understanding of the behaviours or responses which might be seen in children after a traumatic event, and to familiarise themselves with age appropriate responses, care and support and to seek advice appropriately.

Paul Scully

VICTIMS OF CRIME

Nobody ever expects to be a victim of crime, however crime and the experience of crime is prominent in our culture, through television shows, movies, books and in newspapers. High profile crimes attract a lot of attention and may become part of our cultural identity with the intimate details played over and over in the media. Crime and the way it is reported can affect the psychological wellbeing of people and may influence lives. However the experiences of victims of crime often go unattended.

Many victims experience loss, grief and trauma associated with the incident which often has far reaching consequences for their future functioning. Furthermore, victim's experiences within the criminal justice system can significantly impact upon their recovery. Often they will be required to be witnesses or participate in the court proceedings in some way and this experience can be at odds with people's expectations of the criminal justice system. Sometimes offenders are not found guilty and sometimes people's perceptions of justice are not met within a system, which by its very nature must remain neutral.

What do you do when it happens to you or someone you know?

Firstly recognise that there will be a period of shock and/or grief.

- After this period of shock, people may experience a rollercoaster of emotions such as anger at the perpetrator or society, grief for their associated loss, guilt, or anxiety.

- Victims of crime may experience flashbacks, nightmares, problems sleeping.

- For the initial period after the incident you/they will probably feel numb and operate on autopilot for a while.

- A victim of crime may experience significant changes to their lifestyle as they adjust their lives as a response to their experiences.

- There is no right way of coping. We all react differently to events. Sometimes, particularly in cases of homicide, this period of shock may be extended from a few weeks to a year, or longer in some cases.

- Differentiation should be made between the experience of grief and that of depression. It is generally accepted that depression should not be diagnosed until at least 6 months after a major life trauma, as an allowance must be made for the normal human experience of grief.

- When seeking professional support it is best to choose practitioners who specialise in grief, loss and trauma, as these aspects seem to be the recurrent emotional experiences of victims of crime.

- There are often victims of crime agencies in each State that support and service particular types of crime, for example, homicide or rape.

- Victims of crime agencies can be very beneficial for some victims as they provide a sense of belonging and may negate the feelings of alienation and isolation referred to earlier. Many of these organisations are based upon a peer support model in which victims can share their stories and hear others' experiences and methods of coping who may be further along their path of recovery. These organisations are easily accessed via your local telephone book, the Internet — via any search engine, city council, or a GP.

It is important to note that some States may have a compensation or financial assistance scheme that assists victims of crime, and especially violent crime. Information regarding these schemes can be sought from Police personnel and/or the Department of Justice.

Michelle Dyck and Susan Beattie

Education and Careers Issues

- Studying Effectively
- School Refusal
- Career Choice and Change
- Worklife
- Gaining or Re-entering Employment

STUDYING EFFECTIVELY

Effective study is an important skill in preparing for any form of assessment that may be required to gain a job, qualifications or entry into higher education. Although some degree of stress is inevitable, developing effective study skills can help reduce stress, improve your chance of success, and enhance motivation. The following tips cover the practical aspects of preparing for an assessment and offer a recipe for success, rather than stress!

Plan ahead

Taking time to plan ahead and get organised is essential to study effectively and reduce stress. Some ways to prepare for study are listed below:

- Plan to study by developing a schedule that includes dedicated study time. Make sure the schedule is realistic and workable and balances other commitments. You may need to modify the schedule each week according to your situation and goals.

- Set aside a specific place to study effectively. Ensure this space is void of distractions, and has good lighting and ventilation, a comfortable chair and sufficient space for materials. Make a habit of using this space for study only.

- Get organised by gathering all the materials, equipment and information you need before you begin.

- Be sure you understand what you have to do or ask someone to clarify instructions.

- Make a list of what you need to do and by when, and then prioritise tasks to achieve your goals. Try dividing your goals into smaller tasks.

- At the end of each study session, make a note of what you achieved and plan what you need to do in your next session.

Maximise your learning

Being prepared to study is an important step, but being prepared is not enough. Following through with your schedule and maximising your study time is most important! Here are a few ways to maximise your learning, depending on your own learning style:

- Use different sources (e.g., library, Internet, people) to research the topic you are being assessed on. The more you understand the topic, the better you will do.

- Read effectively. For example, preview what you are about to read and then mark/highlight key information as you read.

- Take notes as you are reading. There are many ways you can take notes, such as making a summary of what of you have read in your own words, creating a list of key information, or using diagrams and flow charts to organise information or ideas.

- Make up your own acronyms or jingles to remember important information. Write these memory cues and other important information such as definitions, diagrams or formulas, on sticky notes that you can post above your desk and review regularly. Try moving around the room while you are rehearsing the information you have studied.

- If you are studying for an exam, read and revise your notes often. Work through practice examples for exams and have someone quiz you on your knowledge.

- Be sure to proof read written work and practice oral assessments over again. Ask someone to read drafts of any written work, or to listen to any oral presentations you are preparing for, and ask for feedback.

- Review your study effectiveness regularly. Are you achieving your goals? Do you need to revise your study habits? Do you need help from someone?

Stay healthy in body and mind

Healthy living practices will help you cope with study stress and perform more optimally for your assessment. Be sure to eat well and to get enough sleep, exercise and relaxation while you are studying. Keep your thinking positive/helpful and reward yourself for meeting your study goals. Seek help if you need it.

Diane Barber

SCHOOL REFUSAL

Most children look forward to going to school and enjoy the social interaction, sense of achievement and belonging to a specific community. They may not always enjoy every single part of the school day but in general they like spending time with their teacher, friends at school, learning new things and being challenged.

Other children just dread going to school. For these children, going to school may become so stressful that they have temper tantrums or complain of feeling sick, and indicate they are suffering a stomach-ache, dizziness or chest pain.

Although school refusal has been associated with both separation anxiety disorder and social phobia, the easiest way to think about it is that school refusal is a difficulty attending school associated with emotional distress, especially anxiety and depression.

The issue of school refusal is complex and there is no simple solution. It covers a range of behaviours and it is important to investigate the patterns and underlying causes of non-attendance, so that appropriate strategies are implemented. Parents and schools need to work as partners to overcome the challenge.

Symptoms

For some children, there is an easily identifiable trigger for school refusal, such as being bullied, death in the family, a prolonged illness or move to a new school or suburb. Following one of these events, especially if they are associated with the child staying home with a parent for some time, the child may not want to go to school any more.

The obvious signs are temper tantrums and crying when it is time to go to school as well as vague symptoms mentioned above. Although these symptoms can also be found in children with other medical problems, a reliable sign that they might be caused by school refusal is that they get better later in the morning once the child understands that he is going to be able to stay home.

Other signs that a child's symptoms might be caused by school refusal include that your child:

- Continues to maintain an appetite and gains weight.

- Is physically well (i.e., no fever).

- Doesn't have as many symptoms when they aren't in school (including weekends and holidays).

- Physical examinations by your doctor don't confirm the complaint.

- In general, your child presents as quite anxious and has worries about other things as well.

Managing school refusal

Of course, the main goal in managing school refusal is getting children back in school. Unfortunately, when children seem sick and are trying to stay home from school, it is not always easy to recognise that they are avoiding school. Keep in mind that in almost all cases, anxiety is an overwhelming issue for your child.

What can you do

First of all, a visit to your family doctor or paediatrician is usually a good first step when your child doesn't want to go to school. This can help ensure that your child doesn't have a physical condition causing their symptoms. Do this sooner rather than later.

- Listen to your child with your eyes and your ears. Look for obvious signs of anxiety and talk to your child and the teacher to see if you can figure out what is triggering your school avoidance behaviours (e.g., such as a bully, school performance problems, or friendship issues).

- Make sure that your child goes to school each day, since the more they stay home, the harder it will be to get them to go back to school.

- Make a plan with your child about the drop-off arrangements and insist on your exit strategy: *We will walk together to the gate, you can give me a cuddle then I will leave straight away.* If you expect any further problems then have a pre-arranged back-up plan: *If you make a scene, I will take you to the office and leave you with the principal.* Involve them in the plan and invite sugges-tions to make it easier to follow the plan. Expect them to follow the plan.

- Respond to any protests about going to school using an understanding, positive and reassuring voice: *I know you would prefer to stay home today, but everyone has to go to school and even if it is hard for you, I know you will be able to manage.* Stay calm, confident and matter-of-fact. Use a broken record strategy if necessary, by repeating your response especially if your child escalates the protests.

- On the way to school remind your child of the plan, respond to protests as above and communicate that you expect them to follow the plan. Use the broken record technique if required (*you know you have to go to school*) and keep repeating it. Do not make promises that you cannot keep.

- Above all, make sure that you follow your part of the plan including the back-up plan if required. There may be lots of tears and protests, but continue to communicate your confidence in your child to manage this and exit immediately according to the plan. Ignore the social embarrassment. Be aware that most parents have had some experience of this and therefore, will be understanding. Teachers and school personnel respect parents who act responsibly in dropping their children off, giving a quick cuddle and a brief word of reassurance and exiting without a backward glance.

- Don't hesitate to ring the school to check how your child has settled, but only after you have left the school environs.

- Understand that even though your child doesn't have a physical problem causing symptoms, that doesn't mean that those symptoms aren't real. Your child isn't necessarily making up symptoms such as stomach-aches or headaches. They may just be caused by his anxiety about going to school.

- Consider getting help from the school guidance counsellor, child psychologist or perhaps a family therapist if there are stressors at home, like a divorce, separation, discipline problems, death in the family, new sibling, or a recent move.

School refusal can become very frustrating for everyone involved and especially parents. This can lead to anger and resentment due to the time and energy involved. Keep in mind that your child is already anxious so these feelings will only increase that anxiety. The most important thing is to ensure that your child does not avoid school. If a child is effective in getting the parent to give in, then remedying the situation later becomes so much more difficult. Avoidance only serves to reinforce the anxiety and makes it harder the next day, next week and even next year, despite any promises your child may make. Therefore it is very important that as a parent you try to find out what your child is worried about, how real their worries are, and to help your child devise strategies to overcome worries and return to school.

Vince Dundas

CAREER CHOICE AND CHANGE

Making career choices and decisions is a process — but not necessarily a linear one. Very few people make confident decisions based on epiphanies or flashes of inspiration. You need to be actively involved in every step — you're the one who will be living the choices every day. The decision needs to be yours so don't wait for someone to tell you what to do. A career will usually involve a series of jobs or roles. It's very unlikely you'll be in the one job forever in the modern workforce. Give yourself permission to think flexibly and be open-minded. Gather information from different sources (e.g., the Internet, talking to various people, personal experiences). Most people don't go straight into their ideal job right out of university or school. There are usually transition jobs leading to better jobs. If you wait for the perfect conditions before you act, you might fall in the trap of not taking any action at all and limiting your opportunities. Then you will feel like you are stuck. Feeling stuck in a situation we don't like (e.g., job, relationship, place) can often lead to gloomy or even depressive thoughts. Action and moving forward in some way is a great antidote to this.

To make positive career decisions that you can feel confident about start with two basic types of information. Self-awareness (where might I fit in and what might I be suited to?), and world-of-work awareness (what's out there and what's it like?). The following will help you get kicked off in the right direction (Tip: write your answers down as you go).

Self-awareness

Firstly ask yourself: *During my day, what sort of balance would I like between: People, Tasks, Ideas? What priority would you put on each? What percentage of your day would you like to spend in each mode?*

Then consider the following questions (there's no right or wrong):

- What would you want most from a work environment?

    Work indoors or outdoors? Work at a desk more or be physically active?

    Help individual people or maybe assist an organisation with its performance?

    Have a predictable environment or take each day as it comes?

- What type of work interests you?

  Practical hands-on activities possibly with tools or equipment.

  Helping people and/or the community.

  Being creative.

  Influencing, teaching or managing people.

  Finding solutions and investigating new ways, knowledge or approaches.

  Helping to ensure systems and administration to run smoothly.

- What are your talents, aptitudes and skills? What comes more easily to you?

  Working on practical, hands-on tasks.

  Communicating with and understanding people.

  Working with numbers and facts.

  Being artistic or creative.

  Solving problems.

- What type of environments suit your personality?

  Are you re-energised by lots of people contact or by time spent being quiet?

  Are you a facts and figures type or do you like some ambiguity?

  Do you prefer logical/analytical (right answer) or people-focused decisions (best answer)?

  Do you like structure and timelines or just going with the flow?

What else influences you? What do you value, what is important to you, and what sort of person would you like to be thought of as? What types of career or work would be consistent with these values and priorities?

World-of-work awareness

Next you need to investigate opportunities. Start by reading about fields and jobs of interest. Most vocational colleges and universities have a careers centre with useful information. Try government career information centres in most major cities and some regional towns. There is a mountain of on-line careers information but be careful to use reputable websites. Checkout the following information for careers that you've considered:

- Qualifications and training required.

- General type of activity involved.

- Related careers/jobs.

- Job outlook/prospects/salary range.

- Other sources of information (including brochures and websites of professional associations, training organisations).

- Key employers.

- Go where the knowledge is. Attend careers fairs/expos, university/vocational college open days, trade shows.

- Check out training opportunities at vocational colleges, university and private training organisations.

Alternative Activity (If you have no idea where to begin)

An activity that can help you get started is to get the weekend careers section of a major newspaper and simply start scanning. Make a note of whatever draws your attention or intrigues you (whether you are qualified for it or not) and cut the ad out (try to collect 10 at least). Do you see any patterns forming? Show your clippings to a career counsellor, family member or friend and see if they see any patterns — do the ads have anything in common? Maybe there are a couple of different clusters or groups. Once you have some general areas identified then go back to the activity above and research them. This will at least help you see what interests you.

Prioritising and Deciding:

- From your research above, make a list of the pros and cons of each idea or option. Look at your answers to the self-awareness questions and compare the results to what you're finding out. You might like to discuss this with a careers counsellor, family member or good friend.

- You probably still have lots of questions. Now would be a great time to do some informational interviewing (i.e., brain-picking). Ask knowledgeable people for their advice and insights on:

  Qualifications and getting started.

  Culture and working life.

  Opportunities and career paths.

  How to gain work experience.

  Who are the key employers in the field.

It is important to not ask them for a job at this stage — this will just put them off. You simply want information to start with (and possibly work experience).

- Again, see if you can find someone with whom you are comfortable discussing your thoughts and research. Not someone who will necessarily push their own opinions. You need someone who will listen to your research and thoughts and guide you to a positive choice.

- Take action.

- Be positive — one step at a time — you can do it!

Jacqui Rochester

WORKLIFE

Work is something we all engage in whether it is paid employment, unpaid, voluntary, or work in the family and at home. Work, regardless of its form, contributes to individuals, families and society. Every aspect of our life is influenced by our work. Ideally, we will derive personal satisfaction from work; it takes up a considerable portion of our lives.

The work we do has implications for our lives in general and for the lifestyle we lead. Each of us has only one life and work in its various forms is an integral part of it. Work is not separate from our lives. How we balance work and other facets of our life has often been referred to as work-life balance. Sometimes work, especially paid employment, gets in the way of other facets of our life that matter to us, such as exercise or spending quality time with our family. Balancing work and all of the demands of our daily lives may be challenging, and sometimes frustrating and stressful.

In terms of paid employment, the world of work has changed significantly since many people first entered it, and is still changing rapidly. For example, fewer people will have a job for life and most will change jobs several times. Permanent tenured employment is less available and there is more contract work, project work and part-time work. In this world of work context, personal qualities such as adaptability, resilience, and being open to new ideas are valuable.

In today's world of work two types of skills and knowledge are needed by workers. These are termed employability skills. Some skills and knowledge are particular to jobs. For example, the skills and knowledge required by a plumber are different from those required by a clerk or a social worker. Another set of general skills is transferable between jobs and includes communication, problem solving and teamwork skills, all of which could be valuable to plumbers, clerks and social workers. Skills and knowledge may be developed in initial training and continually refined across our lives.

Because of rapid change, individuals need to keep learning across their lifespan. Initial training and qualifications are important to gain employment, but retaining employment and currency in our field requires us to engage in learning across our working lives. We may engage in formal learning such as obtaining a qualification from a university or technical college or we may learn informally on the job or through professional development activities. Sometimes learning experiences may be provided by employers and sometimes we will need to seek learning opportunities ourselves. Not all of our learning will be work-related. Some will be for the pleasure of learning more about our interests or hobbies.

A result of constant change in the world of work means that most of us will face many work transitions in our lives. Some of these transitions will be planned and some will be unplanned. For example, we may decide to seek employment elsewhere or we may unexpectedly be made redundant. Transition brings with it a range of emotions including excitement, anger, sadness, nervousness and enthusiasm. It is becoming increasingly important that we learn how to manage our progress and transitions across our working lives.

Within a dynamic world of work, self-management is becoming an important skill. Self-management is a proactive process that is continual, rather than a reactive, process prompted by a set of circumstances. If we can find the right job, our whole life may be different. We may have less stress, fewer sleepless nights and actually enjoy going to work. Let us consider some strategies we can employ to self-manage ourselves and our work.

- Know yourself — regularly self-evaluate.

- Understand your personality and interests.

- Know the skills and knowledge you possess.

- Know your strengths and limitations.

- Know what you value in life.

- Know your present and future financial needs.

- Consider the impact of your work on your personal and family life.

- Identify what you are prepared to sacrifice or compromise and what is non-negotiable. Be honest about yourself.

Continually review your experience of work:

- Monitor your experience of work.

- Identify what gives you personal satisfaction and reward.

- Analyse your tasks and roles — break them down into their component parts and identify those you do or don't like — what you like may become an ingredient to look for in future opportunities.

Be proactive

- Keep your CV, portfolio, or resume up to date — include your roles as well as the skills and knowledge you used and acquired.

- Keep records of feedback you receive.

- Be aware of career support services and learning opportunities available to you at work and avail yourself of them.

Keep learning:

- Seek new challenges, look for and take up opportunities — they may help you test future work possibilities.

- Build good relationships with colleagues inside and outside of your workplace.

- Think of future possibilities such as, jobs you might seek and work options such as full-time, part-time, or casual work, job-sharing, and self-employment.

Accept that it is okay to change jobs — the stress of staying in a job you hate may be no worse that the stress of changing jobs.

Be willing to talk to others and seek help:

- Family and friends can provide valuable support.

- Role models, mentors, supervisors, and employers may all be able to assist us explore opportunities, recognise our strengths and utilise our talents.

- Professional career development practitioners are trained and experienced in assisting people with work and learning dilemmas.

- Collegial networks and professional associations may assist us to build networks outside our workplace from which we can gather information, find out about opportunities, develop a broader perspective, and build our profile.

- Work occupies much of our time across our lives and contributes to our enjoyment of life. How work fits into our lives is not something we should leave entirely to chance. Understanding some of the realities of the world of work and developing self-management strategies may assist us lead satisfying and fulfilling lives.

Dr Mary McMahon

GAINING OR RE-ENTERING EMPLOYMENT

This may be your first entry into the employment market, or you may not have been in the workforce for a considerable period of time. Whatever the case may be, you will need to carefully consider your career choice, as well as additional training, skills and technology updates appropriate to your chosen area.

Resumes and cover letters

It is important to customise your resume (particularly when an advertised position is a perfect fit for your skills and employment history). Provide appropriate verbal referees and supply them with details of the position applied for. You will also need to spend time drafting an effective and targeted cover letter for every job you apply for. This is the best way to illustrate your suitability for the role, to create a good impression and to gain that interview.

Job search

Strategies which contribute to a productive and efficient search include utilizing search engines to access appropriate job sites and then narrowing your search criteria so you receive the most relevant listings by researching company information on the web, creating a list of those you would like to work for, identifying appropriate contacts within these companies, and organising your job search materials (e.g., resume and cover letter versions, job advertisements, business cards, company research and contacts). It is also important to stay in regular contact with local recruitment organisations. Regular phone calls will assist with your focus and motivation, illustrate your keenness and assist in keeping your profile to the fore when new job vacancies are listed. Additionally, ensure you make a set number of network contacts (e.g., phone, e-mail) per day seeking information, advice, introductions or assistance, and perhaps voluntary or work experience opportunities.

Social media

Whilst social media sites such as Twitter and Facebook can help you find a job and connect with your networks, when used in the wrong way it can actually jeopardise a job opportunity. Consider carefully what you should and should not post. Private information should not be accessible, so check your privacy settings. There is a lot a prospective employer can find out about you just by Googling your name. Use social media information to create profiles on appropriate sites like LinkedIn or Facebook that will provide a strong positive impression. Whilst targeting your resume for specific positions is great, ensure your resume (job and date listings) match your social media profile. It is important to ensure that your e-mail address and mobile phone message bank are professional and appropriate — an e-mail address such as latenighter@hotmail.com could find your resume in the shredder within minutes.

Interviews

Research the company before you go for the interview, dress appropriately, and practice answering and asking interview questions. Also, prepare answers for behaviour-based interview questions and be ready to provide examples, such as, when you have performed certain tasks or exceeded company expectations. In addition, prepare answers to difficult questions such as why you were dismissed from your previous job. Solid preparation will assist in decreasing your anxiety and increasing your confidence level.

Never denigrate your previous employer to a prospective employer; the only person who will look bad is you. Always send a thank you note or e-mail after the interview that validates your interest in the position and reminds the employer of why you are an excellent contender for the job. Finally be proud of your efforts. Good luck!

Sue McLaughlin

14

Communication, Relationships and Friendship Issues

- Mediation
- Positive Online Social Networking
- Forgiveness
- Dealing with Cultural Differences
- Gender Differences in Communication and Friendship

MEDIATION

Mediation seems to be everywhere these days. It is mentioned in the media, newspapers and in Court and Tribunal systems. Even so, you may think that mediation will never be an issue for you.

However, either you or someone very close to you will be involved in some sort of alternative dispute resolution process at some stage, whether you are in a relationship which is coming to an end, whether you have a dispute with your neighbour, or whether you have a civil dispute in a Court or Tribunal.

You might be asked to be involved in the process, or you might seek it out for yourself. Why has it become so popular? To answer this we first need to understand exactly what is meant by mediation in the first place.

Mediation, conciliation, and alternative dispute resolution, all have similar aims and have similarities in process. Mediation is often described as a process by which the participants, with the assistance of a neutral person, systematically isolate disputed issues, develop options, consider alternatives, and reach a consensual settlement that meets their needs.

Quite simply, mediation is a procedure in which a third person helps people involved in a dispute to resolve it. It often improves the process of decision-making, because the people involved in the dispute actually own the outcome themselves, rather than have an outcome imposed upon them. This is an important point which cannot be stressed enough in a modern world where, let's face it, we just don't like being told what to do. With mediation, the power remains with the participants and not with a decision-maker, such as a Court or a Tribunal. Of course no process has all positive aspects.

With mediation there are no guaranteed outcomes and the outcome might not be exactly what you thought it must be. However, keep in mind the alternative is asking for a third person to arbitrate the decision and sometimes it is better to give a little in order to resolve an issue that is creating problems in your life. Also remember that the other side might just be right about some aspect of the argument!

There are various models of mediation and in the one that is becoming perhaps the favourite is what is called the *facilitation model of mediation*. It focuses on the parties' underlying needs and interests. The idea is to prevent the parties from lapsing into incremental bargaining, by continually emphasising their interests, by drawing attention to commonality. Creative settlement options are encouraged. In this model the mediator is not the one who suggests resolutions, but assists the parties to hopefully find a mutually agreed set of outcomes.

The other models of mediation available all have the ultimate aim of trying to resolve a dispute in a way that creates the least amount of lost energy, or costs for the parties. So what's in it for you if you are asked to be involved in the mediation process?

Mediation has become attractive in our society for the following reasons:

- It prevents escalation of problems.

- Relationships can be preserved away from the conflict of arbitration.

- It focuses on the interests of individuals.

- It is cost effective.

- Outcomes can be flexible.

- It is highly participatory.

So, if you are called to be involved in the mediation process, keep calm and rational, think about your underlying interests and what you want and most importantly, approach it with an open mind.

Keep in mind the following points:

- We tend to overestimate our current position and underestimate the position of the other side.

- We can be overconfident.

- We can suffer from anchoring that is, setting a particular figure or outcome in mind, and choose not budge from it.

- We can all be biased towards keeping the status quo.

- The sunk cost effect — meaning we can be guilty of throwing good money after bad.

- We wish to go along with the crowd and sometimes that can result from advice from our friends, colleagues and relatives (beware of those bush lawyers around us).

- Misestimating the future — we don't estimate accurately the pleasure or pain that maybe suffered in the future if circumstances change dramatically.

- We overestimate the degree to which we think others share our views, beliefs and experiences.

Mediation then generally can lead to positive outcomes for the participants. Try to remain calm during the process, make sure that you explain your side of the story to the mediator and your opponent. Listen carefully to the mediator and what the other side is saying, taking into account what the other side is saying and don't dismiss it out of hand. Do not get aggressive as it will not help the possible resolution of the issues.

It is amazing when people approach the process of mediation with an open mind, how they can find middle ground to solve a dispute, shake hands and move on. It is also amazing to see how the process will not work if people remain negative, obstinate and resistant to the concept of settlement, compromise or simply listening to another person's position. To repeat, an obstinate position will not help later in a hearing before a Court or Tribunal, for example, because it is no longer you in control of the outcome.

Keep in mind the emotional, personal and financial costs of arguing about matters, when they could be resolved to the satisfaction of both sides.

In the end, if the mediation process does not result in a settlement, it has not been a waste of time or effort, because the issues which are in contest will have become clearer and are more defined for a hearing, and settlements might even follow before the hearing because that mediation has occurred.

Sean Barry

POSITIVE ONLINE SOCIAL NETWORKING

Online social networking refers to interacting with people who share interests or activities via the Internet such as Facebook, Twitter, YouTube, LinkedIn, and various dating websites. Online social networking is now used regularly by people of all ages to keep in touch with colleagues, family and friends both near and far. Additionally, these social media are used by many people to make new contacts for various personal and professional reasons.

There are numerous strategies for ensuring that your experiences with online social networking are positive and may enhance your social wellbeing.

Optimise the benefits

If you move to a different geographic area or have less time to meet with friends or colleagues in person, consider communicating with them online to maintain your friendship or relationship.

Inform yourself about security options

Talk to your friends or family about how to use the sites and read up on the options you have to make your personal information more secure.

Use your profile in a positive way

Communicate with people who have similar interests, organise social or professional events, and share information that you are comfortable with having on the Internet.

Be in control of your online interactions

If you are experiencing negative interactions with someone online, stop communicating with them and consider blocking them from access to your profile.

Protect yourself

If you feel you are being bullied by someone, think about how you can prevent that person from having access to your profile and talk to someone for support and guidance about what is happening.

Be respectful of others

Think very carefully prior to posting other people's personal information, including posting pictures or making comments about them, on your site.

Don't be a bully

It is easy to make comments about others that can be hurtful or offensive. Be aware of the potential impact of what you post.

Avoid going online more than you plan

If you think you are using online networking sites too often, restrict yourself to a certain amount of time per day or per week.

Have a process for screening people who request to be your friend

Consider the following — How well do you know them? Why are they seeking to be your friend? What might be the problem with being connected to them? Remember, you don't have to accept every friend request.

Be aware of the information that you post:

- Never share personal information like your mobile phone number or home address as close friends will already have this information.

- Remember that information you post online can stay there permanently, so think very carefully about what you are posting.

- Don't post anything online that you would normally only disclose to a close friend. When communicating online you can be drawn into providing information that you did not intend to share.

- Some aspects of social networking sites are open to all members so only post information in those sections that you are comfortable sharing with strangers.

- Meeting someone face-to-face — if you really want to meet with someone that you have only communicated with online, ensure you meet in a public space, tell someone where you are going and, if possible, take a friend with you.

If your use of online social networking is negatively affecting your work, health or relationships, consider seeking assistance from a friend or helping professional.

Australian Psychological Society (Adapted by Dr John Barletta)

FORGIVENESS

Common reactions when we believe we have been wronged by another person or organisation include feelings of anger, fear, sadness, and loss. Sometimes there are feelings of guilt for no obvious reason or because we think we should have taken action to prevent the event occurring in the first place.

Many people who have been wronged find it hard to let go of what has happened to them and the associated feelings. These feelings can end up consuming them and taking over their lives. Other people will often remark you need to forgive! This can seem like an impossible feat or something that sounds easy to say, but is much harder to do.

Forgiving can be hard to do because of the following beliefs:

- If I forgive, it means I am agreeing with what happened.
- If I forgive, it means I am accepting less for myself.
- If I forgive, it means I have to forget.
- If I forgive, it means it could happen again.
- If I forgive, it means the person gets away with it.

These beliefs are rarely true. In fact, holding on to these feelings only seems to have an impact on the person who is holding onto the feelings. It can often result in difficulties moving on with life due to being continually weighed down by the feelings that often contaminate reactions toward other people and situations. For example, even when there is reason to be happy these underlying feelings do not go away. The feelings may also come out toward other people who have done nothing wrong or very little wrong.

What can you do to help yourself?

Firstly, make a deliberate decision to let go of the feelings. Then try and do the following:

- Make a decision to forgive the person for what they did.

- Recognise that forgiving does not mean that you are worthless as a person. Their actions have nothing to do with your worth, it is about them and their issues.

- Recognise that you are forgiving them not to let them off the hook but to help yourself, to allow yourself to move on and enjoy life more. If you are not convinced, do an exercise listing the advantages of forgiving and compare them to the disadvantages of not forgiving.

- Recognise that forgiving does not mean agreeing with what happened.

- Recognise that forgiving does not mean forgetting what happened — that is impossible.

- Recognise that forgiving does not mean letting it happen again. Holding onto the feelings does not make you any safer or protected; this is an illusion. In fact, people who hold on to anger and other ill feelings seem to attract further negative attention creating more problems, often because people pick up on the anger and think it may be about them.

- If you are struggling to forgive the other person, try and understand why they did what they did. Was their intent to do wrong by you or was it accidental or out of ignorance? We are all human and we have probably all hurt other people or made mistakes that have impacted on others and we did not realise it.

- Recognise that forgiving others is empowering yourself rather than being at the mercy of your feelings.

- Express your feelings toward the other person through writing a letter to be sent to them, or not sent if you prefer. This is a powerful way of letting go of feelings and moving on.

- Finally, the irony is that not forgiving, forever bonds you to the other person in some way — they will always occupy space in your psyche.

If the issue is one of forgiving yourself, you can apply the same points as above, but just ask the questions about yourself rather than another person.

Paul Rushton

DEALING WITH CULTURAL DIFFERENCES

Most countries are culturally diverse, and perhaps you are even a first or second generation immigrant yourself. Perhaps you are in a relationship with someone from a culturally and linguistically diverse background. Your attitudes towards different cultures will influence the quality of relationships you have with others whose cultural background is unfamiliar.

When people move to another country there are several adjustments (also called acculturative strategies) they may use in response to their new culturally different home. Some people who migrate to a country decide to be separate from new culture because it is the easiest way to organise and survive daily living. Some people try to abandon the cultural values of their country of origin and assimilate to the new culture. Some people maintain and value their culture of origin and the new culture. These are people who integrate the favourable aspects of two cultures.

People from mainstream cultures also have certain attitudes toward the cultural behaviour of culturally and linguistically diverse people. You might:

- Expect people from culturally diverse backgrounds to abandon their own cultural values, language, and traditions and assimilate. If you are one of these people it means that you want to have relationships with people from other cultures, but if they are in this country they should be like us.

- Expect people from culturally diverse backgrounds to separate from the mainstream culture. This means you don't mind having people who are culturally different around as long as they stick to themselves, don't jeopardise the cultural status quo, and don't mind them practicing their traditions and speaking another language.

- Expect people to be integrative of the culture, language, values and traditions of their country of origin and the mainstream culture. You value the ability of these people to be bilingual and bicultural.

Whether you identify yourself as a person from the mainstream culture, from another culture, or from two or more cultural backgrounds, you will probably experience acculturative stress. This is experienced when you are unsure and/or unfamiliar with how to behave appropriately with people who are culturally different from yourself.

There are several strategies you can use to reduce this stress:

- By far the most important factor is to focus on the quality of the relationship you have with someone who is culturally different rather than focusing on the differences (e.g., language proficiency, skin colour, cultural traditions, religion).

- Initiate a conversation with someone who is culturally different. Ask them where they are from. Be inquisitive and ask politely and sensitively about their culture. Tell them what you know about their culture even if your ideas about their culture aren't accurate. While some people might be offended at first, if you are sincere or even a little embarrassed, you will usually find your relationship will be based on respect.

- As you build relationships with people from culturally and linguistically diverse people, you will begin to see the commonalities of the human experience regardless of culture and language. In fact scholars who study diverse cultures have found that there are many more commonalities among people of the world than differences.

No matter what culture a person is from, if you offer your help to someone in need, you give yourself the opportunity to develop personally.

Dr Jason Dixon

GENDER DIFFERENCES IN COMMUNICATION AND FRIENDSHIP

There are differences between men and women in aspects of their respective lives, including communication styles and how they form and keep relationships. The major gender difference in communication style is where emotional expression is involved. Feminine traits of being empathic, helpful, warm and sincere very much reflect a relationship role. Masculine traits of being aggressive, competitive, independent and self -reliant reflect more of a task-oriented role.

Women engage in conversation to share and care using equity, support, understanding, inclusivity and prompting. In contrast to this communication style, men engage in conversation to inform, advise, assert status and establish power. Men frequently use speech, devoid of personal emotion, to advise and assert power. Research suggests that men frequently interrupt, and direct and control conversations, whereas women typically disclose more about themselves to a new acquaintance than do males. Research also supports the idea that men experience emotion similar to females, and are very capable of self-disclosure and expressing emotion, but they generally only choose to share with females.

Stereotypic roles for men are more stringently enforced for men by both genders. As a result, many men frequently stay within their perceived gender role due to fear of experiencing negative social consequences from peers and partners. When men are with their same sex peers they are most likely to behave and communicate in a stereotypic manner when they want to get along with peers who are perceived to hold stereotypic views of gender appropriateness. Generally for men to communicate in a more expressive manner they require prompting to self-disclose and are then likely to disclose intimate aspects of their lives.

Both genders can experience emotions in similar ways, but men frequently feel an inability to openly communicate and express emotions. They tend to close down and retreat, particularly when asked to deal with highly emotional situations. Many men will also retreat and batten down during periods when they feel they are under attack, only to engage again when they perceive the incident has passed.

An inability to openly communicate and express emotions can contribute to:

- Depression.
- Anxiety.
- Poor self-esteem.
- Reduced intimacy.
- Diminished relationship satisfaction.
- Alcohol and drug abuse.

It is therefore is important that men learn, practice and are reinforced for good communication to ensure good health, wellbeing and life satisfaction.

Friendships

Men and women who have close friendships consistently report higher self-esteem, self-efficacy, self-confidence, are healthier emotionally and physically, have better functioning relationships, and hold positive perceptions regarding seeking support from others. We all look for validation and caring in our friendships regardless of gender. The majority of friendships are same-sex ones, and both men and women spend approximately the same amount of time with their same-sex friends.

However, friendship styles do differ. Women are generally more involved in each other's emotional life, they actively care for each, and share feelings and thoughts, while men's friendships frequently do not involve so much emotion or disclosure. This is a possible reason men's friendships can be referred to as side-by-side as distinct from women's same-sex friendships which are characterised as face-to-face.

Both genders agree that self-disclosure is indicative of a close personal relationship and research indicates that men are capable of such disclosure and expressing emotion. Despite this knowledge, men generally tend not to engage so freely or easily in self-disclosure. The reason for this may be that, as children, males learn that there are stereotypical roles such as stoicism and independence they are expected to exemplify, and these roles seem to be stringently enforced for men, by both genders. Expressing emotion can result in perceptions of being in need of assistance, dependent, weak, submissive, and incompetent, aspects which both genders perceive to be unattractive in a man. The reason for this may relate to men's fear that disclosure will place them in a vulnerable position where they will be perceived to be weak or inadequate in relation to their peers and that competition is significantly more important to males and their self-concept.

Men's conversations with their mates also differ in content. Women tend to talk about their feelings and just having someone to listen to them is enough to experience strong connections. Men generally do not participate in emotional disclosure and remain more solution-focused and are more likely to cover topics such as sports, work, money or vehicles in conversations with their peers. Men could explore the possibilities of sometimes behaving against type, and notice the rewards that might accrue.

Men are more likely to give tangible support (e.g., assist with a building project, mowing a lawn, working on car, going to the rugby) than emotional support. For men, being mutually involved in activities and spending time together is meaningful, and builds a level of intimacy. Men generally spend their time with their mates being action-focused either doing things or planning activities.

Men have always formed friendships outside the home, in clubs or work environments, and these connections are critical for them. The more men are encouraged to form same-sex friendships, and go on bro-dates, the more likelihood there is that they will maintain good health and wellbeing.

Mike Wood

contributors

Chapter 1 — Personal Wellbeing

Work–Life Balance
John Barletta, PhD, Counselling, Consulting and Clinical Psychologist

Positive Psychology
Optimism
Personal Energy Audit
Bronwen Edwards, DipTeach, Cert IV Personal Training, Lifestyle and Nutrition Coach, Personal Trainer

Building Resilience in Children
Vanessa Spiller, PhD, Clinical Psychologist

Enhancing Happiness and Wellbeing
George Burns, BA(Hons), Adjunct Professor and Clinical Psychologist

Emotional Intelligence
Karen Hansen, PhD, Consultant
Barbara Lloyd, PGDipPsych, Psychologist

Enhancing Motivation in your Child
Andrew Martin, PhD, Educational Psychologist and Research Fellow

Creativity to get Through the Tough Stuff
Lloyd Bond, Creativity Consultant and Educator

Assertiveness
Anne Evans-Murray, MEd, Education Consultant and Counsellor

Managing Financial Challenges
Cate Turton, DipCommServ(Financial Couns), Financial Counsellor

Confidence and Self-Esteem
Paul Burnett, PhD, Professor

Problem Solving and Decision Making
Living the Life You Want
Mark Korduba, MA(OrgPsych), Psychologist

Laughter
Bronwyn Roberts, CLL, Chief Happiness Officer

Perfectionism
Paul Rushton, BPsych(Hons), Clinical Psychologist

Sharing the Care of Children
Phil Watts, PhD, Clinical and Forensic Psychologist

Step-Families
Emily Anderson, MEd(ChFamPsych), Child and Family Psychologist

Adult Children Returning Home
Susan De Campo, RN MHlthSt, Clinical Counsellor

Being a Grandparent
Jan Bond MCouns, Clinical Counsellor

Giving a Baby up for Adoption
Sarah Sherrington, BPhycSc, Counsellor and Child Consultant

Adopting a Child
Mark Bahr PhD, Psychologist and Assistant Professor

Chapter 4 — Children and Adolescent Issues

Child Physical Health and Stress
David McMaster, MBBS FRACP, Paediatrician

Safe Sleeping for Babies and Toddlers
Kelli-Ann Zakharoff, BMid, Midwife and Safe Sleeping Educator

Child and Adolescent Development
Vanessa Spiller, PhD, Clinical Psychologist

Child Safety Around the Home
Bronwyn Griffin, RN GradDipAdvClinNurs(Emerg), Research Nurse

Childhood Anxiety
Children and Adolescents in Transition
Mari Farry, DPsycEd, Educational Psychologist

Shyness in Children
Emily Anderson, MEd(ChFamPsych), Child and Family Psychologist

Anger Management in Adolescence
Mark Korduba, MA(OrgPsych), Psychologist

Child Behaviour Management
John Barletta, PhD, Counselling, Consulting and Clinical Psychologist

Chapter 5 — Health and Wellbeing Issues

Coping Styles when Managing Health Concerns
Sleeping Soundly
John Barletta, PhD, Counselling, Consulting and Clinical Psychologist

Emotional Challenges of a Major Illness
Alan Hobman, RN MSocSc(Couns), Nurse Counsellor

Weight Management and Obesity
Anita Cochrane, MOrgPsych, Psychologist and Dietitian

Pregnancy Health
Gaylene Hardwick, RM BHlthS, Midwife

Nutrition, Diet and Healthy Eating
Anita Cochrane, MOrgPsych, Psychologist and Dietitian

Adjustment to Injury
Mark Korduba, MA(OrgPsych), Psychologist

Using Medicines Safely and Effectively
Jacqueline Bond, BSc(Hons), Lecturer
Lisa Nissen, PhD, Associate Professor

Physical Activity and Wellbeing
Nicola Burton, PhD, Clinical and Health Psychologist

Health Benefits of Strength Training
Returning to Sports
Ammon Re Bradford, Personal Trainer
Tracey Bradford, Personal Trainer

Managing Menopause
Beverley Powell, MBBS, FRANZCOG, Gynaecologist

Managing Chronic Pain
Kellee Waters, PGradDipPsych, CertIV-Fitness, Psychologist and Fitness Coach

Some FAQ for Seeing a Therapist
John Barletta, PhD, Counselling, Consulting and Clinical Psychologist

Chapter 6 — Ageing Issues

Coping with an Empty Nest
Jan Bond, MCouns, Clinical Counsellor

Planning for Retirement
Brendan McManus, PhD, Consultant

Positive Ageing
Caring for Ageing Parents
Coping with Dementia or Alzheimer's Disease
Caring for a Person with Dementia or Alzheimer's Disease
Jenneke Foottit, PhD, Lecturer

Chapter 7 — Mental Health Issues

Keeping your Brain Active and Stimulated
Brain Health
Matthew Bambling, PhD, Clinical Psychologist

Mental Illness and Mental Health
Matthew Hocking, MBBS FRANZCP, Consultant Psychiatrist

Depression
Anxiety
Matthew Bambling, PhD, Clinical Psychologist

Managing the Challenge of Asperger's Syndrome
Minds and Hearts: A specialist clinic for Asperger's Syndrome and Autism, Clinical Psychologists and Psychologists

Depression and Anxiety after Childbirth
Charlene Schembri, DClinPsych, Clinical Psychologist
Jeannette Milgrom, PhD, Health and Clinical Psychologist

Deliberate Self-Harm

Managing Suicidal Thoughts and Urges

Angelo De Gioannis, MD FRANZCP, Consultant Psychiatrist

Katelyn Kerr, DPsych, Clinical Psychologist

Andre Bauer, DipPsych, Clinical Psychologist

Eating Disorders

Yasmin Schaefer, BPsychSc, Psychologist

Emotional Overeating

Kellee Waters, PGradDipPsych, CertIV-Fitness, Psychologist and Fitness Coach

Trauma Recovery

Forrest James, MAnPsych, Psychotherapist

Chris Lobsinger, MSW, Social Worker

Living with a Person Affected by a Mental Illness

Anna Rybak, MRehabCouns, Psychologist

Chapter 8 — Grief and Loss Issues

Recovering from Loss

John Barletta, PhD, Counselling, Consulting and Clinical Psychologist

Supporting Someone who is Grieving

Pregnancy Loss

Jan Bond, MCouns, Clinical Counsellor

Death of a Child

Kristy Jeffcoate, BPsych(Hons), Psychologist

Children's Grief

Elisa Agostinelli, PhD, Counsellor

Brian Sullivan, PhD, Consultant

Parenting Bereaved Children after Sibling Death

Kristy Jeffcoate, BPsych(Hons), Psychologist

Suicide Bereavement

Jacinta Hawgood, MCPsy, Lecturer and Clinical Psychologist

Death and Dying

Venerable Yeshe Khadro, Hospice Director

Facing our Mortality

Brian Sullivan, PhD, Consultant

Elisa Agostinelli, PhD, Counsellor

Sudden Infant Death Syndrome

Linda Male, BPsych(Hons), Counsellor

Recovery After a Relationship Breakup

Karol Misso, MSocSc(Couns), Counsellor

Loss of Employment

Sue McLaughlin, BSSc, Counsellor

Saying the Final Goodbye to Your Pet

Anita Link, BVSc(Hons), Veterinarian

Chapter 9 — Sexuality Issues

Mismatched Libidos

Sandra Pertot, PhD, Clinical Psychologist

Chapter 10 — Stress Management and Time Management Issues

Chapter 11 — Addiction Issues

Chapter 12 — Abuse, Neglect, Violence, Bullying and Crime Issues

Child and Adolescent Abuse and Neglect
Sam Vidler, GradDipCouns, Counsellor

The Problem of Domestic Violence
Men Helping End Family Violence
Brian Sullivan, PhD, Consultant

Becoming Free from Domestic Violence
Betty Taylor, BSocSc, Consultant
Brian Sullivan, PhD, Consultant

Childhood Bullying
Cyberbullying
Marilyn Campbell, PhD, Educational and Developmental Psychologist

Sexual Assault
Sam Vidler, GradDipCouns, Counsellor

Dealing with Traumatic Incidents
Paul Scully, MCouns, Psychotherapist and Counsellor

Victims of Crime
Michelle Dyck, BCCJ, Criminologist and Family Support Coordinator
Susan Beattie, MForMentH, Senior Research Officer

Chapter 13 — Education and Careers Issues

Studying Effectively
Diane Barber, Educational and Developmental Psychologist

School Refusal
Vince Dundas, MEdAdmin, Guidance Counsellor and Consultant

Career Choice and Change
Jacqui Rochester, BA(Psych-Hons), Psychologist

Worklife
Mary McMahon, PhD, Senior Lecturer

Gaining or Re-entering Employment
Sue McLaughlin, BSSc, Counsellor

Chapter 14 — Communication, Relationships and Friendship Issues

Mediation
Sean Barry, MBA, Barrister-at-Law

Positive Online Social Networking
Australian Psychological Society (Adapted by Dr John Barletta)

Forgiveness
Paul Rushton, BPsych(Hons), Clinical Psychologist

Dealing with Cultural Differences
Jason Dixon, PhD, Bi-Cultural Mental Health Consultant

Gender Differences in Communication and Friendship
Mike Wood, PostGradDipPsych, Psychologist

Notes to Self

Printed in Australia
AUOC01n1004310713

257216AU00004B/1/P